THE EMERGENCE OF THE MODERN INDONESIAN ELITE

First published in 1960 by
W. van Hoeve Ltd. - The Hague.
Second impression 1970.

Cover: Founding Meeting Sarekat
Islam Blitar, 1914 (Photograph Collection KITLV).

KONINKLIJK INSTITUUT
VOOR TAAL-, LAND- EN VOLKENKUNDE

REPRINTS ON INDONESIA

ROBERT VAN NIEL

THE EMERGENCE
OF THE
MODERN INDONESIAN ELITE

1984
FORIS PUBLICATIONS
Dordrecht-Holland/Cinnaminson-U.S.A.

Published by:
Foris Publications Holland
P.O. Box 509
3300 AM Dordrecht, The Netherlands

Sole distributor for the U.S.A. and Canada:
Foris Publications U.S.A.
P.O. Box C-50
Cinnaminson N.J. 08077
U.S.A.

ISBN 90 6765 060 9

Printed in the Netherlands.

The Emergence of the Modern Indonesian Elite first appeared in 1960 but is the result of research and writing of almost a decade earlier. My studies for the Ph.D. degree at Cornell University began in 1949. In 1951-52 I was in the Netherlands and Indonesia doing the research for this book, and in 1953 I did the writing. The book should, therefore, be seen as a product of the early 1950s.

When I began to think about writing this book, my conception of the end product was that it would be an acculturation study of how Western ideas and Indonesian ideas combined in the emergence of a nationalist movement in the early twentieth century. As I write these words some thirty years later, the conception seems both vague and grandiose. At the time, however, it seemed quite normally ambitious, for our understanding of both the events and the personalities in the Indonesia of the early twentieth century was much thinner than it is today.

What I knew about Indonesian history by about 1950 was derived from English and Dutch sources. J. S. Furnivall's *Netherlands India* and B. H. M. Vlekke's survey of the East Indies provided the core of information, but did almost nothing to introduce me to an Indonesian viewpoint. I read uncritically in various portions of Stapel's large five volumes and dabbled in Colenbrander's colonial history. I even tried De Kat Angelino's magnum opus, with results that can be imagined. Without background and guidance I struggled through much of Ph. Kleintjes's account of the political/administrative structure of the Netherlands East Indies and gained, I think, some sense of how the colony was managed. None of this seemed to help me in focussing on my research interest. Therefore, it was with great excitement that I heard about and finally obtained a copy of J. Th. Petrus Blumberger's study of the nationalist movement in the Netherlands East Indies. This book, followed later by some reading in his other two studies, was my first systematic exposure to materials that seemed relevant to my research interest. By the time I finished the Blumberger volume my knowledge of events in Indonesia in the early twentieth century had increased enormously as I learned about organizations, people, and events which until then had been largely bypassed in my reading. Also by the time I finished Blumberger I knew that there was work to be done and that I could make a contribution by carrying the unfolding of the Indonesian nationalist movement beyond a recitation of platforms, meetings, and resolutions into the realm of human involvement in a process of cultural change. This new sense of direction has never, however, led me to deprecate Blumberger for his obvious shortcomings. This is partly due to a sense of gratitude for his having opened new windows for me and partly because he was reflecting his station and viewpoint in the environment of the 1930s and could not possibly have known what I did in 1950 about Indonesian nationalism.

The research period 1951-52 in the Netherlands and Indonesia was spent chiefly in talking with persons who had some involvement in the events of the early twentieth century in Indonesia. The use of interviews, developed through my anthropology studies at Cornell University, was made necessary by the paucity of written sources – at least such sources were not known to me or were not available at the time. The persons I talked with were kind and helpful. In addition to telling me about their careers and their feelings (as they recalled them thirty or forty years after the event), they would frequently call my attention to pamphlets or government reports – the latter frequently in their personal possession – that I had not before known about. Mr. A. K. Pringgodigdo even told me about his book on the nationalist movement which was then just published. Between interviews I read as much as I could and sometimes was able to probe more deeply on second or third meeting as I became familiar with the details of particular happenings; this was especially true with Abdoel Moeis and Haji Agus Salim, both of whom were able to recount their past involvements with verve and drama. The real pitfalls for me in such an excursion into oral history became fully evident only when I was back in Ithaca, New York, composing my book. How often I wished to be able to ask just one more question to clarify some point or other.

Early in 1953 with notes from readings and interviews in hand and with lots of ideas buzzing in my head, I was back at Cornell University ready to begin writing. The notion of organizing the material through time periods, as the book is currently arranged, seemed the most logical way to order the materials I had. Since there seemed to be some obvious transitions in the nature of Indonesian organizational developments and in Dutch colonial policy, this type of organization seemed simplest. In thinking through the material, however, I had come to conceptualize a number of thematic changes and developments which I came to view as more important than the short term transitions. However, since these themes were also broadly chronological, I decided to weave them into the shorter term transitions even though this required occasional repetitions and summations as each theme was moved forward.

A number of thematic changes struck me as important, though I was not as well informed on all of them as I would have liked. The changing role of Islam at various levels in Indonesian society was an obvious theme of importance, but I was sharply conscious of my limited insight into and understanding of many of the details. The growth and adaptation of Marxist-Leninist concepts in Indonesian society was another theme that I had to generalize about, but for which I had had only limited exposure. The role of the Chinese community in Indonesia as a factor in stimulating change was readily recognizable to me, but again I had difficulty penetrating beneath the surface phenomena. These themes all have a place in the book but have happily been much expanded and elaborated by later scholars.

Two other themes, about which I felt much more secure on the basis of the materials I had available to me (and which I felt to be of utmost importance), were developed with greater assurance. The first of these themes concerns the expansion of Western-style education for Indonesians. While the number of Indonesians exposed to modern style education remained small, it was quite evident that those Indonesians who rose to administrative posts and who took a leading part in nationalist organizations had virtually all been exposed to some amount of this education. The second theme dealt with the socio-economic background of those Indonesians whom I came to refer to as the functional (administrative) and political (nationalist) elite. They derived, it seemed to me, not from the very highest social classes in Indonesia, but instead from groups just below that level, what one might call the lower level of the upper class, and occasionally from upper middle class status. Their status came to be achieved rather than ascribed, and the road to achievement lay through education. It seems to me, some twenty-five years after the publication of the book, that these two themes are still valid and account for the continued usefulness of this book for students.

The delay in publishing the book was due to a number of factors, chief amoung which was my own feeling of inadequacies in the first set of thematic approaches noted above. Largely due to the encouragement of Prof. dr. W. F. Wertheim and Prof. mr. F. M. baron van Asbeck, both of whom had aided and encouraged me over the years, I submitted the manuscript to W. van Hoeve, Ltd., which was in the 1950s and 60s involved in publishing a number of substantial books on Indonesia. In slightly revised form my doctoral dissertation appeared in print.

By the time the book appeared in 1960, I had already shifted my personal research interest to changes in nineteenth-century Indonesia – a time span that still occupies most of my research time. One of my greatest pleasures, however, has been to witness the expansion of knowledge and growth of understanding of the period covered by the book, namely the early twentieth century. It was my fondest hope that others would improve upon, add to, and shed more light on various subjects which I had touched upon in the book but was not able to handle in the fullest and most competent fashion. This has happened – and certainly would have happened if the book had never been written – but since it was written it influenced, for better or worse, the designs and conceptions of many later researchers.

A number of studies appeared which have expanded and improved upon various of the book's themes and descriptive narratives. Ruth T. McVey's examination of early Indonesian Communism provides details and insights which were not known to me, thereby making available a fuller picture of developments in this area. Deliar Noer's study of the growth of Islam in the twentieth century does what I was not able to do at the time in explicating the backgrounds and changes to various streams in Indonesian Islam. Akira Nagazumi's detailed investigation into the early Budi Utomo added detail and depth to what I had been able to write about this organization. Two biographies of Sukarno added much to the period covered by the book, since these are Sukarno's early years; I refer, of course, to the books of Bernhard Dahm and John Legge. Both these authors with consummate skill bring cultural detail to a biographical study so that the spirit of an individual is shown against the background of his time and place. Sartono Kartodirdjo's studies of peasant movements provide insights into the local aspects of the Sarekat Islam movement which I had sensed but was unable to document in the way he has. E. Locher-Scholten, in a recent work on the Ethical Policy has redressed some of my exuberances by reminding us that this was essentially a Dutch policy in which impact on Indonesians was somewhat incidental.

The above mentioning of various works is little more than a

sampling of the numerous studies, books, and articles, which have appeared since 1960, that broaden our understanding of the events of the early twentieth century in Indonesia. People, organizations, and events that were only dimly perceived in the 1950s are now rolled off the tongues of graduate students as if they were household words. Movements and changes in Indonesian history which were gingerly explored in the 1950s are now apparently well enough understood to form the empirical base for the testing of abstruse theories and methodologies. Indonesian studies throughout the world and especially in Indonesia have made great advances in the past quarter century and will, I expect, continue to do so. It is exciting and satisfying to be part of such an enterprise. It is to the future of scholarship in the area of Indonesian studies that I dedicate the re-issue of this book for whatever it may still be able to contribute in the way of stimulation and example.

R. V. N.

Honolulu, October 1984

BIBLIOGRAPHY

Colenbrander, H.T., *Koloniale geschiedenis.* 3 volumes. 's-Gravenhage: Nijhoff, 1925–1926.

Dahm, Bernhard, *Sukarnos Kampf um Indonesiens Unabhängigkeit.* Kiel: Christian-Albrechts-Universität, 1964.

Furnivall, J. S., *Netherlands India; A study of plural economy.* Cambridge: University Press, 1939.

Kat Angelino, A. D. A. de, *Staatkundig beleid en bestuurszorg in Nederlandsch-Indië.* 2 volumes. 's-Gravenhage: Nijhoff, 1929–1930.

Kleintjes, Ph., *Staatsinstellingen van Nederlandsch-Indië.* 2 volumes. Amsterdam: J. H. de Bussy, 1932–1933 (6th ed.).

Legge, J. D., *Sukarno; A political biography.* London: Allan Lane The Penguin Press, 1972.

Locher-Scholten, Elsbeth, *Ethiek in fragmenten; Vijf studies over koloniaal denken en doen van Nederlanders in de Indonesische archipel 1877–1942.* Utrecht: HES, 1981.

McVey, Ruth T., *The rise of Indonesian communism*. Ithaca, New York: Cornell University Press, 1965.

Nagazumi, Akira, *The dawn of Indonesian nationalism; The early years of the Budi Utomo, 1908–1918*. Tokyo: Institute of Developing Economies, 1972.

Noer, Deliar, *The modernist Muslim movement in Indonesia 1900–1942*. Singapore/London: Oxford University Press, 1973.

Petrus Blumberger, J. Th., *De Nationalistische beweging in Nederlandsch-Indië*. Haarlem: Tjeenk Willink, 1931.

—, *De Communistische beweging in Nederlandsch-Indië*. Haarlem: Tjeenk Willink, 1935 (2nd revised ed.).

—, *De Indo-Europeesche beweging in Nederlandsch-Indië*. Haarlem: Tjeenk Willink, 1939.

Pringgodigdo, A. K., *Sedjarah pergerakan rakjat Indonesia*. Djakarta: Pustaka Rakjat, 1950.

Sartono Kartodirdjo, *Protest movements in rural Java; A study of agrarian unrest in the nineteenth and early twentieth centuries*. Singapore/London: Oxford University Press, 1973.

Stapel, W. F., (ed.), *Geschiedenis van Nederlandsch-Indië*. 5 volumes. Amsterdam: Uitgeversmaatschappij "Joost van den Vondel", 1938–1940.

Vlekke, B. H. M., *The story of the Dutch East Indies*. Cambridge, Mass.: Harvard University Press, 1946.

FOREWORD

This book is essentially a revised version of my doctoral dissertation *Development of the Indonesian Elite in the Early Twentieth Century*, Cornell University, Ithaca, New York, 1954. No effort has been made to incorporate or cite new materials bearing upon this general topic which have appeared since 1954, or to add to the footnoting by citing additional older materials, for it was felt this could go on almost indefinitely and would delay publication into the unforeseeable future. Instead the revision has taken the form of eliminating material which did not seem to bear directly upon the argument, and of reducing repetition. Three studies published since 1954 have made me feel more certain of some of my conclusions and analyses. The material from these studies has not been incorporated into this book since their relationship is tangential, but their presence has permitted me to proceed with less trepidation into the publication of this work on which I personally continue to entertain certain questions of interpretation and analysis. These studies are: C. Geertz, *The Social Context of Economic Change: an Indonesian Case Study* (Center for International Studies, Massachusetts Institute of Technology, 1956); R. M. Koentjaraningrat, *A Preliminary Description of the Javanese Kinship System* (Yale University Southeast Asia Studies, 1957); and Leslie H. Palmier, *Status Groups in Java, Indonesia* (A Thesis submitted for the degree of Ph. D. in the University of London, 1956).

This study is not and was never meant to be an exhaustive study of Indonesian history during the first quarter of the twentieth century. It is rather an interpretation based on wide reading of generally available primary and secondary works, and a careful analysis and evaluation of certain unique sources of information such as conversations with numerous Indonesians and Hollanders during the years 1951 through 1953, and the archive of the late Count J. P. van Limburg Stirum. My main interest in preparing this work was methodological. Traditional colonial history has failed to meet a need of our time and has understandably fallen upon evil days. The historian has reacted by abdicating the function of explaining change in colonial societies to the behavioral scientist whose concepts and methods of analysis do not equip him to function as a historian. As a result no new colonial history has emerged. This work is an attempt to fill that gap.

I am greatly indebted to many persons in Indonesia, The Netherlands, and the United States for sharing their impressions and ideas with me and for giving generously of their time. Since many of these persons have asked to remain anonymous I shall not mention any names here. Some of my conversations with Indonesians are mentioned in footnotes because their views are not available in other forms, while the Hollanders and Americans are not so mentioned because it was usually possible to cite printed materials to substantiate their points of view. All these persons will know who they are, and will, I hope, accept my appreciation of their assistance even though I do not mention their names. Special thanks must be extended to Professor Dr. W. F. Wertheim of the University of Amsterdam and Professor Mr. F. M. baron van Asbeck of the University of Leiden whose encouragement has been a great stimulation throughout. They have both been most generous in offering suggestions, and indicating points of disagreement. Wherever possible I have followed their suggestions, but I have not always felt it possible to do so, and as a consequence they are in no way responsible for the content of this book.

For financial assistance at various phases of the research, writing and publication of this book I wish to thank The Social Science Research Council, the Cornell University Southeast Asia Program, and Russell Sage College. None of these institutions shares any responsibility for the content of this book — this, for better or worse, resides solely with the author. Permission to publish materials from the Ministry of Overseas Territories in The Hague has been graciously extended by Mr. J. Rombach, the Chief of the Minister's Cabinet. The Van Limburg Stirum archive was made available by permission of Jonkheer A. C. D. de Graeff and permission to publish from it was given by Jonkheer W. J. van Sminia. To all who have assisted in the completion of this study the author wishes to express his sincerest gratitude and thanks.

R.V.N.

Troy, New York
October 1958

Contents

INTRODUCTION

The first quarter of the 20th century witnessed an unprecedented growth and development of Indonesia or, as it was then called, Netherlands India. Not all aspects of this growth are treated in this book. The emphasis here is upon social change within this period, and most specifically social change among the leader group of Indonesian society. Indonesian society during this period is one segment of what I have chosen to call East Indian society. This latter would include all persons living in the Indonesian archipelago which, in addition to the Indonesians who were the most numerous, includes Europeans (mostly Dutch), Chinese, and Arabs. Because Indonesians gained political independence in 1949 and created an independent state, this study concentrates upon *their* social and political development. During the years covered by this study the leaders of Indonesian society were not the leaders of East Indian society, for the entire Indonesian population was in a subordinate colonial relationship to the Dutch. Indonesian social development, therefore, occurred in the context of a colonial situation and was strongly influenced by colonial policies, practices and attitudes of the Dutch. This book is an effort to analyze and interpret these colonial policies, practices and attitudes and show their effects upon Indonesian society while at the same time to analyze and interpret the dynamics of Indonesian society with specific emphasis upon the elite of that society.

Glancing beyond the limits of this book to the present-day, it would not be inappropriate to contend that the changes in leadership patterns in Indonesian society during the first quarter of the century formed the social foundation for political independence some years later. Within the scope of this study it can be said that the general course of Indonesian elite development was from a traditional, cosmologically oriented, hereditary elite to a modern, welfare-state oriented, education-based elite. This modern elite is far more heterogeneous than the traditional, but little effort has been made to produce a structural analysis of the modern elite here. Mention is made of administrators, civil servants, technicians, professional men and intellectuals, but in final instance the main distinction made here is between a functional and a political elite. With functional elite is meant those leaders who served, past and present, to keep a modernized state and society functioning, while with political elite is meant those Indonesians who engaged in political activities directed toward various ends but usually involving some alteration of the political *status quo*. The former group served a greater social function through acting as the medium of change than is often realized, while the latter were of more symbolic than practical significance during the period covered by this book.

The expression 'Indonesian elite' may be somewhat misleading. Technically speaking there was no unit known as Indonesia in either a political or a social sense during the years encompassed by this study. Nor were all parts of the East Indian or Indonesian archipelago of equal importance in the developments with which this study deals. As a matter of fact, the island of Java, with its neighbour Madura, henceforth collectively referred to as just 'Java', was the unquestioned focal point of East Indian activity. Not only was Java the political, administrative, and economic center for Netherlands India, but it was also the population center of the archipelago with about 70% of the total number of inhabitants. Most of the people on Java belonged to the Javanese ethnic group who reside mostly in central and eastern Java. In 1900 there were about seventeen million Javanese. But there are other large ethnic groups on Java too: the Sundanese of West Java numbered around seven million at the beginning of the century, and the Madurese of Madura and East Java numbered about three million. In addition to these major components of the population of Java, there were scatterings of other Indonesian peoples from other islands of the archipelago. The upshot of all this is namely that the term 'Indonesian elite' refers to a Java-centered elite composed of various Indonesian peoples – but principally Javanese. This study makes no effort to include social developments of the other parts of Indonesian archipelago during this period whether they be of a similar or of a contrasting nature. Java, and the social developments that occurred there are of primary importance in the emergence of modern Indonesian society, and shall be a primary focus of this study.

The organization of this study is first chronological, and second, topical. The first chapter sketches some of the basic features of East Indian life in 1900. With this as a jumping off point the next three chapters carry developments of change forward in time to 1914, to 1920, and finally to about 1927. The major points of analysis and interpretation are reiterated and developed throughout the study to such a degree that a concluding statement seemed unnecessary. Each chapter has been divided into a few subheadings which, as will soon appear obvious, are only vaguely descriptive and are not intended to serve as descriptive titles of content. The index at the end of this book is recommended as the surest guide for finding scattered points of information.

Chapter I

EAST INDIAN SOCIETY IN 1900

The Europeans

In 1900 Java was a principal part of the Dutch colonial empire. Ultimate control over Java and other parts of the empire had resided, since the middle of the nineteenth century, in the hands of the Netherlands' parliament, or States General, as it is called. Practical control over colonial affairs was in the hands of the Minister of Colonies who was one member of a cabinet responsible for its actions to the States General. The Minister of Colonies carried out the general colonial policy of the government. This general colonial policy was formulated, since mid-century, by public opinion as expressed through the States General. This general policy was relatively constant and was not basically altered by changes of cabinet or parliament. The Minister of Colonies was responsible for implementing the general colonial policy in a fashion compatible with the colonial aims of his party and any other parties included in the cabinet. To assist him in this task he had a Colonial office or a Ministry of Colonies in The Hague in which many persons with colonial experience were employed. These persons were often able to influence the decisions of the Minister of Colonies.

Political parties in the Netherlands were anything but indifferent to colonial affairs. Each political party had its colonial experts, usually men with experience in the colonies, who formulated the party's colonial program and defended it in the parliament and in the press. The colonial program of many parties about 1900 bore little relationship to their position within the political spectrum of domestic politics. Virtually all parties were agreed on a humanizing reorientation of colonial policy at this time, but there were differences on means and methods of applying this new orientation. The most far reaching in their desire for alterations in the colonial policy were the socialists and the conservatives – both of whom had come to regard the prevailing liberal ideology with distrust.[1] In 1900 no political party advocated a termination of the colonial tie between Java and the Netherlands.

By 1900 the Dutch had been on Java for about 300 years. During this time they had tried only a few long term policies in regulating their relationship to the bulk of the island's inhabitants. Basic to each approach toward the colonial relationship was a desire to keep regulation as indirect as possible and an implicit understanding that the relationship must be as profitable as possible for the Netherlands. The Dutch East India Company (1602–1798) had assumed sovereignty over most of Java in order to protect its commercial and mercantile position. The company's chief interest lay in obtaining and exporting and selling certain basic commodities grown on Java. Political and administrative control was ancillary to this major interest, and consequently assumed an indirect form which almost bordered on indifference. During the Napoleonic Wars the Dutch lost control of Java to the English for a few years, and when they regained control of the island in 1816 they discovered that a new system of monetary land tax and more direct administrative control had been instituted. The Dutch attempted to continue the former and to modify the latter, but this makeshift system proved incapable of producing revenue to meet the unusual expenses of war on Java and war with Belgium. In order to raise more revenue the Forced Cultivation System (*Cultuur Stelsel*) was introduced in 1830. This system reverted to taxation in selected produce. This produce was to be grown and partly processed by Indonesians under the supervision of their own administrators and under the watchful eye of European civil servants. The produce from this controlled system was to be delivered to the government in lieu of monetary taxes. During the first decade of operation this system raised great amounts of revenue for the motherland, but during the early 1840's certain unfortunate occurrences within Indonesian society connected with the impact of the system came to light. When the King of the Netherlands lost his personal control of colonial affairs to the States General in 1848, a gradual review of who was making money and how it was being made on Java began to take place.

The Forced Cultivation System collapsed during the 1860's under the weight of internal corruption, under the pressures placed upon it by private business and commercial interests who had grown politically powerful in the Netherlands, and under the ambitions of European entrepreneurs on Java who wished to terminate governmental land control so they might make individual fortunes. The economic rationale was supplied by the dwindling revenues from the system, and the moralistic rationale appeared in the form of illiberal treatment of the Indonesian people whose energies had made the system work. The parliamentary speeches of Baron van Hoëvell and the writings of E. Douwes Dekker (Multatuli) which were directed against various aspects of the system found great response among the people of the Netherlands.[2] During the 1860's the government allowed private enterprise to enter the island of Java. In order to avoid economic chaos or collapse, the Forced Cultivation System was dismembered slowly: by 1870 the major products and plantations had been placed in the hands of private entrepreneurs, but the last vestiges of the system were not swept away until 1917.[3]

After about 1870 the policy of the Dutch government toward Java comes to be known as the Liberal Policy. Under this policy the island (and eventually the entire archipelago) was opened to the penetration of private capital. The wealth of Java was now no longer to flow into the coffers of the government, but instead was to benefit the Dutch middle class who had now also come to control the political process in the Netherlands. From 1870 to 1900 private entrepreneurs made and lost fortunes in Java. Those who were successful became financially powerful – those who failed often became managers for the successful. The economic fortunes in Java were such that by 1900 most enterprises on the island were owned or managed by a nucleus of corporations and banks in Europe. These financial interests exerted great, though not exclusive influence, upon Dutch colonial policy and practice.[4]

The Liberal Policy of the Dutch government toward Java also had a strong humanitarian impulse. After 1870 measures were taken to protect the Indonesian peasant against the full impact of a free functioning money economy.[5] Indonesian landholding was protected against foreign acquisition; a leasehold arrangement was the most that was permitted to non-Indonesian interests.[6] The European civil administration in Java now showed an increasing concern for the welfare of the people of the island. Yet, despite these safeguards, the prosperity of the Indonesian people seemed to be declining, and it was feared that Javanese social solidarity would be affected. Both humanitarian and financial interests were concerned by the decreasing welfare of the Javanese: the former, because of the inability to rectify social and economic injustices; the latter, because of the growing need for markets for produced consumer goods. As early as 1874 the conservative (Anti-Revolutionary Party) statesman, A. Kuyper, was speaking in the States General of a humanized capitalism which would fulfill a moral obligation to the peoples of the East Indies.[8] This urge toward a new orientation of the existing policy grew not only in the motherland, but in the European sector of East Indian society as well.

After 1870 the composition of the European community in Java began to change. This change was largely the result of the rapidly increasing numbers of private citizens introduced into an area that had previously been the exclusive preserve of government civil servants and administrators.[8] The new group of Europeans, working either for themselves or for corporations, began to create for themselves in Java another type of life than had existed under a society made up of government employees. Urban centers became not only commercial centers, but came to be centers of European society as well. Better educated and middle class Europeans brought their Western way of life with them, creating a microcosm of the West in the urban centers of Java. About 1900 European women began to arrive in Java, and from that date forward European society grew more exclusive with regard to other ethnic groups in Java.[9] European society on Java now came to have a new internal solidarity of its own, and also came to have ideas about regulating its own internal affairs on Java and about the colonial policy of the motherland.

The European community on Java was not only concerned about the diminishing welfare of the Indonesian people, but was also greatly irked by the completely centralized control of the government over Europeans in Java. The newly emerging European society wanted to regulate its own internal affairs and demanded from the government a greater degree of financial autonomy and local self government. This demand was principally viewed in terms of the European community on Java, but it was only a short step to envisioning similar rights for Indonesians who through heightened prosperity and increased education would eventually be placed on the road to self government. In 1888, P. Brooshooft, editor of the Semarang newspaper *De Locomotief*, openly voiced the desire for greater local autonomy and improved conditions for the indigenous peoples of the East Indies in an open letter to a number of influential Netherlanders.[10] This started a series of articles against the economic liberalism of the prevailing colonial policy which was culminated in 1899 by C. T. van Deventer's famous article on the 'Honor Debt.'[11] This article called upon the Netherlands to make a financial settlement upon the needy colony as partial recompense for the fortunes that had been withdrawn from Java under the Forced Cultivation System. As of 1900 Van Deventer estimated the sum involved slightly under two hundred million guilders. Attacks on the government were also occurring within the States General where the colonial authority for the Social Democratic Party, H. H. van Kol, took the lead in harassing the government on matters of colonial policy and practice.[12]

From this widespread dissatisfaction with the prevailing policy a new orientation emerged after 1900. This new orientation in the colonial relationship was called the Ethical Policy. It found wide acceptance among all groups, for while continuing to advocate development of the colony by private capital, it also sought to increase prosperity and welfare and to extend autonomy. Such a policy contained something for persons of virtually every political inclination. In addition, the Ethical Policy would also provide the Netherlands with an irreproachable colonial policy toward the East Indies. This was sorely needed, for some foreign powers, viewing the desultory conflict in Atjeh (North Sumatra) which had been going on without decision since 1874, were wondering about the application to other areas of the rule of 'effective occupation' which the Berlin Convention of 1885 had established with regard to African claims.[13] The Ethical Policy would provide the Netherlands with a proper moralistic foundation from which to ward off any foreign claims. The greatest advantage of the Ethical Policy, however, was its ability to inspire Hollanders toward a more glorious colonial future in Java while also opening the way for Indonesians to share in the glory of their own future.

The government which controlled affairs on Java in 1900 and against which the European community on Java was raising its claims for autonomy, was the Netherlands Indian government. It was indeed a centralized government with ultimate control residing in a governor general who stood at the head of an administrative hierarchy which branched down into the local districts. This government had been designed to deal with and control Indonesian society; by default it had for the past couple of decades been obliged to control the newly emerging European society of the urban centers on Java. The administrative corps of the Netherlands Indian government probably had no serious objection to granting autonomy to local communities who were in democratic fashion able to provide for their own needs. Soon after 1900 the legal basis to make this possible was provided (see below, p. 42). The administrative corps for its part was principally concerned with Indonesians, even though its members were part of the European social group and, as such, subject to pressures and influences from that group.

The governor general who stood at the head of the Netherlands

Indian government was appointed by the Crown upon recommendation of the Minister of Colonies. A governor general normally served a five year term though this was not legally prescribed and might be shortened or extended as the situation seemed to warrant. The governor general was responsible to the Crown for the implementation of colonial policy on the spot: he was the supreme authority in the colony. In practice, of course, he was expected to follow the instructions of the Minister of Colonies from The Hague, but his advice as the man on the scene helped in turn to shape these instructions. In actuality his position was an extremely powerful one, for the distance from the motherland allowed him great freedom of initiative. His power, just as that of all administrators, was dependent upon the assistance and cooperation of others — he could not personally supervise all activities. That a governor general was sometimes sheltered from the stark realities of events by subordinates or was subtly influenced and pressured by close associates is probably true. In general, however, most of them managed to have a fairly accurate picture of the state of affairs within the colony. This does not mean they always accomplished everything they wished.

Next to the governor general was a high ranking advisory body known as the Council of the Indies. The governor general was president of this council *ex officio*, but his relationship to its members was that of *primus inter pares*. The Council of the Indies was composed for the most part of high ranking civil administrators with lengthy colonial experience. The degree of reliance the governor general placed upon the Council varied with individual cases.

In general by 1900 it can be said that the Council of the Indies was losing power and importance while the governor general's General Secretariat gained correspondingly. The burgeoning governmental tasks after 1870 found the monolithic Netherlands Indian government ill prepared to deal with them. The first, and for many years only, functioning bureau of the government was the General Secretariat. All correspondence, reports, requests for interviews, orders, legislation and official suggestions directed

to or from the governor general passed through this body. By
1900 it had interjected itself between the governor general and
all his relationships in and out of the government. It was generally
regarded at this time as the most powerful organ of the government.[14] Gradually as departments of government were created
it acted as coordinating agent for the work of these departments.
Not until after the First World War when the creation of the
Volksraad (People's Council) made frequent oral contact between the governor general and the chiefs of departments imperative, did the power of the General Secretariat decrease.

Conducting the actual operation of the functions of state in 1900
were various departments of the government. Each department
had its chief, its staff employees, advisers, and clerks. The great
majority of the persons were Europeans (many were Indo-Europeans); few were Indonesians. In 1900 the departments of the
Netherlands Indian government were: Finance, Internal Administration (which controlled the administrative corps and police), Public Works, Education, Religion and Industry, Justice,
Military Affairs, and Naval Affairs.

Administering the island of Java and forming the sinews of the
colonial government was the European administrative corps.
Since earliest times the Dutch control of the Indonesian population had been based on a concept of indirect rule. The Dutch
were merely to act as advisers, as big brothers if you wish, to the
Indonesian administrators who functioned within the pattern of
the traditional hierarchy.[15] In practice this theory was more
ignored than applied.[16] In order to fulfill the growing demands
of the government upon Indonesians during the 19th century the
European civil administrators had to assume ever more power
and deal ever more directly with the masses of the people.[17] By
1900 the European administrative corps was wielding almost
absolute power throughout Java, over both Europeans and Indonesians.[18]

The enlargement of power of the European administration was
accompanied by a change in the nature of the corps.[19] The Netherlands Indian administration no longer came to be a refuge

for European social outcasts and adventurers, but instead came to be staffed by well-educated sons of substantial middle class European families.[20] These men were eager to advance and assist the welfare of the Indonesian people, and just because of this were often unable to tolerate the indifference and lack of enlightenment on the part of their Indonesian counterparts.[21] The government adviser, C. Snouck Hurgronje (of whom more later) envisioned a solution to this dilemma by providing Indonesians with good Western education so they might extract from Western culture the virtues which would enable them to assume the responsibilities and duties of European administrators. Gradually the Europeans would be entirely withdrawn and an enlightened Indonesian administration would run the country. This notion ran head on into the newly emerging sense of exclusiveness in European society on Java, and also failed to fit in with the increasing amount of governmental concern with the details of Indonesian life after 1900. The growing concern of the European administrators in protecting and shielding the Indonesian common people led to innumerable clashes with the European financial and entrepreneurial interests on Java. These interests began to use their political power to curb the operations and limit the authority of the European administrators. The twentieth century was to witness a gradual diminution of the power of both the European and Indonesian civil administrative corps.

In 1900 there were about 70,000 Europeans on Java. Probably only about one quarter of these were full blood Europeans who had been born in Europe and made their way out to Java. Yet this one quarter contained most of the businessmen and entrepreneurs, most of the representatives of financial interests, and most of the European civil administrators. These were for the most part the people who were voicing grievances and complaints against the government and its practices. With the exception of a few Japanese who had been granted equal status with Europeans in 1899, the remainder, or about 75 %, of the European community on Java was made up of Indo-Europeans or Eurasians. The fifty-odd thousand Eurasians regarded as part of the

European community were certainly not all persons with part European blood on Java. Many Eurasians had been absorbed into the Indonesian population and no longer regarded themselves as European.[22]

The general social and economic position of the Eurasian part of the European community was far from good in 1900. True, some whose fathers had taken an interest in them and provided them with some education had obtained clerical and technical posts with government bureaus and departments or had become artisans and craftsmen in the urban centers. Those so fortunate might be said to make up the middle levels of the European community. But many others, probably the majority in 1900, had been ignored by their European fathers, had been unable to adjust to their inter-cultural position, and had found the government unwilling to do anything for them as a group.[23] These Eurasians had drifted onto the peripheries of Indonesian life where their constant identification with European status, despite their degraded position, prohibited an adjustment. These people became the flotsam of East Indian society. About 1900 the plight of this group was more openly recognized by humanitarian Europeans. Organizations such as the Masons and the Order of Eastern Star and Christian mission groups began to take an interest in the poorer Eurasians. Vocational and technical training schools were started to permit these persons to develop a skill which would enable them to fit into the European community. During the 20th century the Eurasians' situation gradually improved.

In summary, the European community on Java was far from homogeneous, yet there was an apparent striving toward a common cultural base. The common ground toward which increasing numbers of Europeans on Java moved was the common denominator of middle-class European social tastes. Such a common ground, while neither especially good nor markedly evil, did provide a certain solidarity and sense of standards for Europeans removed from their home environment but always envisioning an eventual return to the land of their forefathers. But this social solidarity had the disadvantage of enforcing a marked gulf with the Indonesian community. Even the European civil administrator and plantation manager, through improved communications, could have frequent contact with the urbanized European social milieu. No longer did the European live among the Indonesians on the Indonesian standard as had frequently been the case earlier.[24] This social solidarity sometimes also had the effect of reducing mass sentiments of the Europeans toward the Indonesians to the lowest common denominator. Often little interested in Indonesian life, and finding contact with that life only through household help or hired employees, many of the Europeans developed a certain fear through ignorance of the Indonesian and his ways. Paradoxically enough, those who knew least were often the ones to shout the loudest that they knew the Indonesian, and that his ways were treacherous and deceitful. Naturally not all Europeans believed this — many knew better. But the insecurity within the European community was great enough that sentiments against the native peoples were easily encouraged — rumors, gossip, and petty incidents aggravated all this — until it was impossible for wiser counsels to prevail. A large part of the European community on Java did not hold the Indonesian and his way of life in high regard.

The Chinese and Arabs

Before proceeding to a description of Indonesian society it is necessary to say just a brief word about two other groups within East Indian society, namely the Chinese and the Arabs. Both these groups, like the European, sought to make their livelihood by and through the Indonesians.

The Chinese are the largest non-Indonesian group on Java. In 1900 they numbered about 280,000.[25] Their complex position and situation are not easily summarized, and since they are only peripheral to this study no attempt will be made to do so. Suffice it to say, that they are generally regarded as more 'business-like' than the Indonesians and apply themselves with a directness and zeal that enabled them early to dominate the vast majority of the intermediate positions in the economic structure of the archipelago.[26] By 1900 most of the Chinese on Java were descended from families that had been on the island for generations. Despite this, they continued to look to their former homeland as a source of culture. About 1900, partly stimulated by the recently improved position of the Japanese on Java and partly stimulated by awakening interest by individuals in China in the overseas Chinese, they began to demand certain improvements in their status on Java. Their demands provided a stimulus for some of the latent forces in Indonesian society.

The Arabs, as the term is generally applied on Java, are more than just people from Arabia. Arab is loosely used to describe anyone from the Near and Middle East as well as Indian Moslems. In 1900 there were slightly more than 18,000 Arabs on Java.[27] Most of these Arabs were small business men, merchants, and money lenders — just like the Chinese. Their chief advantage over their Chinese competitors stemmed from their Islamic religious ties with the Indonesian people. The Arabs were known in Indonesia as zealous disciples of the Prophet, and although many of them might have regarded Indonesian Islam as an eclectic faith, they were not above using it when their advantage seemed served thereby.[28]

The Indonesians

Indonesians, in 1900 and also today, recognize two levels in their society. The great masses of agrarian workers, villagers, and townsmen are regarded as the common people. The administrators, civil servants, and better educated and better situated Indonesians in both town and countryside are known as the elite or *prijaji*. Technically a nobility also exists as a separate group, but the Indonesian often includes them rather loosely under the prijaji heading. The prijaji thus corresponds to the group we shall call the elite; to the Indonesian this would mean anyone standing above the great common masses who in some degree or form leads, influences, administers, or guides Indonesian society. Each of these levels of Indonesian society has internal divisions and differentiations, but each is also a self-recognized entity.[29]

About 98 % of the Javanese people belong to the group of the common people. For almost 90 % of these the village determines and is the way of life.[30] The village is the root of the traditional Indonesian life pattern, and it is difficult to overestimate its influence upon the great masses in 1900. The Indonesian village not only controls the basic commodity of livelihood — land, but also regulates tastes and styles, maintains the traditional moral order, provides for the spiritual and religious aspects of its members' lives, cares for its members in times of stress and crisis, and ties each member to the group in a bond of communal solidarity. This communal bond forms the basis of Indonesian society.[31]

The village is socially stratified on the basis of landholding. Control of the land is an essential village function.[32] Landholding on Java assumes different forms in different parts of the island. Western Java has mostly individual landholding, while central and eastern Java have predominantly a system of communal landholding though individual holdings are also known.[33] In no instance, however, is the land held in free dispositional ownership as is known in the West.[34] The individual's rights are almost always circumscribed by community regulations.[35] Despite this fact, the rights to land are usually quite clear, and as long as a family subscribes to the village regulations and continues to exercise its rights to the land, the land will be passed on within that family. A voice in village affairs, an obligation to perform village services, and a higher social status within the village all accompany landholding rights.[36]

The villagers who hold land, especially a piece of wet rice field or *sawah*, are considered the nuclear villagers and are by tradition regarded as the descendents of the founding father and oldest inhabitants of the village. These landholders will also own a house with garden. They are generally the wealthiest villagers. This reinforces their higher status in the village. The village headman, the village administration, and oftentimes the village teachers and religious leaders will all come from this group. They may cultivate their own land or they may rent out this privilege to tenants, but the prestige that goes with landholding remains with the nuclear village group.

Of lower status are those villagers who do not hold a piece of agricultural land, but own only a house and garden. These people either work in nearby industries, or engage in a handicraft, or work the land of others, or do all of these. Traditionally these people are believed to have descended from families who moved to the village after the original inhabitants had settled the area.[37] Many of these families may have been in a village for many generations without acquiring landholding privileges and obligations. Their position within the village is often a respected one, however, and they may be consulted in village affairs when the village elders are seeking a consensus of opinion on some particular matter. Upon the default for any reason of one of the traditional landholding families, it is possible that one of the non-landholding families be moved upward into the group of landholders. The Forced Cultivation which the Dutch applied in parts of Java from 1830 to about 1870 is said to have exerted such strong pressures upon the services of the landholding group in certain localities that they incorporated most of the non-landholders into the inner councils of the village, sharing the land with them and distributing the required work over more hands.[38] This system seems also to have influenced the incidence of communal landholding in central and east Java, and by so doing encouraged an egalitarianism within the village. However that may be, by 1900 there were non-landholding villagers to be found in all parts of Java, and most villages were conscious of a social stratification based on landholding rights.

Lowest on the village social ladder are those people who hold no land and who own neither house nor garden. They build their shelter in someone else's yard and usually work, either as house servant or field laborer, for the person in whose yard they live. This group may have had its origin in the Javanese system of slave holding which was abolished during the 19th century, or in other instances it may have been derived from migratory groups which seem to have been ever present on Java. Whatever the origin, this non-landholding group was the lowest element in the Indonesian social order.

In the regulation of its social and economic life the village has in large measure been a closed, self-determining unit. Its chief purpose has been to provide for its own wants and needs. For many centuries, however, the villages of Java have also had to produce for higher authority. A portion of the village produce served to maintain the higher authorities or was used as a commodity for export. This produce the village passed upward in the form of tribute or rent. It was rent in the sense that Indonesians strongly feel that ultimate ownership of the land resides not with the village but with higher authority, and they are consequently paying for the privilege of using the land. It was tribute in the sense that higher authority was regarded as the preserver and maintainer of the universal, cosmological order, and as such had to maintain the balance in life and prevent calamity. But perhaps even more important than these, the produce which the village passed upward was payment to be left alone in the regulation of its own internal matters, for above all else the village wanted to live its own life and to maintain its own internal harmony.[39]

The person most responsible, in the eyes of the villagers, for maintaining the village inviolate was the village headman. He served as the link between the village and the higher authority. Neither the historical evolution nor the power position of the headman's office has been uniform: variation can easily be found. In general, however, it can be said that the headman is a powerful individual within his limited world. In part his power stems from his membership in one of the nuclear village families, and in part from his intermediary role between village and higher authority. But in largest part his power derives from his mainte-nance of the traditions and way of life of the village, the *adat*, and from his role in maintaining a consensus and a harmony within the village. In all he does he must protect the rights and way of life of the village, and in so far as possible ward off all influences and pressures which might disturb the village harmony.[40]

The headman has not always been successful, however, in keeping the Indonesian village free from outside influence. Higher Indonesian authorities have from time to time exerted very direct pressure and influence upon villages within their domain, and the Dutch colonial authorities had often after 1800 tried to manipulate village affairs. Particularly during the period of the Forced Cultivation System the headman had been drawn more intimately into the process of Western enterprise. After 1870 government compulsion upon village headmen waned, but individual entrepreneurs now sought the headman's hold in gaining land rights or labor contracts from the villagers. It can in general be said that by 1900 Western influence had penetrated Indonesian society down to the village, and had in many instances made the village headman a cog in the Western economic and administrative process. The individual villager had not yet been drawn into these processes on a personal basis.[41]

It has frequently been pointed out that the inclusion of the headman in the Western economic and administrative process had the effect of reducing his dependence upon the support and good will of his fellow villagers. This removal of the headman's dependence upon his traditional power base, it is felt, permitted him to abuse the authority of his office and to assume the role of a small tyrant. That such abuses did occur is beyond question. There are instances of some villages electing incompetents to the headman post in order to reduce the threat of an overly-meddlesome chief, and there are other instances of villagers being exploited by a headman seeking to enrich himself at their expense.[42] Unfortunately there is no indication of the extent of these abuses. In all likelihood they were exceptions rather than a general rule, for the headman must live too intimately with his fellow villagers to risk continuously transgressing against the adat. Most villages probably carried on as usual and the headman remained a power-ful influence, but an influence working for the village. There is no convincing evidence that Indonesian villages were by 1900 being torn apart by outside interference or internal strife.

This is not to say that there were not violent village outbursts on rare occasion both before and after 1900, for these are endemic to Indonesian life. These outbursts or uprisings are usually localized and uncoordinated. They stem from a combination of fears and frustrations stimulated by natural and social problems.[43] Repeated transgressions against the accepted and established order in the village may simply cause villagers to pack up and leave. But these same transgressions under other circumstances, when perhaps combined with natural phenomena such as floods or volcanic eruptions, may lead to a violent outburst against constituted authority. Although irrational in purpose and design, such outbursts virtually never occur without a leader. Leadership takes the form of an individual who, in the name of the Islamic messiah or in the name of the *ratu adil* (proverbial prince whose coming will herald a better life for all), will direct the forces of discontent against some concrete objective such as the local ad-ministration.[44] Such uprisings are not in the main stream of In-donesian religious life, but they come in practice to be associated with a religious-like mystical experience which is not far removed from the daily religious view of the common man.

In 1900 the common people of Java were overwhelmingly Mos-lem. Islam had been superimposed upon a Buddhistic-Hinduistic base which in turn only loosely covered a foundation of spiritual-animistic beliefs developed in early Indonesian society. Islam in Indonesia was quite different from Islam in the Middle East. Indonesian Islam was deeply impregnated with mystical concepts and had made rather sweeping adjustments in order to conform to the existing religious patterns of the Indonesian people.[45] To the Indonesian people, however, who knew nothing of their deviations from the original faith, Islam, as they practiced it, was considered a pure and a good religion and way of life.[46]

Within each village were religious teachers who were viewed as the local religious authority. These teachers had been trained in Koranic schools scattered about Java and might in addition have made the pilgrimage to Mecca. In general they were not well educated but were often possessed of much religious zeal. Oftentimes their zealousness brought them into conflict with the secular authority of the village headman or the supra-village administration.[47] The usual function of the religious teachers of the village was to tend the mosque, if there was one in the village, and to educate the village children. This education consisted of teaching the children to recite the Koran in Arabic, which neither teacher nor pupil understood, and of imparting a few basic rules of the religion.[48] This was the only formal education available to the great masses of the Indonesian people around 1900.

In addition to the religious teachers, each village usually had a number of persons who had made the pilgrimage or *hadj* to Mecca in order to obtain religious merit. Before 1870 relatively few Indonesians had completed this pilgrimage for the trip was arduous and only the most zealous managed it. But after the opening of the Suez Canal, European steamship lines to and from Java passed near the Moslem holyland and consequently the journey became easier for Indonesian pilgrims. Now anyone who had the passage price and the inclination might obtain a high mark of religious devotion by completing the hadj.[49] The result, as might be expected, was that the economically more affluent villagers were able to make the pilgrimage, returning to Indonesia and to their village with the title of *hadji*. This title in itself indicates only the successful completion of the pilgrimage and does not imply any special religious learning, but in general the hadji was especially devout, and was looked up to by his fellow villagers. Thus it came to pass that Islamic religious merit began to reinforce the better situated elements in Indonesian village society. These same elements were often the very ones who felt most strongly the pressures from the colonial government, and it is quite understandable that they should seek comfort and unity in Islam which in Indonesia seemed most distinctly to separate the brown man from the white.

Indonesian Islam about 1900 was undergoing internal struggles and changes. The traditional religious teachers (known as the orthodox group) who had taught the mystical, eclectic type of Islamic faith common to Java, were being challenged by purists and progressives who had been stimulated by doctrines emanating from Egypt and the Middle East. These Reformists, as they were called, had essentially two major aims. First they wanted to rejuvenate Islam so it would not succumb before the Western advances in science and learning.[50] They proposed to do this by restudying basic Islamic doctrines and interpretations to make it possible for Moslems to move in new directions. They were convinced there was no incompatibility between modern science and the true faith.[51] Second they wanted to purify Islam and to increase the zealousness of its adherents. This in the case of Indonesia called for the removal of mystical and pre-Islamic practices which had such a strong hold on the orthodox Indonesian Moslems.[52] In some places, such as the Minangkabau area of the west coast of Sumatra, the concept of a purified and reformed religion gained a foothold at about the turn of the century,[53] but in most areas it was firmly squelched by the orthodox, home-trained religious teachers who saw in reformism only a threat to their own position. Faint internal stirrings were beginning to occur in Indonesian life, however, as a result of this religious difference.[54]

The majority of Indonesians who lived in the growing urban centers were also part of the common people. Here too there was social stratification, but instead of being based on land or wealth it was based on the individual's nearness to symbols of power and authority. The house servants of leading European and Indonesian families were regarded as the highest level for it was believed they somehow shared in the prestige and success of their employer. Next highest were those persons who worked for a government agency, regardless of their position. Lower on the scale were those Indonesians who had small private businesses or enterprises. Most of them had suffered economic decline during the 19th century and were looking toward reviving Islamic sentiments to raise both their economic position and social status. At the bottom of the heap were day laborers, migrant workers, coolies and peddlers who lived from day to day.

All these urban dwellers were, to greater or lesser degree, torn out of the context of their traditional Indonesian life pattern. They lived in native quarters in which life was anything but Western, yet also lacked the coherence, harmony and solidarity of village life. They lived on the fringes of Western culture, for the cities were creations of the West and were maintained by Western commerce and enterprise, and they adopted many of the superficial aspects of the Western way.[55] This urban group was one source of a new Indonesian social phenomenon, the marginal man; at best an imitator of Western ways, but more than likely unable to orient to the new, and equally unable to return to the old.[56] From the lower elements of this urban society a proletarian mass gradually emerged.[57] Here grew the mob so feared by the European and so pampered by the irresponsible demagogue. Here was the element ready to harken to the cry of the agitator, but always melting before the symbols of authority.[58]

Above the common people of Indonesia stood the prijaji or elite. Less than two percent of the total Indonesian population, they had attempted to maintain homogeneity and purity of blood by following a rigid system of social identification. By 1900 this restrictiveness, for various reasons, had broken down. It is wisest not to attempt to identify the prijaji by either exclusiveness of customs or purity of blood. In practice the most usable criterion for distinguishing the prijaji is social function — they provided cohesion to Javanese society above the local level and provided the intellectual, cultural and cosmological basis of Indonesian society. In a word, they fulfilled the functions of an elite.

In 1900 the prijaji, if we exclude the nobles whose functions were very restricted and generally became even more so, consisted principally of administrators. These were the people who were and had been running the country under the Dutch civil administration. But the prijaji in 1900 were a changing group, for within its ranks were increasing numbers of civil servants and individuals who might best be classed as intellectuals and professional men. A certain number of such persons had always existed, but about 1900 they were coming to be somewhat more Western in their education and training and in their conception of service to state and society. These divisions within the prijaji group are far from clear-cut and are not in any sense exclusive. It is thus not only conceivable but highly probable that a single individual might fall in more than one of these categories. It would not be unusual for an administrator also to possess the qualities of an intellectual, or a civil servant to be both an intellectual and professional man.

Since the prijaji were changing, and since this change will become a dominant theme in all that is to follow, the present description will focus on what the prijaji had been and what they had become by about 1900. It has sometimes been assumed that all the prijaji of Java are descended from kings. This is not true, for in times past powerful vassals or successful adventurers were able to assert political control over parts of Java and assume the role of prijaji for the inhabitants. The titles of rank such as 'Raden' or 'Raden Mas' came in time to be associated with certain administrative posts rather than with pure lineal descent from an ancient noble family. It is true that the nobility at the princely courts of Jogjakarta and Surakarta remained honorary heads of all the prijaji in a cosmological sense, but it is also true that by 1900 much of the cosmological aura had evaporated for many of the prijaji. They had for generations been accustomed to look to the Dutch colonial government as the actual source of political power.[59]

The Dutch East India Company during the 17th and 18th centuries had extended its direct control over most of Java. There was no attempt made to displace the local Indonesian authorities as long as they proved cooperative with the new regime. The Dutch East India Company assumed a position above the prijaji and expected that the tribute which had always moved upward through the Indonesian administrative system would now simply move one step further upward into their hands. This tribute for the Dutch took the form of forced delivery of commercial products which they in turn sold on the world market. The Indonesian administration in turn found itself more and more supported by the armed might of the Company. Some of them felt no longer dependent upon the goodwill of the Indonesian people and began to abuse their powerful position by making personal gain at the expense of their countrymen. Before 1800 the Dutch, with occasional exceptions, remained indifferent to these internal Indonesian matters.

After 1800 this indifference to local politics on the part of the Dutch, and also the English who controlled the island from 1811 to 1816, began to change. A twofold purpose motivated this change: first, the abuses of power by some of the prijaji had become so flagrant that widespread suffering among the common people occurred; second the colonial government hoped to deal more directly with the masses of Indonesians by replacing the tribute system with a direct monetary land tax. An attempt was made to disengage a number of the prijaji from the administrative system, and to increase contact between the colonial government and the village. For various reasons this plan proved unsuccessful in practice.[60] In 1830, under pressure of falling colonial revenue, a new colonial policy was initiated.

The Forced Cultivation System *(Cultuur Stelsel)* was introduced in 1830. Among other changes, it put the prijaji back into the administrative hierarchy in a form somewhat reminiscent of the East India Company days. Now, however, the prijaji were expected to operate in a much more rationalized, bureaucratic fashion, and their primary function was made the supervision of the production of selected crops. Dutch administrators were interspersed among the prijaji to keep an eye on the controlled operation of this new tribute-passing economy. This is the formal beginning of the type of supervised, indirect rule which saw a Dutch adviser next to each of the higher ranks of the Indonesian administration. The Dutch government tried to make it appear as if the prijaji were reinstated to their old authority and even went so far as to give guarantees of hereditary rights, but in reality they had been extracted spiritually and concretely out of the feudalistic, Javanese cosmos and placed within a rudimentary form of modern administrative state. The life of the prijaji was more affected by the West than any other Indonesian group. Changes among the prijaji were gradual and uneven for there was no pervasive uniform system that controlled change. Daily contacts and conversations between prijaji and European administrators, daily observation of European customs and styles, and elemental education in European schools and homes were the media through which change was wrought. Individual circumstances and personalities determined the receptiveness and speed of this process.

The removal of the Forced Cultivation System and the introduction of private capitalist enterprise during the 1860's led to further changes in the position of the Indonesian prijaji. For one thing the administration became more rationalized and the indirect control of the Dutch advisers became more formalized. A regular promotional hierarchy for both European and Indonesian administrators was established. The young Indonesian prijaji began his official career as a *mantri*, an office which might involve secretarial or police duties at the local level. Then assuming all went well he would become a *Sten Wedana* (Subdistrict head), *Wedana* (district head), and finally *Bupatih* or Regent who headed an area known as a Regency. In 1900 there were somewhat over eighty Regencies on Java. The European advisers were known as *Contrôleur* at the district and subdistrict level, Assistant Resident at the Regency level, and Resident at the Residency level which included two or more Regencies. This rationalization of the administration was accompanied by a change in function from plantation supervisors to efficient humanitarian administrators. This change in function obviously required a change in training and education of the prijaji.

The Dutch government developed an interest in education for Indonesians about the middle of the 19th century.[61] A few Indonesians selected from the highest elements of society were permitted to attend European primary schools which had existed on exclusively Java since 1816. In 1848 money was set aside for the first Javanese schools. These schools were designed to train scribes and administrators and drew their students exclusively from those prijaji families whose hereditary rights made them eligible for such positions.[62] These schools were far from sufficient and the practice of bringing young prijaji into the homes of Europeans to be trained in European traditions and manners continued. Some European families took this responsibility seriously, but others regarded the Indonesian as incapable of assimilating formal education and treated him as merely another servant about the house.[63] If the young prijaji learned anything at all it was to be discreet and to cater obediently to the will of his European master.[64] In 1879 the Hoofdenschoolen or Chiefs' Schools were established.[65] These were specifically designed to train the sons of Regents for administrative posts. Although an improvement over the earlier school forms, and far preferable from an efficiency viewpoint to the local Moslem schools, they were qualitatively and quantitatively far from adequate.

The changing position of the Indonesian administration may possibly have had the effect of pulling its roots out of Indonesian society and drawing it toward the West.[66] Actually it is easy to exaggerate the amount of change that had occurred among the prijaji by 1900. Certainly outward forms had changed for some, and a few were deeply affected by the West. But most Indonesian administrators continued to regulate their private lives on traditional patterns and make their adjustments to the West outwardly.[67] It is doubtful, despite the efforts of the colonial government in the late 19th century to reduce the signs of prestige and symbols of office of the Indonesian administration, that the common people of Indonesia noticed much difference in their administrators by 1900. Where these changes and alterations *were* noticed, however, was among members of the lesser prijaji families who themselves aspired to the top administrative posts. Here among the lesser prijaji were persons willing and anxious to take advantage of the social change within the administration to improve their own status. More than any other group, the lesser prijaji came forward to challenge the prestige and power position of the higher prijaji.

These lesser prijaji consisted for the most part of younger sons and near relatives of the Indonesian administrators and nobles. In times past, these persons would have looked forward to gaining a foothold in the administrative hierarchy either through force or through natural displacement. The guarantee of hereditary rights given the higher prijaji by the Dutch, and the more settled conditions prevailing under the *pax Neerlandica* of the 19th century, appreciably limited these opportunities. At the same time the phenomenal population growth on Java during the 19th century increased the number of prijaji, but did relatively little toward increasing the number of available administrative posts. These lesser prijaji were reluctant to seek work outside the government since government service carried the highest prestige in Indonesian society. Force of circumstances, however, compelled them to look outside the positions of the traditional administrative hierarchy. An expanding governmental service outside the traditional hierarchy for which education would serve as the key for entry was to become the answer to their dilemma.

In 1851 the colonial government established a teachers' training school to supply teaching personnel for the Javanese schools which had been started just a few years earlier. In the same year the expanding government health and hygiene program sought to solve its need for semi-skilled medical workers by setting up the so called 'Dokter-djawa' School for training vaccinators.[68] The position of teachers and vaccinators was not initially regarded as of much consequence in the Javanese social structure.[69] Sons of the higher prijaji did not aspire to these positions, and the government had to dredge up students from elsewhere with such stimulants as scholarships and promises of governmental status. Many of the students for these schools came from lesser prijaji situations, and some even came from merchant and village families.[70] These semi-professional schools underwent various changes during the 19th century which in general tended to increase the content of the education offered.[71] By the end of the century this type of education had produced the prototype of the civil servant and intellectual of the 20th century. Also by the end of the century most of these persons were coming to be viewed as prijaji of some standing by the common people of Indonesia, even though they were often not descended from the higher prijaji families. Their position of service within the expanding governmental structure entitled them to be included within the elite group of Indonesian society. A few Indonesians, either trained in these semi-professional schools or educated in one of the growing number of missionary schools, even began to seek entry into some of the bureaus and technical services of the central government where Eurasians and Europeans predominated. Throughout the 20th century the expanding governmental services would seek people with formal Western training to fill posts within the rationalized bureaucratic structure. Educated Indonesians who filled these posts would automatically be drawn into the prijaji or elite category — most of them, however, were already of prijaji status and were seeking to improve their position within the prijaji group. For some the prijaji classification might have lost all meaning as they became imbued with ideals of service to state and people, but this group probably remained a minority during the early twentieth century, and most were interested in the personal and social prestige attached to their new bureaucratic role.

When the first vaccinators and teachers went out to work, their position was often ambiguous. Their education and training were often superior to that of the Indonesian administrator under whom both tradition and the bureaucratized government had placed them.[72] Small wonder that the European administration often sought to deal directly with them and to bypass the Indonesian administrator. How natural that they should be the group most sensitive to the dwindling stature of the administrators of the higher prijaji group. A feeling of growing resentment often characterized their attitude toward their nominal superiors of the higher prijaji.[73]

A desire to rectify the deteriorating position of the Indonesian administrator in the eyes of his European colleague and his better educated Indonesian brethern, underlay the plans and proposals of Dr. C. Snouck Hurgronje, who since 1891 had been an adviser to the Netherlands Indian government.[74] Snouck Hurgronje's idea was to make the best in European culture available to Indonesians through an extensive educational program. This he felt would create among Indonesians a sense of enlightened self-interest which would enable them to understand what Western culture could do for them. Through this 'association' of Indonesians with European culture, a self-stimulating, efficient and progressive Indonesian society loyal to the motherland was to emerge. Since the plan was too extensive for full and immediate application, it was to begin by providing the Indonesian administrators with better educations.

In 1893 the government took a moderate step in this direction by revamping Indonesian primary education. This education had failed to meet the needs of either the young administrators of the future or the entrants to the semiprofessional schools. To meet these needs and at the same time fulfill the desire of a small but growing number of the common people (particularly in towns and cities) for a basic secular schooling, the government created two types of Indonesian primary schools. These schools were known as the First Class Native Schools and the Second Class Native Schools.[75] In both schools instruction was to be given in the indigenous language, but here the similarity ended. The First Class Native Schools were intended for sons of the prijaji and students going on to the semiprofessional schools. Here the course of instruction was longer, the teachers better trained (usually they were graduates of the teachers' training school), and a wider curriculum was offered. The Second Class Native Schools offered a rudimentary course of primary instruction which was designed to do little more than meet the fundamental needs of a basically literate society. By the end of the 19th century neither of these schools had found its way into the villages of Indonesia.

Chapter II

The Acceleration of Change, 1900–1914

The Ethical Colonial Policy in Theory and in Practice

In the Netherlands the vital issues of the Ethical Colonial Policy seemed to be less concerned with humanitarian and moral principles, upon which practically everyone was agreed, than with financial arrangements between motherland and colony. Van Deventer's debt of honor had envisioned not only support for the needy colony but had also called for separation between metropolitan and colonial finances. This latter issue met opposition more on method than on principle. With H. van Kol, the colonial authority for the Social Democrats pushing from within the parliament,[1] and Van Deventer, who upon his return to Holland in 1897 had joined the Radical Democrat Party, exerting pressure from the outside, the East Indies was finally relieved from its share in the Netherlands' national debt in 1903. This was, of course, only one facet of the new policy, yet an important one, for money was the key to its implementation.[2] The following year, 1904, the financial position of the East Indies was somewhat improved when the motherland granted a credit of forty million guilders — this was a much watered-down honor payment — in order to cancel some of the colony's debts.

The elections of 1901 changed the political picture in the Netherlands. The Liberal Party which had controlled politics for fifty years found itself out of power. Concern with the pocketbook (the Liberals had undertaken social projects), and with religion (the last half of the 19th century had been devoted to maintaining a religious neutrality), had brought to power a coalition of rightist and religious groups which were determined to return to Christian principles of government. Van Deventer, the man of liberal optimism, had not been elected to a seat in the parliament and had to continue working from the outside: he was able to make his influence felt. The annual message from the throne in September 1901 reflected the Christian spirit as the Queen spoke of an "ethical obligation and moral responsibility to the peoples of the East Indies." The message went on to express concern over the depressed economic condition of the East Indies and asked that a commission be formed to investigate this matter. From this is dated the Ethical Colonial Policy.[3]

Life was breathed into the motherland's handling of the new policy when in September 1902 A. W. F. Idenburg assumed the post of Minister of Colonies which had been left vacant by the death of T. A. J. van Asch van Wijk. Idenburg, a military officer recently returned from the East, had shown himself to be a staunch supporter of the Christian parties, but had taken a moderate attitude toward the expansion of mission work in the colony. He faced difficult problems. Crop failure and famine in several districts of Java called for immediate action and also necessitated explanation to the Social Democrat Van Kol, who had visited the stricken areas and based his concept of Javanese prosperity on what he had seen there. Immediate measures of relief were taken, but the Minister was far more concerned with what could be done to prevent a recurrence of such disasters. Idenburg pointed out that,

> During the past twenty years the population (of Java) has increased by 45 percent while the area of sawah land increased only 23 percent (productivity 28 percent).... The average production per person is thus declining. The number of farmers who do not own their own land is increasing. The number of persons seeking their livelihood in other fields of endeavor is increasing, but their average income is declining. All these facts justify the conclusion... that Java is in a period of transition... from a pure agricultural community to one in which industry comes forward to take a place next to agriculture.
>
> And when one recognizes this fact as the general cause, then the direction in which one must seek general improvement is obvious.
>
> Under the first rubric of means one will then try to advance industry to the advantage of the native people.
>
> The second category concerns means for enlarging the productivity

of agriculture in general; that is, increasing and improving the irrigation works. My attention has been drawn to the trivial amount expended for this purpose during the past ten years. Further there must be more intensive cultivation and curtailment of agricultural usury through the extension of better agricultural credit. Where overpopulation seems to be the chief problem one's thoughts are automatically led in the direction of emigration.[4]

Minister Idenburg showed an acute awareness of the problems facing the East Indies in 1902, and although one may disagree with his analysis, his sincerity and willingness to face the problems cannot receive other than praise. Implementing these concepts was a slow procedure. The Indies needed money but many legislators objected in principle to an honor debt — far better to make a loan without interest. For the financial as well as the moral aspects of the new policy the speeches and writings of Van Deventer became a powerful motivating force.[5] He was able to popularize and eulogize his own thoughts and concepts as well as those of other men-of-good-will, thus creating a zeal and sense of mission which pervaded the new policy. With good cause Van Deventer has been called "the father of the Ethical movement."[6] He placed the welfare of the indigenous peoples above all else and was the most active antagonist of the poverty of Java which he blamed on exploitive practices by the Forced Cultivation System and sugar planters.[7]

When in 1904 Minister Idenburg wished further information about the reduced prosperity in Java he commissioned Van Deventer and other colonial experts; G. P. Rouffaer, E. B. Kielstra, and D. Fock (all men inspired by the Ethical principles) to draft for him a summary of the situation pending the more complete report by the commission working in Java on the matter.[8] The Van Deventer report which appeared in the same year did much to bring home to persons in the Netherlands the regression of the Javanese economy and living standards, and succeeded in quieting those voices which tended to minimize the situation.[9]

The report made proposals which the Minister was prepared to follow, but his best efforts did not gain the approval of the Liberals and Radical Democrats. Irrigation, agricultural credit, and emigration received attention, though not in the degree that the most advanced advocates of change wished. But the key to all change, education, was ignored. To Van Deventer and his followers there could be no improvement without adequately trained indigenous personnel to carry the burden. To Van Kol, the Ethically inspired but penniless Idenburg's best efforts were fruitless. Placing Dutch colonial policy before the 'Nemesis of History' and decrying the fact that 'the duty has been too heavy for us,' Van Kol was not beyond citing Mirabeau's famous words, "la misère, la hideuse misère est là et vous, vous déliberez,"[9a] in order to gain the financial support for the new policy. No one was quite certain what the great misery was, but the parliament was stampeded into extending credit to the colony.

Nineteenhundred and five was an election year, a year that placed Van Deventer and enough other Radical Democrats in parliament to take a major hand in cabinet formation. Now the Liberal D. Fock became Minister of Colonies — he stood prepared to advance and expand native education. It would take years to accomplish what was envisioned but the groundwork for the new policy had been laid in the Netherlands by 1905.

In the East Indies the opening years of the 20th century found men already at work advancing the spirit of the Ethical Policy. These men were not interested in the slogan-making which occupied the politicians in the motherland. During the 19th century some Hollanders had already been concerned with the welfare and status of the native. They had directed their personal efforts toward improving conditions. K. F. Holle (d. 1896) was a humanitarian with a true concern for the people of Java. Through his advice to the government and through his direct assistance in agriculture to the Sundanese people, he serves as an outstanding example of a number of administrators who gave their best efforts to improving the conditions of the land and people whom they had come to love. Another outstanding more scholarly example is the previously mentioned Moslem and Arabic authority, C. Snouck Hurgronje, who during the 1890's had gained an intimate knowledge of the life and customs of the people of Java. His value to the government as Adviser for Native and Arabic Affairs led to the creation of his post as a permanent office within the Netherlands Indian government.[10] Snouck Hurgronje's ideas were popularised at the University of Leiden where he became a professor (1906). His students and disciples continued to advise the government on native affairs throughout the 20th century. His concept of educating the native elite in the best Western traditions had a far-reaching influence on Indonesian society where many of his protégés became leading figures (see below, p. 47).

Another who assumed initiative was the Assistant Resident of Purwokerto, W. P. D. de Wolff van Westerrode (d. 1904) who, building upon the work of his predecessor in office, laid the organizational foundation for local Savings, Loan, and Agricultural Credit Banks to relieve the usurious debts under which the villagers struggled.[11] His work formed the basis for a government credit system which would soon come into being (see below, p. 73).

Often termed the first Ethicus in practice was J. H. Abendanon, in 1900 made Director of Education in the East Indies, who with the help of his wife stimulated a self-awareness among young Indonesians. The young Abdoel Moeis, later to be one of the leaders of the Sarekat Islam organization, was one of the intellectual coterie which met in the Abendanon home in Batavia.[12] This same atmosphere stimulated the correspondence of the daughter of the Regent of Japara, Raden Adjeng Kartini.

This correspondence, reflecting the first glimmerings of Indonesian women's emancipation, ultimately led to the creation of girls' schools. These schools produced Western educated young women who shared a changing social life with the educated Indonesian male elite. Probably no man was so sincerely motivated by a love for the Indonesian people as was Abendanon. His thinking was too advanced for many of his fellow Hollanders, however, and in 1904 he was reassigned to the motherland.[14] Although his wings were clipped, he continued to befriend Indonesians studying in the Netherlands, guiding and helping them in many ways.[15] Here have been mentioned but a few of the persons inspired by the true spirit of implementing the material and spiritual advancement of the Indonesian people. F. Fokkens,[16] P. H. Fromberg,[17] and others could also be mentioned, but enough has been said in illustration of those humanitarians who needed no official policy to stimulate them towards new goals for the peoples of the archipelago.

The journalistic message for the Ethical spirit in the East Indies was carried by P. Brooshooft, editor of *De Locomotief*. *De Locomotief*, a Semarang daily, was owned by and spoke for the East Indian importers. Under the guidance of Brooshooft and his successor, J. E. Stokvis, this newspaper became the leading tribunal of the Ethical Movement. Writing in 1901 Brooshooft showed acute insight into the realities of the world and the nature of the Ethical Policy when he deplored the theatricals of politicians. He aptly said that "The real spirit that must typify the Ethical Course is a true sense of justice — the feeling that we give the Javanese, who is dependent on us against his will, the best that we have for him — the noble spirit of the stronger to handle the weaker with justice."[18]

Had ethical and humanitarian ideals been the sole criterion for a follower of the Ethical Policy, it would be relatively simple to evaluate the sincerity of individuals and the effectiveness of measures. But these ideals form only a general framework within which politics were conducted, and are therefore insufficient to explain the deep-seated differences which arose under the new policy. The greatest differences in meaning and intention which arose under the Ethical Policy resulted from inherent consequences of applying the policy within the existing East Indian social framework. These differences can best be illustrated by the misunderstandings surrounding three words frequently used to describe East Indian social relationships: 'unification,' 'association.' and 'assimilation.'

The term 'unification' came originally out of the legal world. Prior to 1900 it was used to describe attempts of jurists to cull all ordinances and laws from various parts of the East Indies that were related to one particular matter and affected one particular part of the society into one category. After 1900 the meaning of 'unification' altered. Henceforth it came to refer to the attempts to unite the legal systems and legislation for all parts of the East Indian society into one code. Specifically this would embody a unity based upon the principles of European (Dutch) law. Thus the judicial system would become one, the judges would sit for all parts of the society, and there would be a single codified law for all residents of the East Indies. This new understanding of unification was no longer limited to the legal world, but came now to include other facets of the social relationship. The advocates of unification advanced this unity concept in relation to the civil service, education and taxation. What they envisioned was the disappearance of all discrimination within the East Indian social order. Their ideal was to see all duality disappear from the archipelago. Many of the staunchest advocates of this policy were convinced that all that separated Indonesians from Europeans was education and superstition.

The terms 'assimilation' and 'association' also have legal connotations and are in a very real sense subheadings of the term 'unification'. Unification by assimilation would be unity on a European basis as described above. Unification by association implies unity only in so far as this could occur naturally, preferring diversification as long as unity would only be of special benefit to one group.[18a] Both these terms have wider meanings, however, and are employed to refer to cultural problems. Here 'assimilation' refers to a displacement of Indonesian culture by the culture of the motherland through administering, educating, and legislating the colony as if it were an integral part of the motherland with all inhabitants equal in all respects. 'Association', on the other hand, while wishing to make the metropolitan culture available to the colonial peoples for their future prosperity and well-being, implies a strong inclination to respect the indigenous culture and an unwillingness to force change.

From the above definitions it will already be obvious that there could be many variations of opinion. All believers in unification, assimilation, and/or association, considered themselves integral parts of the Ethical Movement. Yet it was exactly here, on these points, that those persons who were not completely convinced of the wisdom of the Ethical Movement and yet could not find it in their hearts to think or speak of themselves as non-ethical, formed opposition.[19] It was far easier to oppose unification, for instance, than the good intention of raising indigenous prosperity. It would be no trick to show that 'assimilation' was not desired by the little man of Indonesia; it almost certainly was not. One could become the spokesman for the little man, could resist change as fiercely as he, could lament the destruction of his integrated life, and could in this manner oppose other parts of the Ethical Movement.

The determination of a criterion for anti-Ethical sentiments is not that easy, however, for many very sincere Ethici were concerned with the lot of the common man in Indonesia and did what they could to cushion the impact of the West upon his life (see below, p. 80). One must be careful not to garner all opponents of radical changes in village life among opponents of the Ethical Policy. Nor is it entirely possible to find one segment of society holding a completely divergent view with regard to the Ethical Movement. In general, however, the most active opposition came from the insecure and small European lower middle class, from the Indonesian-born Europeans (the *sinjo*), and from certain sectors of the Indo-European (Eurasian) group.[20] Concepts of racial superiority were most prevalent among these groups and usually account for an unwillingness to consider unification.

To most well-intentioned men, however, the differences resolved themselves into a matter of tempo of change rather than disagreement on principles.[21] Those who came to be regarded as 'Ethici' were pushers, they wanted to keep ahead of developments, they sought to stimulate, they were imbued with a dynamism, they were motivated by optimism and self-assurance. For the first two decades of the 20th century they set the pace. No one policy or measure is as significant to the Ethical Policy as is this spirit and *elan* which seized its leading proponents and infected many others. "But how glorious is the aim that we pursue! It is: the formation out there in the Far East of a social entity which is indebted to the Netherlands for its prosperity and higher Culture, and thankfully recognizes this fact." (C. T. van Deventer).

Others were less certain that this goal could be attained, or at least favored a more gradual policy. It would perhaps be best not to push matters, for "man glaubt zu schieben und wird geschoben" — far better to move slowly in this weighty matter of Western impact and acculturation. Close contact with the realities of the daily colonial situation was enough to bring many men around to this latter point of view. The pushers, the intense men, slowly gyrated into the upper spheres of government in both motherland and colony. From on high their decretals drifted down to the men who stood squeezed between reality and theory: here the discrepancy between fact and fiction became ever greater.[22]

Indication has already been given (see above, pp. 7 & 9) of the economic motivation behind the Ethical Policy. In a word, it was in the best interests of European (Dutch) manufacturers, importers, and entrepreneurs to carry through many of the aims of the Ethical Policy. Certainly there was not complete agreement among all sectors of the economic and financial world on all aspects of the new policy, but in general they were astute enough to realize that heightened prosperity on Java would be to their advantage. The Ethical Policy also continued to include private capital in the plans for the development of Indonesia.

As a result of this economic aspect of the Ethical Policy, men with strong Marxist convictions have viewed the entire policy as a capitalist-imperialist trick.[23] As economic determinists, they have felt that everything proposed and implemented by the Dutch government was for the benefit of the financial and capitalistic interests of the Netherlands. They viewed the Ethical Policy as only another means of keeping the Indonesian people economically servile, culturally sterile, and politically stupid. These ideas began to gain a certain response from dissatisfied or disoriented persons in Indonesian society.

Chief target for these economic determinists was the sugar planters who seemed to have the most direct and most insalubrious influence upon Indonesian society round and about their factories. During the first decade of the 20th century, following upon the decision of the Brussels Convention of 1903 to remove protection from European-produced beet root sugar, sugar plantations and sugar exports became of increasing importance for the Netherlands Indies.[24] Next to the tin calf a confectionary calf now stood, and many were the followers of the new idol. Powerful representatives of the sugar industry were able to gain concessions and resolve grievances where smaller entrepreneurs of an earlier day had been powerless. The economic determinists cried that the Ethical Policy had sold out to the vast revenues provided by the sugar industry, but the information presented by the other side — sugar — raised considerable doubt as to the absolute validity of the critique.[25] The sugar question, like scores of similar disagreements, came to be a relative matter; so much depended upon what one understood by 'good,' 'progress,' 'dualism' and other such terms.[26] Complaints against the sugar industry diminished until after the First World War, but other issues were continually at hand to receive the abuse of those who for one reason or another were opposed to the colonial relationship.

The most consistent airing of complaints against the existing state of affairs came from the European part of East Indian society. In the twentieth century this came to resemble ever more closely the society of the motherland. The latest thoughts and ideas of the West came to be felt in the colony and all phases of Western thought came to have some representation in the colony. After 1900 one can find support for almost any opinion in the writings and utterances of some member of the European segment of East Indian society. It is, of course, not possible to determine with statistical accuracy what effect this change in the European part of East Indian society had upon the Indonesian section of that society, and particularly upon those Indonesians who stood in close relationship to the West, but the influence must have been exceedingly great — much greater than is generally recognized. Within the opinions and expressions of European society are found the essence of practically every grievance, complaint, and demand expressed by Indonesians in the course of the 20th century.[27]

In order to implement change and to institute more efficient methods of government a primary consideration is effective control over the existing organs of control within a given area. At the beginning of the 20th century the Dutch had such control on Java and Madura but only in small scattered enclaves on some of the other islands. Most of the native rulers, sultans, chiefs, and other potentates, of the 'Outer regions' had been loosely bound to the Netherlands by 'long contracts' which had left them free to regulate their own affairs with the exception of those powers which the Dutch had specifically claimed for themselves.[28] Dutch control outside of Java was ill-defined.[29] With increased interest in colonial expansion among the European powers, with a heightened desire to bring the benefits of the West to the native peoples, and with Western economic penetration into many of these loosely controlled areas, a need for more effective controls became increasingly apparent.[30]

Slowly at the beginning of the 20th century, and at an accelerated rate upon the termination of the organized struggle in Atjeh (ca. 1904) — 'pacification' operations in the area continued for some years — the Dutch began to re-negotiate their contracts with the Indonesian chiefs.[31] These new 'short contracts', as they were called, which sometimes were forced upon reluctant rulers, placed all power in the hands of the Dutch except for what they saw fit to delegate to the ruler.[32] In comparatively short time Dutch control of the outer islands became a legalistic reality which could stand international scrutiny. It was General J. B. van Heutsz, famed Atjeh fighter, who during the early years of his term as Governor General (1904–1909) was most active in extending and securing Dutch hegemony in the East Indies. His name was enough to throw the fear of God into any local chieftan who might resist re-negotiation. Where this was not the case, as on Bali, to cite one instance,[33] Dutch arms served as a strong persuasive factor.[34] After about 1904 one can realistically speak of the Netherlands East Indies as a geographical-political entity with territorial extension and political hegemony throughout the East Indian archipelago.[35] Modern Indonesia is a direct territorial continuation of this modern bureaucratic state created in the early twentieth century.

At the same moment that the Netherlands Indian government was drawing together its strings of power throughout the archipelago it had plans for decentralizing that power. Decentralization had been in the air for some years. Originating in the European colonial community, the desire for self-regulation of local affairs finally won the approval of politicians in the homeland. Here, as originally probably not intended, the concept was broadened in scope until its theory extended beyond any one segment of the society. The proposal was strongly advanced by D. Fock of the Liberal Party in 1901,[36] and in 1903 was harmoniously passed by the Parliament of the Netherlands.[37] Money was set aside by the central government for local affairs. Local councils were to have executive power over this money. Powers of the central government were distributed to lower administrative organs — not to the previously-existing bureaucratic organs — but to newly created local citizens' councils.[38]

With the Decentralization of 1903 a far reaching process was inaugurated which extended to many aspects of East Indian life. It is doubtful if the original proponents of the law were fully aware of the forces they released upon the East Indian scene. For instance, the modification of the laws which regulated political assemblage to allow gatherings of the local citizens' councils, also erased the legal barriers to the formation of other organizations of various form. The first councils were formed in the larger cities. Council membership was restricted by appointment and later by franchise limitations so that Europeans kept control.[39] However, councils were also created in districts and Regencies, and here Indonesian members predominated. Membership was, however, carefully regulated so that Indonesian civil servants and administrators were most generally seated on these councils.[40]

Despite this control, these councils served as political training grounds for many of the Indonesian elite and also managed to bring these Indonesians into closer contact with the methods, aspirations, and thought patterns of the West. They emphasized individuality and regarded questions of membership, jurisdiction and rights on a Western basis. The councils, it is true, had little contact with the masses, but this was not immediately intended. The important fact is that they were instrumental in stimulating a political awareness in the particularly Westernized and elite part of Indonesian society. Through and by means of these councils questions of autonomy, self-administration, and the removal of Western tutelage were brought to the fore and gained a growing number of interested followers.[41] Almost all members of the Indonesian elite came in increasing measure to have some feeling, be it ever so vague, on these political issues — issues which were raised because of and by means of these local councils, an institution of the West, desired by men of the West, and intended to serve primarily the formulators. Once again no accurate estimate can be made of the influence and extent of the thoughts and sentiments thus aroused, but it seems safe to say that the growing self-consciousness and inner awareness of the Indonesian elite was advanced by measures such as these.

These upper strata of Indonesian society which were most directly affected by the promises and apparently logical consequences of the decentralization procedure, were also the ones who were best able to see and feel the shortcomings of the process. Through their Westernized training they for the most part had had some contact with the liberal social philosophy of the West, and as marginal groups they came to feel rather early the bankruptcy of that system of Western thought. They could not help but notice the failure of the underlying principles of Western liberalism to apply to their own situation. As the European and Indonesian social groups grew further apart in daily contact and understanding, the colonial relationship assumed an ever growing dualistic character. Cries for assimilation and association were lost in the realities of a daily existence that could not be shorn of petty hatreds, insecurities, jealousies, and individual differences. The growing Indonesian elite began feeling more strongly that they were discriminated against: they resented what they were and what they had been, some grew humble and some grew bold, almost all found their situation somewhat less than satisfactory, but practically none had more than the vaguest notions of what might be done to alleviate these circumstances. For the most part they sought further strength in the institutions and methods of the West and the more these were denied them the greater was their frustration. They knew just enough of the West to view its culture with mystical awe and unconcealed hope; none of them were enough at home in the West to choose wisely and independently from the multitude of cultural courses that were offered them. All stood open to the wiles and dictates of clever leadership, a leadership which they felt could only be produced by the ways of the West. Against the actions and policies of the colonial government which had created them they gradually began to direct their resentments, but their goal remained an improvement of existing circumstances within the new realm which they were busily creating for themselves. Practically none of them envisaged a new life outside the confines of the existing system.

The effect of Decentralization was also felt by the European civil servants. True, it was here that it was meant to be felt, for power had been taken from the civil servants and either completely or partially dispensed to the councils. But the effect of this was somewhat different from what had been anticipated. The European civil administration had stood in close contact with the people, in some instances even closer than the indigenous administrative hierarchy, and had been viewed, as they had considered themselves, as protectors of the common people. With the advent of councils and establishment of specialized branches of government (see below, p. 72ff.), the virtually absolute power of the civil administration was curtailed. No longer were the Contrôleur and Assistant Resident able to exercise their protective influence as they had earlier.[42] The Indonesian villager, laid bare to influences he neither liked nor understood, turned to the administration for protection, but the civil administration could stand only helplessly by while newly created agencies attempted to deal with the problems of the masses. The situation worsened after 1904. The pressing need for European administrators brought persons into the service who were interested more in career and retirement than in actual service to the people. The result of transfer of power and growing professionalism was a gradual reduction in prestige of the European civil administrative corps.

The indigenous administrative corps which had become closely tied to the Western system of governing found itself moving in the same direction at an even more rapid rate than in the 19th century. The theory that the native administrators should be completely indoctrinated in the Western way of governing so that they could assume more responsibility in the regulation of Indonesian affairs remained the guiding theory, but practical considerations ruled this theory almost invalid. The increased concern of the government with the minute details of life and welfare of the Javanese people resulted in the activities of administration far outpacing the training that was afforded native administrators. The European administrator came to have ever less faith in his 'younger brother' as a medium for implementing a welfare policy. In a multitude of small things the native civil servant was made to feel inferior and incompetent — it is certainly not strange that he could not act with the zeal and inner motivation that resulted from an inspired humanitarianism and sense of progress which came so naturally to the men of the West.

It was indeed a dilemma for the government, for in advancing welfare and decentralization policies they had to limit the authority of the only group of persons in the archipelago upon whom they could count if matters went badly or got out of hand; namely, the corps of European and Indonesian administrators and civil servants. For almost a score of years the government wavered and tacked with seeming lack of absolute policy — now supporting their administrators, now pulling the rug out from under their feet. The high point (or low point depending upon one's point of view) came in 1913 when the government issued the famous *hormat* (honor, distinction) circular.[43] The purpose of the circular was to remove some of the last remaining vestiges of traditional prestige from the Regents and high-ranking Indonesian administrators. Thus a concession to the growing self-awareness and sense of individualism of the Western educated Indonesian *nouvelle élite* was naturally a further reduction in the prestige, and consequently also the power, of the native administration. But a further insight into the mood and confusion of the government is provided by the most interesting secret 'instructions' to the European administrators which accompanied the circular and which, like the main body of the circular, were soon common knowledge. The government pointed out in the secret instructions that the European administrators had in the past occasionally abused their powers, that this must stop, and further that they had not always been treating the native administrators with a respect that was due their high positions.[44] In such manners did the government weaken and lessen the prestige and power of its administrative corps.

The government, for its part, often felt that the administration had been blocking its best efforts to promote a wise native welfare policy. Undoubtedly there were conservative elements in the administration who had not been pushing the government's Ethical Policy with great enthusiasm, but the confused actions of the government which were motivated by a desire to please all groups and to be democratic to the point of stagnation only served to weaken the government's position in the eyes of all groups.[45] It was a futile attempt to be democratic in a situation that was at its foundation undemocratic; it was a condition beyond the scope of the Western liberal social philosophy and no solution could be found within the mental frame-of-reference of the well-intentioned Europeans in the government.

Indonesian Social Change

Despite the above noted discrepancies in the application of the welfare and reform measures embodied in the Ethical Policy, the underlying assumptions of unification and association continued and remained the hope of many of the Ethici for strengthening the entire colonial system.[46] These aims were advanced principally through increased and improved education for Indonesians. In 1900 the Chiefs' Schools were reorganized so that their curriculum would compare favorably with other secondary schools, being re-christened Schools for Training Native Administrators (o.s.v.i.a.).[47] Unfortunately since the other secondary schools underwent various reorganizations about the same time, the osvia found itself once again behind the others. Efforts continued to be made by the prijaji class to send their sons to European schools in the Indies so that they would learn Dutch and be in line for a better position in the government service.[48] Such tendencies were furthered by opening the European Primary Schools to Indonesians shortly after 1900 and by the efforts of some Europeans such as Snouck Hurgronje to get the sons of leading families into the European educational system and thus advance the association process.

Snouck was instrumental in winning over a part of the Bantem (West Java) aristocracy to Westernized education and was happily successful with his experimental pupil Achmad Djajadiningrat, later Regent of Serang and high government functionary, whom he helped into and through a European secondary school in Batavia.[49] At this time, early in the 20th century, the presence of an Indonesian at a European secondary school was rare, but this was soon to change.[50] Achmad's brother, Hoessein, also followed the path of Western education and was an even greater success for Snouck Hurgronje: Hoessein followed in the academic tradition of his mentor, finally completing his studies in literature and liberal arts at the University of Leiden.[51]

The process of developing Western-educated Javanese leaders at first met with a lack of cooperation and sometimes open resistance on the part of the Javanese parents. They feared the adverse effect this might have upon the social standing of their children and feared it might do them more harm than good. By 1906, however, the government had had greater opportunity to show its intentions and this resistance disappeared; after this date there is an increased and active desire on the part of the upper class Indonesians for Westernized education.[52] Even after the need for outside stimulation had waned, Snouck Hurgronje continued to take individual interest in the sons of some of the leading families. About 1906 he took the later Regent of Tjianjur and Bandung, Wiranatakusumah, out of his class in the OSVIA and sponsored him through the Dutch secondary school in Batavia which provided a better education. Unfortunately Wiranatakusumah never graduated because his interests in the occult and hypnotism consumed too much of his study time, but he did assume high office and became one of the leading figures in West Javanese life.[53]

For the young protégés of Snouck there were frequent gatherings at the mentor's home — the sons of Regents and Sultans assembled there. Although they were few in number they came to form a strong nucleus of Indonesians who were deeply inspired by a liberal social philosophy and as such took a major part in many of the developments in the East Indies during the colonial period. The personal interest and attention of Snouck Hurgronje served to bring his protégés rather strongly under the influence of Western culture. Snouck was not the only European who took this sort of personal interest in a group of Indonesians, The name of Abendanon has already been mentioned (see above, p. 35), and such names as Engelenberg, Van Lith, Hardeman, and others might be included, but they remained at all times a small group. From the point of view of the retention of the colonial ties this is unfortunate, for Europeans of this sort were long remembered and much respected by the Indonesians whom they helped to gain a deeper understanding of Western culture.

During the early years of the century some sons of nobles were able to study in the Netherlands. Especially the sons of the House of Paku Alam found their way into the European educational system. Birth was, of course, a leading factor in making this possible. The Paku Alam Study Fund and the assistance and stimulation received from the Free Masons helped make the possibility a reality. Pangeran (Prince) Notodirodjo, administrator of the House of Paku Alam from 1901 to 1907, was the motivator behind much of this. At the turn of the century, Koesoemo Joedo, of the Paku Alam House was already pursuing his studies for the higher civil service in Leiden (1900–1904).[54] He was soon followed by Notodirodjo's son, Noto Soeroto. The latter became an Indonesian poet and protagonist of an East Indian Commonwealth based upon the strength of a superior elite group, much as Plato had envisioned his Republic. At the same time, the son of the Regent of Japara (and brother of Kartini), Sosro Kartono was also studying at Leiden. Soon dropping his studies for mystical pursuits, he became a faithhealer in Indonesia where his fame spread far and wide.[55]

Doctor Abdul Rivai was also in the Netherlands at this time. Rivai was a Sumatran (Minangkabau), who through personal friendship with a Dutch teacher managed to receive Westernized education and to pass through the 'Doctor-djawa' School. After a most successful private practice in Medan, Rivai, a blunt man who loathed established conventions, went to Europe to continue his studies. To his chagrin he found that Dutch universities had no provision for accepting credit on his work done in the Indies. Unable to continue his studies, he turned to other pursuits and came to lean heavily upon the friendship extended by Lieutenant Colonel Klockner Brousson, soldier, writer, and man of influence. Together they started the weekly magazine *Bintang Hindia* (Star of the Indies).[56] Governor General Van Heutsz, favorably disposed to this effort, encouraged the publication through a subsidy and by advising all civil servants to subscribe. Klockner Brousson was now in the East to handle distribution and translation of the periodical there. Rivai, left to himself in the Netherlands and seeing the opportunity offered by the rather wide distribution of the periodical, began to dabble in political and social questions which touched upon the essence of colonialism. This was not what was wanted — pressure was exerted. In 1907 Rivai wrote his swan song under the name of Ta Sen Ang (Unhappy) about politics and the rights of the Indonesian people. That snuffed out the *Bintang Hindia*, one of the first Malay language organs founded upon Westernized journalistic concepts.[57] Rivai's voice was the first of many to be raised in protest against apparent discrepancies in liberal democracy which seemed unable to allow the ultimate consequences of its own ideals. Rivai went to Ghent, Belgium, where he *was* permitted to apply his previous training and experience toward a Medical Doctor's certificate which he received in a few years time.

Gradually more Indonesians came to the Netherlands to study. When another of the sons of Notodirodjo, Notodiningrat (presently Professor Raden Mas Wreksodiningrat) arrived in Delft (1908) to study engineering he found about thirty other Indonesian students in the country.[58] For social contact they formed the *Indische Vereeniging* (Indies Club) in 1908 — a cultural organization, but also a podium from which new thoughts and ideas could be disseminated.[59] Already at an early date these young Indonesians became aware of the fact that in the Netherlands they were treated far better than in their homeland; now for the first time their individual integrity was respected: they were no longer made to feel like second-rate people.

Educational facilities for Indonesians on Java, once the initial resistance to Western instruction was overcome, grew rapidly and came to affect far more people than the educational possibilities for Indonesians in Europe. Within this educational expansion and development can be found the roots of the social change which affected the Indonesian elite. As Dutch control was extended (see above, p. 41) and as new agencies of government were created (see below, p. 75), the need for a Western educated Indonesian bureaucracy became ever greater. Where previously the prestige posts in the Indonesian hierarchy had been awarded on the basis of birth, the new colonial policy made education supplemental to birth, and in time and in certain instances made education the chief criterion.

This in turn resulted in a greater diversification of the Indonesian elite. Whereas in 1900 the prijaji group had been mainly nobles and administrators, by 1914 it contained increasing numbers of civil servants, government technicians, and intellectuals who shared the elitist role and who in the eyes of the Indonesian common man of the village were included within the general designation 'prijaji'. There was certainly competition among the old and the new prijaji, especially for leadership and control of the desires and aims of the common man, but there was still much common ground on which both groups could feel as one. During the early twentieth century the broadening leadership pattern of Indonesian society was almost exclusively a development within the prijaji group, and a sense of social distinctiveness remains a strong force among the elite.

One of the leading sources for members of the new elite was the 'Dokter-djawa' School which underwent reorganization (1900–1902) and emerged as the School for Training Native Doctors (s.t.o.v.i.a.). Stimulation for improvement of the school at the turn of the century had come from the Deli (East Coast of Sumatra) planters who were vitally interested in better, yet cheaper, medical personnel. Workers on Sumatran plantations were for the most part imported into Sumatra under contract from Java, for the local labor supply was insufficient to meet the needs. Since the supply and maintenance of labor became a far more pressing problem than was the case on Java, the planters placed great emphasis upon the health of their employees.[60] European doctors were difficult to obtain and expensive to retain. The Deli planters saw the solution to their problems in the training of Indonesians to a point where they would be capable of carrying most of the work of full fledged medical doctors. Under the leadership of Dr. H. F. Roll and backed by the Department of Education the medical training course was expanded. The school now offered six years of instruction to follow three years of preparatory work for most students.[61]

Since the position of native doctor was not highly regarded in Indonesian society various inducements were used to attract students. Already in 1891 it had been decided to allow all young men expressing an interest in the 'Doctor-djawa' training to enroll in the European primary school system free of charge.[62] This inducement was paired to a signed promise by the parents that their son would go into government service for a number of years upon completion of his training.[63] This was necessary because salaries for doctors in government service were comparatively low and private practice was alluring. In 1904 inducements were raised by promising students a monthly salary of 150 guilders upon graduation with the opportunity to rise rapidly to three times that amount.[64] But even this was not considered great compensation for the amount of effort required in the training process.

The 1900–1902 reorganization had made a European Primary Education and a working knowledge of Dutch mandatory for entry to the STOVIA. The school could now accomodate two hundred students, twenty-five being admitted every year. After 1904 the degree from the STOVIA could gain the holder entry to a medical school in the Netherlands at an advanced standing so that it would be possible to obtain the European Medical Doctorate Degree within a year and one half after completion of the STOVIA course. Also under the revised training plan the various grades in the STOVIA were equated to academic ranks in the regular secondary education system. Thus the first year of the STOVIA now became equivalent to the end diploma of the School for More Extended Lower Education (M.U.L.O.), etc. In 1913 the course of instruction was extended to seven years to make the STOVIA equal to the Netherlands Indian Doctors' School (N.I.A.S.) which had been founded in Surabaya in that year.[65] The graduates of both institutions now received the title Indies' Doctor. Constant supervision was exercised over the STOVIA students — the requirements for classroom work as well as personal conduct in and out of school were rigid. In the first fourteen years of the 20th century there were only 135 graduates from the school. This represents a rather high casualty rate among aspiring Indonesian Doctors.

Those students who did not complete their medical training, or the majority of those who started, usually did not fare badly. A few years of the medical school was sufficient to provide them with enough educational backing to win good positions in the civil administrative corps. After the Dutch territorial extension, which culminated in 1904, the administrative corps needed many more people to serve in the territories that now fell under more direct administration. They were happy to take many of the failures from the STOVIA and start them in the administrative corps at a fairly good rating.

To most of those who dropped from the STOVIA the government service provided an adequate and contented life.[66] For some, however, government service did not succeed in healing the torn roots which were still tender from being transplanted from one culture to another. Abdoel Moeis, for instance, after not succeeding in the STOVIA tried government service as confidential clerk for the Director of Education, J. H. Abendanon. Upon his employer's departure for Europe, he found himself reduced in rank and unable to make his peace with the Indo-Europeans whom he encountered in the service. He turned to Rivai's *Bintang Hindia* in the capacity of translator for the Malayan language edition. After that periodical's collapse, he again went into government service, but within a few short years found the routine so distasteful that he sought employment elsewhere.[67] This time he turned to journalism, first for a European newspaper, then as co-founder of an Indonesian journal, in which capacity we shall hear more of him (see Chapter III). Another of the STOVIA failures was Soewardi Soerianingrat, member of the Paku Alam House, who tried to find contentment in both government and private service but could find no satisfaction in the Western cultural world. His struggle for a solution forms one of the most significant and interesting developments in Indonesian growing self-awareness. (see below, p. 60 and Chapter IV).

Those who completed their training were assured of economic security, if nothing else, for their income was adequate though far from luxurious, and there was more than enough work for them to do. After their years in government service they might go into private practice where they would receive greater monetary recompense. But all this was not always what satisfied: life set other requirements and created other problems which could not be met by economic stability. Western ways superimposed upon Eastern foundations were bound to create repercussions.[68] Dr. Radjiman Widijodiningrat, for instance, who had received his 'doctor-djawa' title in 1899 and who in 1909 went to Holland and became a full fledged physician, was deeply concerned with his dizzily swaying cultural position. Not that the status of doctors within Javanese society troubled him, for this was gradually improving, and he, as court physician to the Susuhunan of Surakarta, suffered no lack of prestige. Yet before going to Europe he had delved into Western philosophy and had fallen strongly under the influence of the Kant-Hegel-Bergson trend of thought, be-cause here he found a connection with his Javanese thinking. Also before his European tour he had become a member of Annie Besant's Theosophical Society which through its concepts of universal brotherhood, syncretic religion, and the mystic potencies of life and matter was able to gain a wide following among the more educated Indonesians. While in Europe he became strongly attracted by the teachings of Karl Marx: in the doc-trines of this thinker he found words of meaning for the people of Indonesia and soothing balms for his own inter-cultural po-sition. He could never find enough satisfaction in the theory of the class struggle, however, to become an inspired follower and advocate of thoroughgoing socialism.[69] Dr. Radjiman was not alone in his searchings for a firm foundation upon which to build his inner life (although his strong mystical tendencies were ad-mittedly somewhat unusual). Other doctors were seeking an answer to the same problem. They too had been rooted out of their Javanese cosmos and had only taken shallow root in the Western tradition of which their training and observation had only permitted a grasp of the materialistic aspects.[70]

Many of the young doctors, and this is particularly true of the period up to 1914, were irritated or annoyed by the treatment they had received while students at the STOVIA. The rules of the STOVIA required that all Javanese and Sumatran non-Christian students wear native dress while in attendance at the school. The purpose behind this is problematical — it may have been a means of opposing assimilation or association, but, if so, was certainly not a government policy; it may have been a desire to force the young doctors to keep their places within indigenous society where they in last analysis would have to find their field of operation; or it may have been an attempt at keeping them satisfied with the relatively small salaries they would receive in comparison to the higher ranks of the Indonesian administration whose education was inferior.[71] Whatever the reasons behind this ruling, the result was that a great many of the STOVIA students became dissatisfied with their treatment and came to regard it as a mark of their inferior status in the eyes of Europeans.[72] The fact that they had all been through European primary school where they had been permitted to wear European style dress only served to make the restriction more galling. Deepest resentment toward the forced wearing of native attire seems to have arisen in those students who were from the lower ranks of the Indonesian prijaji. They could never hope to aspire to socially eminent positions within the traditional patterns of their own society.

The STOVIA was only one institution which provided advanced education along Western lines for younger sons of the prijaji who could not find places in the administration. In addition there was the Veterinary School started in 1907, the Law School founded in 1908, the Agricultural Secondary School started in 1903, and the Teachers' Training Schools which after 1906, with the advent of village education and the use of Dutch in the First Class Native Schools (see below, p. 68), had to provide a higher quality teacher. All these schools provided Indonesians with advanced Westernized education; all graduated a semiprofessional Indonesian who in the early years of the century came to form the intellectual component of the Indonesian elite. All these schools also fall outside the scope of the rituals and procedures common to traditional Indonesian life. And all formed a facet of that phase of the Ethical Policy which sought to strengthen the socioeconomic position of the Javanese and make him better able to build the structure of his own economic welfare. Yet not one of them was equipped to help its Indonesian graduates to cope with the tremendous psychological and spiritual problems which followed as an aftermath from education that was tuned to a non-Indonesian way of life.[73]

In this milieu the seed which bore the first Indonesian organization on Western lines was nurtured; that organization was the *Budi Utomo* (Beautiful Endeavor). From its formation in 1908 some writers date the Indonesian nationalist movement, and others date the 'awakening' in this part of the world. Both are right, yet both are misleading. The Budi Utomo was nationalist only in the most limited sense of the word — it envisioned the advancement of one particular cultural group — but originally at least it had no pretensions about establishing a nation. The 'awakening', if one examines this much abused term, occurred much earlier and the Budi Utomo was representative of those elements of Indonesian society which were already quite 'awake'.[74] What makes the Budi Utomo an innovation is that it was the first Indonesian organization on Western lines.[75]

It has already been observed that the life of Java was organized about the village or desa, and in the case of the prijaji class about the court or town of the higher authority. This life was based on traditional ties or adat; horizontally egalitarian, the chosen head being *primus inter pares*, vertically authoritarian with great respect for higher authority backed by religious, mystical and mythical sanctions. Within this organizational pattern all life was contained — Javanese life knew no other organizational pattern; there was no life outside the pattern.[76]

There were peripheral organizations which seemed to deviate from the normal pattern, yet these always stood in close interrelationship with the traditional pattern of life. Such, for example, were the *sinoman*, organizations of young people, which were particularly active where the desa structure was weak (such as in the Surabaya area).[77] Sinoman were formed for mutual cooperation and assistance in event of feasts, ceremonies, etc., and although standing outside the normal sphere of desa life were formed along desa lines.[78] Similarly some of the economic co-operative organizations which were formed, particularly through outside stimulus (see below, p. 88), fell outside the traditional hierarchy. Usually they were formed among groups that already existed on the fringes of traditional life but were based upon factors long operative in the Indonesian concept of life. Further might be mentioned some of the mystical orders of the Moslem religion whose extent and influence have been so little explored, but again these for the most part tied closely into the animistic concepts which underlie much of Javanese life.[79] Yet none of these organizations stood in so unattached a relationship to the traditional aspects of Indonesian life as did the newly formed Budi Utomo.

Budi Utomo appears on the Indonesian scene as an organization based upon a free and conscious united effort by individuals.[80] Seeking legal recognition (which was received in 1909), the organization came to stand before the Netherlands Indian courts of law in the same capacity as a private European individual. The organization evolved a program and a purpose which lay outside anything found in the Javanese cosmos, or for that matter even capable of being formulated in the traditional Javanese cultural pattern.[81] Membership was selective and had little bearing to indigenous relationships, except of course that the organization in its early years was dominated by intellectuals. The organization shows, in outward aspects at least, the effect of Western attempts to change Indonesian economic and social life. The membership was quite logically composed of persons who stood in close contact with Western thoughts and actions. How far inner-organizational regulations were based on traditional customs and relationships is difficult to determine — respect for age and authority seem to have wielded a certain influence — but to the outer world the organization presented a Western-looking front.[82]

Reasons for the emergence of this style of organizational form are many. Western concepts undoubtedly had penetrated to many of the organization's founders who felt that to be effective an organization must follow Western patterns. Probably

with the growth of decentralization the Indonesians had had
ample opportunity to witness the formation and growth of European organizations founded to advance particular interests.
Furthermore Western law and legal concepts made provision
for the birth as well as for the felicitous nurturing of organizational life, and provided an atmosphere conducive to the pro-
pogation of ideals above and beyond the local level.

In avowed purpose the Budi Utomo was predominantly Java-
nese-cultural. It sought the stimulation and advancement of the
Javanese people (whom it regarded as the Javanese, Sundanese,
and Madurese language-groups, all of whom had adopted a form
of Javanese culture) toward a more harmonious development.
It sought to strengthen them to face modern life by rejuvenating
Javanese culture. Throughout its life (Budi Utomo lost its formal
identity in 1935) the organization never lost its cultural role, but
there were times when other influences challenged this primary
purpose. One such occasion occurred in the formative period
of Budi Utomo's existence and illustrates the sentiments that
were alive in Indonesian society at that time.[83]

The spade work for the Budi Utomo was done by a retired
doctor-djawa, Mas Wahidin Soediraoesada. He wanted to establish a scholarship fund to aid promising Javanese students.
The ideal was strictly Western in means as well as end, and
although exceeding the bounds of local particularism was Java-
centric. In 1906 Dr. Wahidin toured Java contacting many of
the lesser civil administrators in an attempt to gain their support,
but nothing positive came from this. Not until he turned to the
students in the stovia did his ideal begin to bear fruit. Here
the idea of scholarships for Javanese students was expanded into
the concept of a General Javanese Union, and as first step toward
this ultimate goal the Budi Utomo was created among the young
medical students in Batavia in May 1908. This was more than
Dr. Wahidin had envisioned, and his concept was lost beneath
others that seemed more imperative.[84]

Dr. Wahidin, who has only recently again been elevated to the
rank of national hero, faded from view as the leadership fell into

the hands of some of the young medical students. Particularly Raden Soetomo, descended from a lesser Javanese prijaji family, and Goenawan Mangoenkoesoemo and his brother Dr. Tjipto, sons of a Javanese school teacher, played an important part in the creation of the organization. Soon chapters of the Budi Utomo were formed at the Veterinary and Agricultural Schools, at administrators' schools and at the teachers' training schools. In Jogjakarta a chapter was formed consisting primarily of Javanese civil administrators and members of the princely families, particularly of the House of Paku Alam.[85]

In order to achieve a General Javanese Union (*Algemeen Javasche Bond*) it was decided to hold a congress in October 1908 to coordinate efforts toward this larger and more encompassing goal.[86] At this congress the older and more authoritative elements from the Jogjakarta chapter took over the reins of the organization from the younger members who still had to devote much time to their studies.[87] In the same move any tendencies to engage in political activity were nipped. For the most part such political ambitions nestled among the younger members of the organization who were still students at the STOVIA, as well as among a small group of energetic and purposeful intellectuals who were no longer tied by scholastic examinations and classroom procedures. Among this latter group were Dr. Tjipto Mangoenkoesoemo and Soewardi Soerianingrat. They took the lead in concerted opposition to the conservative Javanese elements who sought to impose cultural limitations on the organization.[88]

Men of an entirely different mold, Dr. Tjipto and Soewardi opposed the cultural policy of the Budi Utomo for varying reasons. In how far they saw at this time that the cultural policy of this Javanese organization was guided by men who sensed the threat inherent in Western culture, and as a consequence sought a strengthening of their own culture in the face of outside incursion, it is difficult to say. Certainly in the years before 1914 they were convinced that the cultural approach was the approach of weakness and compromise — they favored more direct action. With daring courage they sought simultaneously to imitate the methods and to destroy the power of the West. Interestingly enough, within a few years Soewardi was to conclude that the best approach to the problems facing Indonesians was through their own cultural tradition. But Soewardi as a Javanese noble was a strong bearer of Javanese culture and was always assured a position of status. At this time (1908) he favored more direct political action to combat the influence of the West. This feeling was based on certain personal experiences with European society through which he had developed a healthy hatred toward the dualistic and discriminatory aspects of the East Indian social structure.

Dr. Tjipto never turned away from the path of political action. A lesser prijaji only through the acquired status of his father and through his own professional training, he had had only low status in the traditional Javanese cosmos and consequently could find no comfort in this traditional culture.[89] An ambitious man, he secretly coveted position in the very culture pattern which denied it him. Turning to cynicism he rejected the Western cultural pattern, which not only had provided him with a medical training, but had abused his pride by making him suffer the indignity of native dress and by refusing to accept him as equal at all times and at all occasions.[90] As a soul adrift, he threw himself into the anti-plague campaign (1910–1911) and won decorations from the Dutch government for his valor, but the ribbons proved only hollow honors and did not open doors to the better life he desired.[91] He took to condemning the colonial relationship, but was also not above abusing and ridiculing Javanese traditions and manners. He sincerely desired a better and freer life for the people of the Indies, refusing to believe that current policies and practices of either Dutch or Indonesians were leading to that goal. He hated many because they were of higher birth and disliked others because they compromised and failed to carry steadfastly the ideal he had built for himself. He was perhaps the most sincere man that Indonesia has ever produced, but he was an idealist who had the un-Indonesian trait of not being able to compromise between ideals and reality. He was a most difficult person for anyone to work with harmoniously.

The younger men, for whom Dr. Tjipto and Soewardi acted as spokesmen, found themselves opposed by a strong group of conservative Javanese who had to consider their position in society as well as in government service. This conservative group was uncertain in its attitude toward Western innovations, but it was not prepared to be stampeded by a few hot-headed intellectuals who had only the vaguest of positive ideas. Using their traditional prestige and authority, this elder, more conservative group managed to gain control of the Budi Utomo. Having really neither cultural nor political aims, this group was most interested in a mutual protective and socially elite organization. The retired Regent of Karanganjar, Raden A. Tirtakoesoema, was chosen to head the organization at the October 1908 convention. To all appearances everything was arranged to glide smoothly forward into calm and sterile waters.

But the membership among the younger, more Western-oriented part of the Budi Utomo increased more rapidly than among the elders, and the younger men grew restive under the tight reined policy. Most of these younger men like Dr. Soetomo, Dr. Goenawan Mangoenkoesoemo, who was better able to adapt to life in higher circles than his brother, Dr. Radjiman, and Mas Dwidjo Sewojo, a product of the teachers' training school, desired neither the conservatism of the old guard nor the advanced, practically suicidal thinking of the Tjipto-Soewardi group. Instead they formed the nuclear group for a cultural policy that would seek to direct Indonesian life into new lines. The stimulus for this policy came from Indonesians of higher training and education who now began to consider themselves the intellectual segment of the elite as distinct from the traditional hereditary elite of nobles and administrators.[92] Within this group of young intellectuals the most constructive and most consciously-dynamic element of the new Indonesian leader group was founded. Their concrete goals and ideals were vague; they varied with the situation and were formed to meet specific occurrences. In general they envisioned a general betterment of life for all Indonesians and a raising of standards in the manner of the Ethical Colonial Policy.[93] They either did not have, or did not voice, specific proposals toward independent nationalism — a degree of self-administration or self-government was about as far as any of them thought.

Gradually the intellectual group favoring progressive cultural action came to dominate the Budi Utomo and drew it out of its conservative husk. For most of the conservative prijaji this was too much. Irked by this trend as well as by the restriction of their privileges by the 'hormat circulaire' (see above, p. 45), they formed the *Regentenbond* (Regents Union) in 1913 which advanced their aims of greater local autonomy and greater recognition of their traditional position. The Budi Utomo now came to be dominated by young cultural progressives such as Radjiman, Dwidjo Sewojo, etc. who strongly favored retaining the cultural mission of the organization. Their support came not only from their own group, but also from some of the members of the high Javanese nobility (especially the House of Paku Alam) and the members of the lower civil service and lower prijaji families. In 1911 Prince Notodirodjo was chosen to head the Budi Utomo. In the original settling process the conservative Regents were not the only group to drop out of the organization: what had been too radical for them had been too conservative for the radical group headed by Soewardi and Dr. Tjipto. They too now dropped out of the Budi Utomo in order to seek a more radical following elsewhere.

They had not far to search. Support for the more radical tendencies of the young Javanese came from an Indo-European, E. F. E. Douwes Dekker. At the time of the creation of Budi Utomo Douwes Dekker was associated with the *Bataviaasch Nieuws-blad* (Batavian Journal). He was largely responsible for this newspaper coming to be regarded as the voice of Young Java in European circles.[94] Douwes Dekker was an adventurer who had not yet passed the half-way mark in a life of seventy active years. He was a distant relative of the famous Multatuli but lacked both the strong neuroses and compelling brilliance of his ancestor. His life assumed meaning because he was a dedicated man; the resoluteness with which he pursued his convictions was exceeded only by the insuppressible egotism with which he cast himself in the role of genius.[95] The strongest conviction of his life, and the one for which he had recently entered the lists after a delayed return from fighting with the Boers in Africa, was the creation of a united and independent Indonesia. In his mind was first formulated, and by his voice and pen was first openly advocated, an Indonesia free of colonial ties, uniting all the peoples of the East Indies who were under Dutch rule.[96] He was indiscreet and courageous in consistently and openly advancing this ideal. He served as a rallying point for dissatisfied and disaffected Indonesians and Indo-Europeans, and was able to crystallize their sentiments into a program of positive revolutionary action. For all this, his influence upon the young dynamic Indonesian elite remained indirect, and he always remained outside the inner group of Indonesian leaders.

Douwes Dekker advocated an East Indian rather than a Javanese or Indonesian nationalism. He envisioned the creation of a nation composed of all persons who associated themselves with the freedom of the archipelago; no racial limitation was placed on membership in the *Indische Partij* (Indies' Party) which he created in 1911.[97] Devotion to the common fatherland was all that was required, and all forms of political action to achieve the eventual aim of independence were allowed.[98] The party had no social or cultural emphasis; it was strictly political. It wanted an independent Indonesia — once this was achieved, other matters could be resolved.[99] Douwes Dekker was joined by Dr. Tjipto and by Soewardi in the years before the Indische Partij was officially formed and this triumvirate came to form the nucleus of the party. The party received some support from the association principle which was the ideal of many persons who joined its ranks. The cultural counterpart to the party became the Theosophical Society which had a remarkable influence on many disoriented Indonesians, but there is no indication of formal concerted action between the two groups.

Douwes Dekker's program for implementing his ideals is difficult to ascertain from the ranting journalistic efforts in the short-lived party journal *De Expres*. Apparently he wanted the educated elite of Indonesians and Indo-Europeans to control the government. In reality this would have meant almost complete control by the Indo-Europeans, for they were in general a better educated group than the Indonesians. Douwes Dekker was probably not unaware of his party's Eurasian slant, but his program of equal rights and equal citizenship attracted a number of dissatisfied Indonesian intellectuals and civil servants. The greatest support for the party, however, came from the Indo-European group.

Through Douwes Dekker and his party this Indo-European group clamored loudly for equal status and equal pay for all racial groups in the archipelago. It may seem paradoxical that the Indos desired equality with Indonesians, but there was cold logic behind their demands. When the Netherlands Indian government offices instituted systematic and detailed bookkeeping early in the century, it became necessary for the Department Chiefs to keep a careful eye on their expenditures. For many years it had been the practice to hire Indonesians only for the lower positions in government services. These Indonesian personnel were hired on a salary scale that was much lower than the European, for it was thought that the native needed far less income to maintain his standards than was the case with the European. After the turn of the century, however, a growing number of educated and skilled Indonesians began to compete for higher positions than those usually filled by this group. The dualistic salary scale remained in force, however, even for these higher positions. Thus, all factors being equal, the Department Chiefs found themselves pressured by budgetary considerations to hire the less-expensive Indonesians in preference to the Indo-Europeans who were on the European salary scale. Private enterprise followed much the same pattern. As a consequence, those Indo-Europeans who competed for positions with Indonesians were being bested in the economic struggle. Many of the higher civil servants in the Dutch colonial government were Indo-Europeans and would probably have preferred to hire fellow Indos, but they were bound by their budgetary regulations. Here the dual relationships of the colonial status seemed to have a reverse impact.

Through the Indische Partij the duality of colonialism was strongly condemned.[102] The party's program made many Indonesians aware that they stood in an inferior position to the Europeans — the fact that Europeans were paid more had always been accepted as one of the norms of life. Now Indonesians came to question this. Should not equal work be equally paid? Douwes Dekker was eminently successful in advancing this one particular point — so well did he lay the groundwork that even without his presence (he was exiled in 1913) the concept was carried forward. In 1918 a law was passed which established a unitary salary scale for many positions, regardless of the employee's ethnic origin.

The Netherlands Indian government was, for obvious reasons, not inclined to look with favor on many aspects of the program of the Indische Partij. This party was revolutionary. Small wonder that the party's request for legal recognition was denied by Governor General Idenburg.[103] This in itself did not halt the flow of propaganda which the party leaders were issuing through their party organ, De Expres. To stem this the government tried Douwes Dekker, Dr. Tjipto and Soewardi on charges of 'journalistic excesses' and exiled all three from the East Indies in 1913.[104] In retrospect it is easy to accuse the government of hasty or unduly severe, or even unwise action, in this trial and ensuing exile. Certainly the immediate result was to bestow the status of martyrdom in the cause of Indonesian freedom upon the three men and raise them to symbols of resistance to colonial oppression. And a rereading of the pertinent materials on which judgment was based,[105] fails to make a strong and convincing case for the government. Yet from the government's point of view there was probably much more involved than some journalistic indiscretions. The government at this time faced mounting criticism on the implementation of its Ethical Policy from groups in the Netherlands, while also facing growing dissatisfaction among its own European and Indonesian administrators because of their loss of authority under decentralization policies. At the same time the government was confronted by a growing Islamic movement (see below, p. 82), and by a fear approaching hysteria on the part of some colonial Europeans toward the newly awakened Indonesian political and organizational consciousness. In short the government was confronted by diverse pressures which could best be allayed and resolved by taking decisive and uncompromising action against the clearly revolutionary threat of the Indische Partij. The wisdom of the government's action must remain a moot point.

The extension of Western secondary education which underlay much of the action and reaction of such organizations as Budi Utomo and the Indische Partij was only a part of the Dutch program in the educational field. Educating the broad masses of Indonesians was also an essential part of the Ethical Colonial Policy with eradication of illiteracy and raising of prosperity as the primary aims. Generally the Ethici thought in terms of education on a Western basis and were not adverse to using education as the lever to assimilate the indigenous peoples into a higher and 'better' way of life.[106] Van Deventer envisioned a rebirth of Indonesia through good education; Van Kol spoke of 'light rays' that would penetrate to the most remote desa; and Abendanon viewed education as the tie of friendship and trust which would bind all people who walked the path of progress.[107] None of them was seriously concerned with the effect of education upon Indonesian culture. Underneath these idealistic expressions lay the goal of education as viewed by the Ethical Program: an economic strengthening within the scope of a Western inspired civilization.[108] The people's education aimed at preparation for more efficient work in indigenous agriculture and crafts — it did not seek to create new skills and vocations; it sought only to prepare the ground for indigenous prosperity within the framework of the existing economic system. Only in the advanced institutions of learning, such as have been discussed above, was specialization in Western skills and techniques encouraged.

D. Fock who became Minister of Colonies in 1905 regarded education as one of the most essential features of the Ethical Program. To determine its needs he had J. E. Jasper investigate the status and prospects of mass education on Java and Madura. Jasper, whose report was submitted in April 1906, accurately noted that the Second Class Native Schools met the needs for a basic general education, but felt that the numbers of these schools should be increased to extend the Westernized educational system. Jasper noted the slight demand for education from the villages and saw that the pressure for education came from the prijaji class and urban groups.[109] The second class schools seemed sufficient to meet the most modest demands of the groups that were the most vitally interested in Western style education. Building his thinking about the Jasper's Report, Fock, in the budget for 1907, proposed to more than double the 675 existing government schools by adding 700 Second Class Native Schools.[110] Fock, a careful budgeter, felt he could defray the expenses for this project through the revenue derived from tin exports.[111]

At almost the same time that Fock and Jasper were thinking of expansion of the Second Class Schools, the attention of Governor General J. B. van Heutsz came to rest upon the problem of education. He viewed the problem in a different light than Fock and Jasper, and as a man of action set about to implement his ideas despite any deviating opinions from other quarters. Van Heutsz saw that the opening of the European Primary Schools to certain classes of Indonesian students (which had occurred about 1903) had resulted in so great an increase in the enrollment of these schools that they were in danger of being swamped under the added burden.[112] Evidently there was a demand for Western language education which was not being met in the indigenous school system. The aspirations for civil service positions which placed a premium upon Dutch language ability, and the prerequisites of specialized-advanced schools which now made a European primary education part of their entrance requirement, had made the curricula of the First Class Native Schools obsolete.

In 1907 Van Heutsz set out to reorganize these First Class

Schools to bring them into line with the requirements of the time. Two years were added to the curricula and some Dutch language training was provided.[113]   These changes were still not entirely adequate, but were the beginning of a revision process that ultimately led to the creation of Dutch-Native Schools (*Hollandsch-Inlandsche Schoolen*) in 1914. The course of instruction was raised to seven years, and the education and the final diploma were equated to those of the European primary schools. In this manner did the government meet the demands of the better-situated groups in Indonesian society whose growing demand for Western style education for their children had resulted in the overcrowding of European schools.

But Van Heutsz was also interested in the problem of educating the Indonesian masses, and started in May 1906 to experiment with a basic village school. In 1907 he instituted the desa school in Java. This new creation affected both the budget of the government and the general education program quite differently from the extension of the Second Class Native Schools proposed by Minister Fock. The purpose of the desa school was to bring the rudiments of reading, writing and arithmetic to the villagers, and as such was a vital step forward in the plan to eradicate illiteracy. The plan was to have the initial costs and partial subsidies for operation for these schools borne by the government and to have the village, in so far as possible, contribute to the upkeep and part of the operation of the school. The village schools would be a much lighter burden on the Netherlands Indian finances than an increased number of Second Class Native Schools.[114] The discrepancy between Minister Fock's Second Class School plan and Governor General van Heutsz's desa school plan was resolved by adopting both plans on a modified basis. The extension of the Second Class Schools was not as great as originally envisioned — a reformed plan provided for only 345 of these schools. The number of desa schools did not advance as rapidly as had at first been expected either, yet progress was made; by the end of 1909 there were 723 desa schools, and by 1912 there were more than 2500.

Over and above the resolution of immediate problems associated with the establishment of desa schools — such as constructing schools, supplying teachers from the graduates of Second Class Native Schools, and convincing villagers of the value of the schools — no simple judgment can be rendered on the success of the desa school program. The schools attempted to operate in a sphere where there was no great urge toward education. The program sought to fill a gap that was only seen by the more far-sighted, well-intentioned men of the West. It was part of a great literacy program, but it was never quantitatively adequate to cope with the immense work it had set out to do. Not thousands but tens of thousands of new desa schools were needed each year. Yet it is doubtful if either the human or material resources were on hand for such expansion.[115] As it was, the program could barely keep pace with the growing population, and the literacy rate (Roman script) during the period under discussion remained below five percent. The schools themselves attempted to operate in an environment where there was no great urge toward instruction with the result that the acquired skills often were soon forgotten. For the more adaptable pupil the schools offered no opportunity for further study.[116]

The Second Class Native Schools were equally remiss in supplying further educational opportunities, but here the shortcoming was far more serious. The graduates of these schools usually sought a new life and new employment within the Western sphere while those who had attended the desa school usually returned to their normal village life. Between the Second Class Native School and the village school the line between Western and non-Western education can perhaps best be drawn. Westernized education carries with it a rational approach which differs markedly from the Javanese life pattern still predominating in the villages.[117] The instruction in the desa school both in methods and subject matter had little impact upon the cosmological orientation of the Javanese villager.[118] The Second Class School, however, not only taught more advanced material, but also removed the student from the traditional environment dominated by the Javanese culture pattern. It placed those Indonesians who came into contact with it in the anomalous position of having to orient to two worlds, while its subject materials carried the pupil's mind far beyond the confines of village life and presented him with skills that he could use outside that life.[119]

With all this came the entry of individualism into the lives of the students: individualism in accomplishment, effort, and initiative[120] — this again stood in contrast to the group-efforts and easy-going atmosphere of the desa schools. Neither the Second Class nor the desa schools were indigenous to the Javanese life pattern, but the Second Class Schools were able to instill some of the thought patterns of the West in the student along with the material of instruction.[121] The teachers in the Second Class Native Schools were trained in the Westernized Teachers' Training Schools and followed Western techniques in teaching.[122] The tragedy of the Second Class Native Schools lies in the fact that these schools raised in the pupils an appetite for success and advancement in the Western dominated colonial realm, but did not supply either the diploma or the prerequisites for satisfying this hunger. The graduates of these schools formed a large part of the dissatisfied group of semi-intellectuals in Indonesian society.

In the years 1909–1910 native education received further stimulus and criticism from the colonial specialist of one of the right wing parties, H. Colijn. In 1909 the right wing parties once again gained control of the Netherlands' parliament. Former Minister of Colonies, A. W. F. Idenburg, was sent to the East Indies as Governor General, and J. H. de Waal Malefijt, a man of staunch religious convictions, became Minister of Colonies. Colijn, an ex-military man, had just recently returned from the East Indies. There he had been in close relationship with J. B. van Heutsz, who had appointed him to the post of Adviser for the Outer Islands. He had been elected to parliament in 1909. Rapidly he won for himself the position of the most authoritative voice on colonial affairs for the right wing parties. When these parties were in power, which was much of the time in the 20th century, his opinions played a large part in shaping Dutch colonial policy. Colijn was closely allied with the large and growing capitalist interests (he was later to become one of the directors of the Bataviasche Petroleum Maatschappij, Royal Dutch Shell) and strongly favored further development of the archipelago's economic potential (particularly in the outer islands) through Dutch capital. In the years preceding the First World War, and especially the years following 1909, the East Indian economy experienced a tremendous capital growth. In 1909 there were 232 new companies founded with 47 million guilders capital — in 1910 some 290 more with 74 million guilders capital. Dividends for those years ran as high as 20 and 30 percent.[123]

Colijn was especially concerned with the costs involved in administering the East Indies and about the fact that so little progress had been made toward placing greater administrative responsibility in the hands of Indonesians. Administrative reform (read simplification) had long been under consideration, and after numerous proposals and counterproposals was finally effected by constitutional change in 1922 (see below, Chapter IV). At this time, however, Colijn lay the blame for the Indonesians' failure to assume greater administrative responsibility at the door of native education which he felt afforded no access to higher private and public positions.[124] His criticism of the First Class Native Schools helped lead toward improvement in the formation of the Dutch-Native Schools which were created in 1914 (see above, p. 68). Colijn's criticism struck deeper than educational structure, however, for he noted with some alarm that the sense of 'drive and duty' so essential to the West was often lacking among those Indonesians who had enjoyed Western style instruction.[125] The reasons for this phenomenon, which Colijn probably observed correctly enough, resided in complex patterns and relationships of the Indonesian culture. Colijn sought a much simpler explanation, however, and fastened blame on the lack of Christian religious instruction in government schools. He felt the government policy of religious neutrality in education was responsible for a moral breakdown among Indonesians and underlay their inability to adopt Western attitudes. He exerted pressure in an effort to gain greater religious emphasis in the education system, but met with firm resistance from the bulk of the Europeans in the East. Government subsidies were extended to schools founded by church groups, but the government schools retained their religiously neutral position. The growing pressure for religious instruction in Western style schools was soon to have its repercussions within Indonesian society (see below, p. 85).

The purpose of all this education as envisioned in the Ethical Colonial Policy was to allow Indonesians to take a more active role in their own political, economic and social future. Political control, in addition to the decentralization procedure already discussed (see p. 42ff.), was also to extend to the bureaucracy where an 'Indonesianization' of the administrative corps was envisioned. The government's increased concern with all phases of East Indian life had resulted in greater numbers of Indonesians being taken up in the expanded Netherlands Indian government structure. But at the same time there were also increasing numbers of Europeans in the government service who had to supervise ever more details in the multiplying branches of service. As a result there seemed to be very little progress toward freeing the Indonesians from their tutelage. In fact the very reverse seemed to be the case and many educated Indonesians were growing embittered by the constant and continuing amount of minute supervision to which they were subject.[126] After 1914 steps were taken to relieve the supervisory concern of Europeans with the functioning of Indonesian society, but in the years covered by this chapter administrative supervision was at its height.

Reforms and Their Effects

The growing concern of the Ethical Policy with all aspects of Indonesian life affected not only educated Indonesians in the administration who chafed under supervision, but came to affect all levels of Indonesian life.[127] This effect was so deep and so manifold that all its aspects cannot be discussed here. A few examples of the impact of government services and welfare programs will have to suffice.

The program of credit extension is a good example of the impact which the government policies had on Indonesian life. Native consumer credit had been granted through pawn shops which until late in the 19th century were controlled mainly by Chinese and Arabs. Under the then existing system of licenses and franchises the government had only slight control over the activities of the pawn shops, and abuses had crept into the system. In 1900 it was proposed that the government take over operation of the pawn shops. After testing the feasibility of this plan and finding it successful, government pawn shops were instituted in Java and Madura in 1904.[128] The government pawn shop service needed semi-intellectual employees, and recruited them largely from the graduates of Second Class Native Schools. This type of employee could hardly be regarded as part of the elite group of Indonesian society, yet they were even more distant from the agrarian element. In ambition and view of life the majority identified themselves with the upper, non-agrarian classes, and many felt their future to be intimately involved with a Western style welfare state. These semi-intellectual employees were important to the government, for governmental plans and proposals had to be implemented through this group which the government hoped would stand in closer proximity to the Indonesian masses than the Indonesian administrative elite. This hope may not have been well-founded, but at any rate the government, during the first quarter of the 20th century, was prepared to concede much to these semi-intellectuals. In general the government retained their support, but they were a volatile group with chronic dissatisfactions.

In meeting the problem of credit extension the government took more positive stepts than instituting a system of pawn shops: the Peoples' Credit System (*Volkscredietwezen*) was started to operate primarily in the vital area of agricultural credit. Prior to 1904 when this system was inaugurated the peoples of Indonesia did have a rudimentary credit system which included:

(a) assistance and savings establishments (prijaji banks), (b) cooperative burial and 'rotating kitty' funds, (c) village sheds for dispensation of rice and other essentials, and (d) organizations for feasts and celebrations such as the previously mentioned sinoman. These institutions were not strongly enough financed or organized to meet the monetary requirements imposed upon villagers by the penetration of Western influences into rural life.

The system which the government instituted in 1904 was chiefly patterned after the previously existing institutions, but was strengthened by governmental financial backing and by Westernized organization. Special employees of the *Volkscredietwezen* as well as the regular civil administrators now began to advance the use of and extoll the benefits of this credit system among the rural population.[129] The government credit system was composed of three types of credit and savings institutions.[130] The village grain sheds (*lumbung desa*), operated on the local level, were stocked with rice through communal effort, then in turn loaned rice wherever necessary against interest rates calculated in produce.[131] The *lumbung* tended to stabilize the price of rice the year around and countered the practice of speculators and dealers of buying rice at low prices at harvest time.[132] Their operation was kept almost entirely outside the realm of money economy: in this capacity they served to absorb many shocks of the penetration of Western culture into Indonesian rural life.

Secondly, the village, or desa, banks also operated on the local level. These loaned money in small amounts for local needs. The original capital was usually borrowed from a district bank. The small loans were repaid with a monetary interest and also a slight surplus which then became the borrowers share in the bank. In this manner the desa banks became local holding corporations, and in due time only shareholders or persons introduced by shareholders could borrow at the desa bank.[133] In these banks the penetration of money economy was carefully controlled through an institution carefully patterned on some of the cooperative aspects of Indonesian life while standing under close and constant Western supervision.

Lastly, the district or regency banks (*Volksbank*) were institutions which attracted and loaned money from and to all parts of the population. These banks were generally directed by a European and were started with funds loaned by the government; by nature they were largely philanthropic. The primary purpose of these banks was to loan money to Indonesian companies and associations. The Ethici hoped that these banks, along with other measures, would lead to the formation of an Indonesian entrepreneurial class, but during the first quarter of the 20th century they had only slight success in achieving this goal.

The Volkscredietwezen attracted numerous well educated Indonesians who used employment in this service as a step toward higher posts in the civil administration. Pangeran A. A. Koesoemo Joedo, of the House of Paku Alam, for instance, graduated from Leiden in 1904, being qualified to join the European administrative corps. However, his chances for advancement there would have been limited, so in 1906 he accepted an offer to join the Volkscredietwezen.[134] He remained with the credit system until 1916 when he became Regent of Ponorogo.[135] Other Indonesians with lesser education joined the service in the lower posts and were drawn into a new orbit of life.

What was to be yet another influence upon the rural masses of Java was the creation of the Department of Agriculture, Industry and Commerce in 1905. This new branch of the Netherlands Indian government machinery was primarily concerned with agriculture.[136] Rapid progress was made in expanding the operation of this department, and removing concern with Indonesian agriculture from the hands of the civil administrators. One of its primary tasks was agricultural education. Using the graduates of the Secondary Agricultural School in Buitenzorg (Bogor) as teachers, a series of Indonesian farmer schools were started (1912) which educated villagers in better farming methods for their particular area.[137] This work was a natural complement to the Agricultural Information and Extension Service which started in 1911. This service used both European and Indonesian agricultural experts to disseminate not only information but also better seeds and seedlings to farmers.[138]

Another area in which the Netherlands Indian government began actively to operate at the turn of the century was the opium production and trade. During the 19th century the government had farmed out opium privileges to private individuals — mostly Chinese. The humanitarian sentiments underlying the Ethical Policy were offended by the abuses which had invaded the system. In 1894 the government began experimenting, first in Madura, later in parts of Java, with government control of the sale and production of opium. This proved so successful that in 1904 the government control was extended to all of Java.[139] The *Opium-regie* became another government service that required workers and employees, and once again these were sought among the Indonesian population groups, and more specifically among those persons who had had some degree of Western style education.[140]

Here have been mentioned only a few of the institutions which formed the swelling stream of increased government activity. Paradoxically, a government attempting to decentralize, economize, and simplify its administrative cares was compelled to do more and more, and to do that better and better. It extended its influence into ever more fields while augmenting the numbers of its employees.[141] The above examples have but scratched the surface of the gigantic process of forming the East Indian colony into a modern administrative state. The growth of the civil administration in the outer islands since 1904 when the semi-independent rulers came to stand under closer government supervision, and the extension of education with all teachers in government schools standing under governmental control, also formed part of the same process. Consider the unmentioned services such as Peoples' Health and Medical Extension Service; Post, Telephone and Telegraph Systems; Railways and Tramways; Taxation and Finance Bureau; Bureau for Popular Literature; Archeological Service, and others which formed part of the government's activity. Add to this the burgeoning private enterprises such as plantations, factories, oil refineries, inter-island shipping, banks, and most other institutions that typify modern Western life. All these employed Indonesians in increasing numbers.[142]

Those Indonesians who were drawn into this system were removed ever further from their traditional patterns of life and thought. These were in large measure the Western educated Indonesians recruited mainly from the lesser prijaji group and those villagers who had received some Western instruction in Second Class Schools.[143] These, along with displaced farmers who had gravitated into urban and plantation centers, formed a semi-Westernized element of great fluidity. As a group they were exceedingly ambivalent both as relates to their position within Indonesian society and to their attitude toward the West. Some of them resented the West for its destruction of old patterns and traditions and for the insecurity which follows upon changes of a life pattern — they sought to find alleviation for the tempests that buffeted them in a strengthening of the cosmos they left behind. Others disliked the West because it did not seem to go far enough, did not include them fully enough, and did not enforce a strong, rigid pattern of life. But the great majority of them neither hated nor praised; they simply accepted the ebb and tide of a changing life as it swirled round them, seeking merely to gain whatever advantage they could. The contradictions and forces inherent in the West remained an enigma. They knew only their daily life and were not given to speculating on forces they could not comprehend. Beyond the confines and immediate goals of existence little appealed to them.

Below this semi-Westernized group swarmed the great rural masses who can not be ignored as a factor in the process of forming the ideals and aims of the Indonesian elite. Javanese village life was certainly not unaffected by the rapid expansion of governmental services, nor by the changes that were occurring within the Indonesian elite group during the early years of the 20th century. Rural sentiments and thought patterns were not oblivious to changes in the world about them; rural life tended to be conservative, but it was alive, it reacted to stimulants.[144]

Most notable of the measures affecting village life in Java and

Madura was the Native Community Regulation of 1906. It was the result of general changes in European thought closely associated with the Ethical Policy. During the late 19th century official thinking was inclined to direct policy toward the individual Indonesian rather than to the village. This tendency resulted in the official removal of certain restrictions which the government felt stood in the way of the growth of Indonesian individualism: i.e., private land holding was encouraged; individual land contracts were required; feudal services were replaced by a head tax (1893);[145] etc. These stimulants remained operative wherever they seemed to render satisfactory results (viz. West Java), but in general this attempt to stimulate individualism fell far short of its mark. In practice men of the West and institutions of the West found it far more expeditious to deal with the Indonesian masses on a village basis than on an individual basis. Government and private enterprise faced the same problem — they could accomplish nothing by ignoring the social and economic solidarity of the village.

When early in the 20th century it was learned that villagers were being required to perform village duties which looked very much like the abolished feudal services, it was decided to investigate.[146] C. J. Hasselman, a member of the European administrative corps, was delegated to look into the matter. Hasselman will never go down in history as an Ethicus, yet his report laid the cornerstone for a policy that permitted implementation of many ideals of the Ethical Movement. He was not so blinded by slogans and mottos that he failed to distinguish the realities of the situation he set out to investigate. He concluded that what the Europeans had judged as 'oppressions' were not regarded as such by the villagers. Indonesians needed far more protection against individualism than against the village government which strove to strengthen corporate village life and build up their village community.[147] That this report was accepted and acted upon shows (1) that the individualistic aspects of liberalism were not *ipso facto* adopted into all aspects of the Ethical Policy, (2) that the East Indian government was prepared to sacrifice temporarily Indonesian individualism in the hope of advancing some of its major objectives, and (3) that these views were widely enough held to make this modified policy acceptable. If the village defied individualism then the thing to do was to use the village (as a corporate body) to achieve the desired goals of improvement and advancement. The Native Community Regulation of 1906 did just this.[148]

The Native Community Regulation recognized existing conditions by acknowledging the desa head as representative of the desa.[149] It affirmed his place in the administrative hierarchy by making him responsible for the satisfactory conduct of local affairs[150] — but always under supervision of the head of the local administration: i.e., the European Contrôleur.[151] The regulation went even farther; recognizing the village as an instrument of welfare which would accomplish on the local level the great aims of the Ethical Policy, it sought to use the village to effect welfare, prosperity, and an economically buoyant population.[152] In order to achieve these ends village services might be levied on the inhabitants.[153] The reasoning behind this policy was further elucidated in the commentary to the official ordinance.[154] Here it was stated that "the village needs the help of Government to protect its rights against the individual."[155] The Community Regulation of 1906 obviously bolstered the communal ties of the village while simultaneously preparing the way for careful supervision of village life and welfare.[156]

The practical application of the Community Regulation, although foreseeable, seems to have eluded the eager and well-intentioned minds of the theoreticians and politicians. The local European administrator was to fulfill a supervisory and regulatory function which would gradually diminish as those village activities directed toward increased welfare became stabilized. In theory his role of direct and personal supervision of local affairs was as great or greater than it had been before. But in practice his function and the function of the Indonesian administration was restricted by the growth of civil bureaucracy designed to further Indonesian welfare and prosperity. At one time the administration had interpreted and applied government regulations to the village, but now the administration was only a cooperating agent for the host of European and Indonesian specialists who descended upon the village with the mission of building up indigenous welfare.[157] (see above, p. 44)

> Before long almost every village had its Village Treasury, to provide funds for everything that the Controleur or Assistant Resident thought the village ought to want; school, village bank, paddy bank, stud bull, pedigree goat, bazaar and so on. At the same time the people were educated in business principles, and numerous registers were prescribed for the headman, clerk and village priest; but, with anxious care lest democracy should be sacrificed to efficiency, an elaborately democratic machinery was constructed, with periodical 'Village Meetings,' at which resolutions should be formally adopted by a due proportion of villagers duly qualified to vote; likewise, for the conservation of village lands and customs, all matters relating to them were carefully placed on record.[158]

Furnivall's description of the pressures and changes that came to be felt in Indonesian villages is correct, but his emphasis upon the civil administration as the agent of change is not altogether accurate. Many of the newly created government agencies were greater stimulants than the local administrators. Moreover, European administrators were a heterogeneous lot, not to be simply classified as a group precipitating forced welfare policies and imposing changes upon the people. Some, newly arrived in the East, may well have been overly zealous in advancing the program of the Ethical Policy. But many of the older administrators viewed these attempts at change skeptically and attempted to modify the government's intense efforts toward influencing village life. Their experiences in close contact with Javanese life led them to fear that the process of inducing change would go neither as simply or smoothly as seemed to be expected.[159] Since their numbers did not increase as rapidly as those of the younger men, they fought what for some years appeared to be a losing battle to bring a greater sense of reality into the application of a welfare policy. Their struggle was not alleviated by the fact that the Netherlands Indies became a modernized bureaucratic state after 1900. Orders and policies tended to be carried out in a stereotyped manner. Certain ideas and certain patterns found favor — others were discouraged. What was considered good and proper was adhered to regardless of suitability to the actual situation. Bureaucrats knew what was expected, and in securing their own futures were not inclined to tamper with established procedures. They sought to do well in what was expected of them. Adversity was not appreciated, the machine had to run smoothly.[160] Small wonder that both those who followed the acceptable pattern and those who sought to modify it suffered from the limited vision permitted by the mental blinkers of a modern administrative state. Despite all this, the oppositional struggle was not to be in vain; weaknesses in the prevailing policy became too obvious, and when disruptions in Indonesian life seemed on the increase, the policy was modified (see Chapter IV, p. 244).

The practical application of the Ethical Policy in the villages became intimately associated with gentle pressure, or *perintah halus*, exerted by members of government agencies and administration.[161] This was deemed necessary in order to bring the welfare measures to the villages. The villages, meanwhile, desired nothing so much as to be left alone. There is little doubt that many of the changes would never have been realized without constant urging by men in authority.[162] With the welfare aim predominating thought and action, many European civil servants found it increasingly difficult to work smoothly with the indigenous administrators.[163] Either because they hesitated to disrupt integrated village patterns or because they feared the threat to their dominance inherent in the welfare policy, many native administrators failed to give whole-hearted support to the policy. It was not something that fit into their pattern of life. The 'hormat circulaire' of 1913 (see above, p. 45) was indicative of the growing disrespect on the part of Europeans for members of the indigenous administrative corps, stemming from their reluctance to implement changes vigorously. It was indeed unfortunate that those very elements of Indonesian society which should theoretically have been drawn into the closest association with the Western orbit of life were repulsed through the overpowering compulsion of applying a welfare program.

Meanwhile the villages grew more restive under the government's pressure for change and improvement. Their uneasiness usually took the form of uncomprehending bewilderment rather than active resentment.[164] Yet occasionally their resentment took violent form. Most of this violence occurred in the outer islands where the Western impact was more sudden than on Java. But even on Java the violent Samin movement which flamed up sporadically from 1905 to 1914, and which has been attributed directly to interference by the administration with all sorts of internal village affairs, indicates a growing restiveness under the program.[165] Increasing numbers of villages seemed to be losing faith in the civil authorities who had traditionally regulated their lives, as these authorities now seemed unable or unwilling to stem the tide of change.[166] Where this attitude prevailed the villagers usually turned away from the secular authorities and sought strength and solace in their religion: Islam.[167] This meant that the religious elements in Javanese village life were strengthened vis-à-vis the secular elements.

This growth of Islamic sentiments during the 20th century is a reflection of the position and function of religion in Indonesian life. To the Indonesians Islam was much more than a religion — it was a way of life. As such, it came more and more to stand for everything that was indigenous as opposed to foreign. Islam came to be a factor of unity within the growing self-consciousness of Indonesians, and at the same time came to be a criterion of national solidarity, of brown man against white.[168] The solidarity and security provided by Islam had little to do with the internal Islamic dispute between Reformism and Orthodoxy (see above, p. 22), for the majority of the people were interested in the life pattern supported by the religion, not in the doctrinal disputes of scholars and teachers.

At the same time that Indonesians were turning to Islam as a bulwark against the social pressures and changes being set afoot by the Ethical Policy, the government began its efforts to further Christian activities in the archipelago (see above, p. 71). The Netherlands parliamentary elections of 1909 had given the conservative, religious parties a substantial majority in the States General, and a Christian fervor seemed to seize the policy makers in the motherland.[169] The Governor General A. W. F. Idenburg (1909–1916) was a member of one of the religious parties from whom much help was expected. Within the States General the Radical, Liberal and Socialist colonial authorities, Van Deventer, Fock and Van Kol had lost their seats, so the Minister of Colonies J. H. de Waal Malefijt (1909–1913) had a free field on which to play his policies.

In the years after 1909 Christian mission groups rapidly extended their activities in the archipelago. Missions which operated in the broad realm of welfare and economic advancement among the Indonesian people were given assistance by the State.[170] Limitations on the number and location of missions were removed so that new areas of the archipelago were opened to Christian missionary activity. Finally the missions established schools whose program of instruction was comparable with the government schools. These Christian schools were almost immediately recognized by the government and were subsidized on the same basis as any school that met the government's standards. The failure of the Christian parties to introduce religious instruction into the government's public schools has already been noted (see above, p. 72), but such restrictions did not of course apply to the Christian mission schools. These schools increased in number on Java, but especially on the 'outer islands' of the archipelago, and had a great influence on the development of the Western educated elite group. For our purposes in this study the Christian schools will be grouped with the government schools as dispensers of Western style instruction — the chief differences resided not so much in the method or content of instruction as in the requirements for admission, the Christian schools in general taking students from all levels of Indonesian society.

In addition to mission work the government also attempted

to further Christian principles in the daily operation and administration of the East Indies. An example of this is the 'Sunday Circular' and the 'Market Circular', both of which were issued by the Governor General in 1910. The 'Sunday Circular' suggested that it would be inappropriate to conduct State festivities on Sunday and especially requested all administrators and civil servants to refrain from official or semi-official activities on Sunday. The 'Market Circular' sought to restrict the holding of Indonesian markets when these fell on Sunday — this happened rather frequently since the Javanese market operates on a five day cycle rather than a seven day week. Despite the fact that the Governor General had carefully circumscribed his circulars in an attempt to avoid all injustices and to soothe all grievances, both these measures antagonized both the Europeans and the Indonesians on Java.[171]

Most vociferous in raising the cry of clericalism in government was the European press in the Indies. The great majority of Europeans in the East Indies did not make religion one of the cornerstones of their lives; they were of that group in Western culture which lives under Christian inspired principles without actively participating in, or seeing the need of, organized religion. They looked askance upon the activities of the missionaries and now feared that their own freedom of indifference would be shattered. Actually their fears went far beyond the sources of original provocation. But perhaps the Europeans in the Indies, or better said perhaps the journalists among them, felt that the desires of superiors would be applied indiscriminately by some shortsighted administrators. Or perhaps they saw in the Minister's measures the establishment of a principle which they wanted to nip in the bud.[172] Or they might even have feared the untoward effect that a heightened Christian religious activity could possibly have upon the Islamic peoples of the Islands.[173] Whatever the motivation, they raised a tremendous clamor against the religious measures emanating from The Hague. This cry in the European press, probably more than the actual circulars or the suggestions they contained, succeeded in arousing the fear in many Moslems that a great Christian drive would expel Islam from the archipelago.[174]

Spearheading the Islamic opposition to the Christianizing policies of the government was a Reformist Moslem organization named *Muhammadijah* founded by one Hadji Achmad Dachlan. Dachlan had been in the Middle East earlier in the century and had studied at the centers of Reformist teachings. He had returned to his home in Jogjakarta and made himself very unpopular by pointing out that the directional orientation of the main mosque in town was due West which was not exactly the direction of Mecca. This aroused such resentment among the Orthodox teachers that the Sultan of Jogjakarta 'exiled' Dachlan back to Mecca for awhile. Upon his return he decided to advance his Reformist concepts in a calmer manner and toward more important ends. In May 1912 Dachlan founded the organization Muhammadijah in Jogjakarta with the aim of countering missionary activities in that specific area and also advancing the Reformist ideas in Islam. Dachlan proved to be a most persuasive teacher and his organization began slowly but steadfastly to make headway. Its practical program took a leaf from the book of the missionaries and was directed toward social work. Schools, foundling homes, clinics, hospitals, and other humanitarian institutions completely Western in inspiration were founded by the Muhammadijah. Membership was solicited on an individual basis without pressure of fears and superstitions so often applied in Indonesian religious life. The organization operated under a Western style charter and was soon granted legal status by the government — this was tantamount to official recognition in the eyes of most Indonesians, although in Western jurisprudence it indicated only a particular position under the law.[175]

Of more immediate prominence than the Muhammadijah was another Islamic organization, the *Sarekat Islam* (United Islam), officially founded in 1912, too, and also perhaps in part a result of the government's emphasis on Christian principles, but in background, inspiration, and purpose quite different from the Muhammadijah. The Sarekat Islam is most outstanding for the immediate and startlingly rapid growth which it enjoyed. Certainly the revived interest in religion was a factor without which the Sarekat Islam would have remained a small, local organization, but other forces were also present to induce its phenomenal growth. Since the Sarekat Islam *did* become the brightest star in the Indonesian organizational firmament during the second decade of the 20th century, and since the leaders of the organization strove for leadership positions in the whole of Indonesian society, it seems desirable to study its formation and early development (which will be done in this chapter) and its further development and decline (which will be handled in Chapter III).

Shortly after 1900 groups of Arabs and West Coast Sumatrans, who through geographical position, religious inclination, and economic adaptability stood closely allied with each other, began to feel threatened in the economic position they had gained on Java. They were primarily merchants and local wholesalers, and had in general not suffered the severe economic ills which afflicted Javanese manufacturers and workers who could no longer compete with European produced materials. The Arabs and Sumatrans had adapted rather well to the new economic pattern, becoming one of the media through which Western and Indonesian products were distributed to the people. About the turn of the century they were subjected to strong economic pressures from the Chinese within the archipelago.

Alerted by the new mood emanating from the Chinese homeland toward the end of the 19th century, and quickened by the vision of a strong China which would take an active interest in the overseas Chinese, the Chinese in Java had begun to demand improvement of their status. The fact that the Japanese had been placed on equal footing with Europeans in the archipelago in 1899 was particularly galling to the Chinese. Prior to this time European status had been available to those desiring it as individuals, but had, on a group basis, been limited to Christian peoples. With the elevation of the Japanese to European status the criterion for this position was changed and complicated. European status came to be based upon social conditions of the homeland, political grandeur of the homeland, form of legal code in the homeland, race, and religion. The Chinese resented the superior position granted to the Japanese, and since as a group they are not tongue-tied, the Chinese lost no time in declaiming how they felt.[176]

One of their first demands was the abolition of the 'pass system'. The Netherlands Indian government had for years imposed travel restrictions upon 'foreign orientals' in the islands, restricting them to certain sections in the cities and towns. When a Chinese wished to travel beyond the confines of his assigned locality, be it for business or for pleasure, he had to have a pass from the civil authorities. These passes were a hindrance upon the freedom of movement of the Chinese and acted as a brake upon their commercial activity. The complaints of the Chinese were answered by the abolition of the pass system on Java about the turn of the century — the growing Dutch commercial interests needed the Chinese as middlemen and supported their request.[177]

The next grievance concerned the position of the Chinese with regard to Westernized education — they were left on the peripheries without being granted quotas in any of the new educational developments. As a result they initiated their own schools (in 1901 the Tiong Hwa Hwee Koan was founded), but quickly found their demands met by the government with the creation of the Dutch-Chinese Schools (H.C.S.) in 1908. As regards legal status, the Chinese were brought within the bounds of European commercial and criminal law, but retained their own private law. They continued to be regarded as Foreign Orientals in familial and social matters.

At the same time that concessions were made to the Chinese, certain economic plums dropped from their grasp. Pawn shops, loan operations, and opium franchises which had been largely in the hands of Chinese were taken over by the government. Only in loan operations did the Chinese, along with Arabs and better-situated Indonesians, remain operative, for their close personal contact with the rural masses gave them a decided advantage over the government-sponsored desa banks and other credit agencies. The action of the government freed much Chinese capital for reinvestment. Many Chinese began speculating in sugar and helped sponsor the great sugar boom of the pre-war years. Other Chinese sought to place their money in local industries, small shops, and commerce.[178] In so doing they trod heavily upon the economic domain of the Arabs, Sumatrans, and a handful of Javanese merchants and entrepreneurs. Chinese industriousness, perseverance, and money were now free to move all over Java.

The Arabs and Sumatrans saw the need for concerted action against the Chinese. Sometime around 1904 or 1905, the exact date is not certain, an organization for mutual help and assistance, named *Jam Yat Khair*, was formed in Batavia. Actually very little is known about it. Composed almost entirely of Arabs and West Sumatrans, the organization was primarily for economic protection and cooperation, yet it also reflected the strong religious sentiments of its component elements.[179] It stood prepared to support almost any organization in the Indonesian world which showed strong Moslem leanings.[180] Arabic schools were sponsored and teachers brought from Arabia to teach in them. In 1908 the Jam Yat Khair sponsored an educational organization of young Indonesian Moslems which received the name of Sumatra-Batavia-Alcheira.[181] It also stood behind endeavors in the field of journalism. A conscious effort was made to win over any Indonesians engaged in enterprise or commerce to cooperate with the movement. In this the organization met with some success and its membership and branches increased.

Probably influenced by the Jam Yat Khair was one Hadji Samanhoedi, batik dealer in the princely lands of Surakarta. Samanhoedi was one of a handful of Indonesian merchants who felt not only his classless position within the Javanese social hierarchy, but also felt the stimuli emanating from the formation of the Budi Utomo in Jogjakarta, from the revived interest in Islam, and from the increased activity of the Chinese.

The batik industry was at this time (ca. 1910) a cottage and small workplace industry. Wholesalers and middlemen (Arabs, Sumatrans, and an occasional Javanese) dispensed the cloths, dyes and waxes, and in due time collected and marketed the finished products. Finely woven cotton cloths known as cambrics which served as a foundation for the entire batiking process were supplied from the mills of Europe, having already in the last century displaced the native woven cloths. The cambrics reached dealers through Chinese middlemen. Early in the 20th century aniline dyes began to replace the indigo and other native produced dye stuffs. Now the dye also became an import product and was handled by the Chinese. It was felt that the Chinese were gaining an ever firmer hold upon the batik industry in which their control of the essential import commodities gave them an advantage.

At the same time those Indonesians whose self-awareness was stimulated through frequent contact with the West began to resent the old prerogatives over persons and property claimed by the local nobility of the princely lands. For both economic and social reasons the Arab-Indonesian merchants of Surakarta decided to organize. Hadji Samanhoedi took the initiative in forming what was in essence to be a benevolent and protective organization.[182]

As Samanhoedi himself had neither time nor talent for the creation of an organization he set out to find a director-organizer. His choice fell upon someone who had had experience with commercial organizations: Raden Mas Tirtoadisoerjo. Tirtoadisoerjo represented a small, disorganized segment of Indonesian society whose training had drawn them out of the orbit of Indonesian life and whose pride and self-consciousness did not permit them to find contentment and security in the service of the colonial government. Born of the prijaji class, son of a Central Javanese official, Tirto was educated in one of the Administrators' Schools (osvia). After completing his training he was, as is customary, placed in one of the lower posts of the government service with normal chances of periodic advancement. For some reason — perhaps a general dissatisfaction with the work, per-

haps a feeling that he deserved more, or perhaps an affront by a
superior — Tirto soon left the government service to seek his
fortune in other fields. Private enterprise usually welcomed educated personnel, but Tirto undertook to try his hand at journalism. With the moral and financial support of the Arab-Su-
matran commercial interests in Batavia, Tirto founded an Indonesian commercial journal, the *Medan Prijaji* (Nobles' Forum)
which was published in Bandung. As the paper enjoyed moderate
success, Tirto was encouraged to found some Indonesian commercial organizations. In 1909 he founded the *Sarekat Dagang
Islamyah* in Batavia and in 1911 a *Sarekat Dagang Islam* (United
Commercial Islam) in Buitenzorg (Bogor). In 1911 he was asked
by Hadji Samanhoedi to come to Surakarta (Solo) to organize
an Indonesian commercial organization among the batik dealers
there.[183]

The relationship between Tirto and Samanhoedi seems to have
been blighted at birth and rapidly atrophied. Tirto felt the Solo-
created Sarekat Dagang Islam to be a branch of his earlier organizations; Samanhoedi felt it to be his project. Despite their differences, membership grew rapidly. Dues were low, entry was accompanied by an enticing secret pledge and a semi-religious oath
of trust, and membership came to have a certain mystical-
mysterious aura. Strong traces of Western organizational procedure were in evidence, but many of the mutual-aid aspects of
Indonesian life were strongly emphasized.

Tirto's general concept seems to have been to use these commercial organizations as a lever toward activating Moslems to
strive for advancement. This was combined into concepts of a
brotherly relationship between members, and mutual assistance
bolstered by all the legal means of Western jurisprudence to
raise the standards of the people.[184] The 'Sarekat Islam' of which
Tirto first spoke, although he did not specifically apply the name
to the organization, was to work toward the prosperity and
greatness of the entire land — Java. The concept of membership was reminiscent of the Indonesian social order with its variation of rank and obligation. There were to be special, extra-

special, administrative, and regular members, but at the very bottom were the working members (*wargo rumakso*) who had to perform all sorts of duties, but who would be helped and protected by the organization. As the masses of Indonesia formed the solid core of the social order, so the working members were to form the core of the organization.

From almost the very first, something seems to have gone differently in the Surakarta organization than in Tirto's earlier commercial organizations. Perhaps it lay in the nature of the Solo area. This area with its strong ties to traditional Javanese life was the scene of increased Christian missionary activity and a heightened Islamic counterplay. Here also the Chinese entrepreneurs were seeking to penetrate some of the last remaining bastions of indigenous economic life. The growth in membership forced the organization out of the strictly commercial category and led it into activities over which it had little control. What to the merchants had been a matter of economic competition with the Chinese was interpreted by the young militant members of the Sarekat Dagang Islam as a racial threat which had to be met by force. Chinese began to be attacked in the streets; shops and warehouses were damaged; open violence began to be the order of the day in Surakarta and Surabaya. Soon the 'fighting forces' of the potentates of Surakarta became involved in the rioting and the disturbances reached such proportions that the Resident of Surakarta had to issue a decree curtailing the activities of the organization (August 10, 1912).[185]

Meanwhile the top leaders of the organization were busily extending their operations despite their inability to control the membership in the Solo area. Tirtoadisoerjo continued his activities with his organizations and newspaper in Batavia, Buitenzorg, and Bandung. The Surakarta organization also started a newspaper, *Sarotomo* (Guided Force), which was printed in Jogjakarta and also edited by Tirto. Samanhoedi was backing his brother, Hadji Amir, to found a branch of the Sarekat Dagang Islam in Bandung under the name of *Darmo Lumakso* (Million Duties?).[186]

Shortly before the rioting in the Solo area resulted in the decree curtailing activity, a sharp controversy arose over the newspaper *Sarotomo*. Either because Tirto had mismanaged funds or because the journal cost more than anticipated, the venture collapsed soon after it began. The relationship between Samanhoedi, who was evidently displeased with the general nature and results of the organization in its tumultuous state, and Tirto was now completely shattered. The Resident's curtailment was followed by an investigation which failed to find serious delinquencies on the part of the organization. Within two weeks Samanhoedi was preparing to reorganize his commercial organization in the Solo area. He first had to find another organizer, however, for the relationship with Tirto had been broken.

Samanhoedi's choice for organizer now fell upon another Javanese of prijaji birth, Raden Umar Sayed Tjokroaminoto. Tjokroaminoto, like Tirtoadisoerjo, had attended the Administrators' School (OSVIA), did not like government service, and sought his future elsewhere. It is told that he became associated with a travelling *wajang* show (Javanese puppet performances) and became noted for his impudence and fearlessness. The stories that circulated about his outspokenness and courage in flaunting established authority may well have been the deciding factor in Samanhoedi's selecting him.[187] Upon receiving the request to act as organizer for Samanhoedi's commercial group, Tjokroaminoto went to Surakarta to survey the groundwork that had already been prepared. It may well be that at this time he already saw the tremendous potential inherent in the popular appeal which Tirtoadisoerjo's efforts had had among the common people. At any rate, he joined forces with Samanhoedi, and upon his return to Surabaya, where he had conducted his previous activities, issued the legal statutes of the new *Sarekat Islam* of Surakarta in his name and that of eleven Solo merchants and Sultan's employees (September 10, 1912). Thus was officially founded the Sarekat Islam, one of the most lustrous of 20th century Indonesian organizations.

According to the new statutes, the purpose of the Sarekat Islam was (a) advancement of the commercial spirit among the indigenous population; (b) assistance to members who were in difficulty through no cause of their own; (c) advancement of the spiritual development and material interests of Indonesians, and by so doing assisting in raising their standards; and (d) opposition to misunderstandings about Islam, and advancing the religious life among Indonesian peoples in accordance with the laws and customs of that religion. This was to be accomplished by means which did not conflict with public order and common decency. There were to be only regular and honorary members. Almost immediately (September 14, 1912) the new statutes were sent to the Netherlands Indian government for recognized legal status.[188]

A comparison of Tjokroaminoto's statutes with the earlier efforts of Tirtoadisoerjo shows that the later work of Tjokro manifests a greater degree of Western influence and is more in line with the practical needs of organizational life in the newly developing social order. The fact that the legal advice of a European lawyer's office in Surabaya was carefully followed may have had much to do with this. The earlier effort to approximate Indonesian society in the organization's categories of membership (with even a place comparable to feudal service) is dropped; the concept of a brotherly relationship is supplanted by assistance in case of need. The necessity of commercial stimulation was more strongly emphasized in the newer statutes (probably much to the satisfaction of Samanhoedi), and the Islamic appeal, which had proved to be such a powerful welding force, was strengthened. Samanhoedi, who was elected first president, had every reason to be satisfied with his choice of organizer. Little did he realize that the organization which he regarded as his progeny would within a few years outgrow the purpose of economic advancement and protection for which it had been conceived.

In January 1913, a Sarekat Islam Congress was held in Surabaya, and from that time the popularity and membership of the organization swelled. The foundations for operation and growth within Surabaya had already been prepared by an Arab dominated commercial combination, similar to those already mentioned in other cities. The activities of this group, centering about the Setya Usaha Company, sought to weld a strong commercial organization centering about a newspaper issued primarily to provide Islamic merchants with an advertising medium. This paper was later to grow into the organ of the Sarekat Islam.

The tone of the new Sarekat Islam toward the government was clearly enunciated at the 1913 meeting by Tjokroaminoto, now vice-chairman of the parent organization, when he said, "We are loyal to the Government; we are satisfied under Dutch rule; it is not true that we wish to create unrest; it is not true that we want to fight — who says or thinks this is mentally deranged — we do not wish this, a thousand times no!" This attitude was quite understandable.[189] Apart from the fact that the organization had applied for recognized legal status, the entire movement was following the only type of advancement and progress that its leaders knew: namely, the dynamic concepts of the Ethical Colonial Policy. The influence of the West is obvious in the actions and aims of the Sarekat Islam leaders. Their desire to improve the living conditions of the Indonesian people blended smoothly with the government's program. At this time the government and the Sarekat Islam were moving in the same direction. Only somewhat later would the divergences in their paths become apparent.

Of tremendous importance for the existence of the Sarekat Islam was the strength of the religious appeal made to the people. The Arab merchants had been quick to realize the inherent advantage of their common religion with the indigenous population and were prepared fully to exploit this factor in order to limit the power of their Chinese competitors. Now, however, the spirit was seized upon by the rising Indonesian leaders, and carried even further — it became the basis of a popular appeal; it became a factor that led to the astonishing popularity of the Sarekat Islam.[190] All the pressures in early 20th century Indonesian life — from the Dutch Ethical Policy, from Islamic Reformists, from the writings emanating from the religious centers of the Near East, from the breakdown of traditional patterns of life, from the changing hierarchy of obligation and respect — led to in a renewed reliance upon Islam. The Sarekat Islam used the religious part of Indonesian society, whether Orthodox or Reformist, to strengthen its hold in the villages and urban centers.

The religious appeal caused the organization to grow rapidly. Chapters were founded in all the large cities. In Batavia, where previous organizations had laid the groundwork, the Sarekat Islam soon claimed over 12,000 members. A new sense of self-awareness, often manifested in an overemphasized impudence to compensate for an earlier humbleness, seemed to seize many Indonesians. This caused all sorts of stories and rumors to go the rounds of the European community in which a growing fear and dislike for this new aspect of Indonesian life soon developed. These sentiments were fanned and exploited by the conservative European press in the Indies so that much of European society was kept in a constant state of tension and distrust.[191]

The greatest growth of the Sarekat Islam was not in the large cities, however, but in the rural areas (particularly East Java) where in the early years tremendous numbers of villagers flocked to meetings and joined the organization by the hundreds. Here was amassed the great bulk of the organization's membership. Many of these people joined because of mystical reasons (see below, pp. 114–5).

Meanwhile the Netherlands Indian government watched developments in the Indonesian world with anxious eyes. Anxious on the one hand lest the movement would get beyond control or would direct itself against the government, and anxious on the other, lest it would die a rapid death from overexertion. The government could not ignore the problem of the Sarekat Islam: the organization had asked for legal status. The man to face the problem was Governor General Idenburg. Idenburg was one of the outstanding proponents of the Ethical Policy; he saw that changes were occurring in Indonesian society and was pleased, for he had long worked toward creating a new awareness among Indonesians. He also saw that new leaders were coming to the fore as representative of the new sentiments at work in Indonesian society. He had for some years been an advocate of extending the Decentralization Law of 1903 by forming a Colonial Council in which the leaders of the various Indonesian groups could participate in framing policies.[192] Now Idenburg was faced with an organization which claimed to speak for the Indonesian masses and whose leaders would have liked nothing better than to influence the government in the formulation and implementation of policy. Yet Idenburg had certain doubts about the Sarekat Islam. What was the great appeal of this organization and for whom did the leaders speak? Could a central group, however well-intentioned, control local chapters spread throughout Java? Was the Islamic appeal pan-Islamic, and if so, was it a threat to constituted authority? Was the rapid growth a threat to the stability of the Sarekat Islam? The result of this questioning attitude was an uncertain stand by the government with regard to the Sarekat Islam.

Governor General Idenburg adopted a paternalistic, protective attitude toward the young Sarekat Islam.[193] He upheld the organization in the face of the civil administration and stood prepared to consider all legitimate grievances. But his protective instinct caused him on June 30, 1913, to refuse legal recognition to the central body of the Sarekat Islam.[194] At an audience granted the Sarekat Islam leaders just a month earlier, Idenburg had shown deep sympathy for the movement and had shown a warm personal friendship toward Tjokroaminoto.[195] His reason for refusing the recognized legal status, which in the eyes of the Indonesians was tantamount to disapproval, was that he feared that the Central Sarekat Islam would not be able to assume responsibility for the various branches of the organization.[196] There is little doubt that Idenburg was sincere in his decision to withhold legal status, and it can be argued that by so doing he saved the Sarekat Islam from a series of legal complications which might have led to either its suppression or its rapid demise.[197] That Idenburg was not unfavorably disposed toward Indonesian movements such as the Sarekat Islam is clearly shown by a personal letter he wrote to A. Kuyper less than a week after his refusal to grant legal status. He writes:

That which goes by that name (moral degeneration) is nothing more
than that the native begins to reflect about himself and his environment.
It is the beginning of his 'awakening.' And this does not have to be
a degeneration (and up to now it is not such: I dare all to prove
the contrary) but it is the end of the *taillable et corvéable à merci*. We
must be pleased by this even though it gives us certain difficulties; we
wanted it so — at least so we said — and advanced it through our
education...[198]

Later in the year 1913 the Sarekat Islam held another convention in Surakarta. At this meeting the tone was more embittered, and it was decided to keep civil administrators out of the
organization in so far as possible. This was related to the feeling
among the Sarekat Islam leaders that their aims ran counter to
those of most of the civil administration. The civil administration
reciprocated in this feeling. At the same convention it was decided
to keep all non-natives out of the movement. Neither of these
resolutions was ever strictly applied, yet they could be called upon
whenever it seemed auspicious to do so.

Through meetings and rallies the name and popularity of the
Sarekat Islam continued to grow. Innumerable grievances
were raised and the Netherlands Indian government usually had
one or more of its advisors on hand to feel the pulse beat of
public opinion.[199] Yet the Sarekat Islam, in the years before the
First World War, remained exceedingly confused in aims and
attitudes. Its leaders, no doubt as surprised and amazed as
everyone else by the tremendous expansion of the organization,
had not yet adapted themselves to their new role and position.
Their growing awareness and further activity will be discussed in
the following chapter.

Meanwhile certain changes had occurred in the motherland,
which, although not affecting the general scope of the Ethical
Policy, did influence certain aspects of the colonial relationship.
Nineteen hundred and thirteen was an election year. The liberal
and radical parties which had undertaken the election of 1909
separately were now united in a Liberal-Radical Concentration
(*Vrijzinnige Concentratie*). Together they took exception to the
colonial activity of the right wing government, and as a single

plank in their joint platform took issue with the religious attitude of the government in power.

> Through forced Christianization the motherland threatens to alienate the native peoples of our colonies. The tendency to supplant govern- ment schools with schools of Christian sects transports the school con- troversy to the Indies. Our possession of our colonies is threatened as a result of measures that are diametrically opposed to years of tested colonial guidance.[200]

An increase of 40 % in the number of church sponsored schools since 1909, an increase of almost 300 % from 1910 to 1912 in the subsidies granted to church sponsored normal schools, and an enrollment of teacher trainees almost equal to the government schools, seemed to lend weight to the Liberal-Radical concern about present policies.[201]

The Liberal-Radical Concentration won 35 % of the seats in the Second Chamber of the Netherlands States General in the 1913 elections. This made it the largest single group in the par- liament and as such it was called upon to form a cabinet. Due to lack of cooperation from the Socialist left, this proved impossible and recourse had to be taken in an extra-parliamentary, or busi- ness, cabinet. This new cabinet was formed by P. W. A. Cort van der Linden who regarded his mission as the creation of a cabinet which would stand outside all political parties, and yet would represent public opinion as expressed in the elections. In this cabinet the post of Minister of Colonies was filled by Theodore B. Pleyte of the Radical Democratic Party, one of the component groups of the Liberal-Radical Concentration.

Pleyte was a lawyer who had practiced in the East Indies and had been associated with the legal office of his close friend C. T. van Deventer, who along with Van Kol and Fock was now again seated in the parliament. The Minister had taken an active hand in advancing the election slogans directed against the colonial regulations of his predecessor, and everyone looked for the turn of the wheel which would start the new direction in colonial affairs. They looked in vain. Pleyte's first official move was to retain Idenburg as Governor General, his second, was to declare that election slogans must not be taken too seriously. Undoubtedly the Minister felt somewhat hampered by the lack of a party government. Only on a point close to his heart, the school question in the East Indies, did he feel obliged to turn away from the old course. Even here, however, he sought compromise rather than a radical departure from the policy of actively advancing religious education. Deciding not to tamper with the subsidy regulations for education, Pleyte was insistent about making religious courses in all subsidized schools elective, thereby granting the pupil, or in practice his family, the right to decide whether religious education would accompany the secular. The Christian parties of the Right had to remain content with this compromise.

From this time forward the dynamism of Christian missionary activity in the archipelago is curtailed. Never again would the European or the Indonesian groups in the East Indies seriously have to fear the activity of the Christian church. To a few ethical, religious-neutralists like Van Deventer and Fock, the damage had already been done, for they regarded much of the Sarekat Islam activity as a reaction to the intense missionary activity.[202] Certainly they had no ill-feelings about the existence of the Sarekat Islam, but they deplored those sentiments within the organization which were directed against Christianity and consequently also against Western culture. These Ethici wanted to see the Sarekat Islam guided by a Westernized, ethical spirit which would through self-motivation accomplish what the Ethical Colonial Policy had been attempting from outside.

The years immediately preceding the First World War saw the full blossoming of the Ethical Colonial Policy. When Van Deventer, after an absence of fifteen years, returned in 1913 to his much beloved East Indies he could marvel at the progress which had been made in all fields of endeavor, and particularly at the new *elan* of the Indonesian people. The advances made in the first years of the 20th century, when viewed in retrospect, surpassed the dreams of the most optimistic of the Ethici. Certainly much remained to be done, but the measures already taken in the fields of health, education, agriculture, credit, transport, administration, and others, bade fair to change the entire complexion of Java. The tide of the times was certainly with the leaders of the Ethical Movement. Prosperity which was so tediously sought at the beginning of the century seemed miraculously to have returned.[203] Few people bothered to read the conclusions of the laboriously prepared volumes of the 1904 Prosperity Investigation which were completed just before the war.[204]

It was certainly a grand and glorious mission — this task of helping the Indonesian people to help themselves to the greatness of Western culture. In the motherland and in the colony men stood prepared to help and to guide the Indonesians on the paths that would lead them to the better life, the nicely circumscribed and formalized life of the West, the life which offered material pleasures never before known to man. It was certain to be good for Indonesians as it had been good for Europeans. A small but growing number of Indonesians came to identify their welfare with the West and they too began to seek improvement and democracy. In this latter, they were often disappointed, but the Ethici could point out that when Western integrity, industriousness, and individualism filled the hearts and souls of the Indonesians, then too, would there be occasion for independence. Not today, or even tomorrow, but in the future. It was a sincere, honorably conceived vision of a great cultural and civilizing task.

In less than a decade the dream had dissolved.

Chapter III

Rampant Radicalism and Steady Growth, 1914–1920

The First World War and the Growth of the Sarekat Islam

The World War (1914–1918) deeply affected the Netherlands and her colonies. Neither the motherland nor the East Indies participated directly in the war, but they could not escape its effects. With its land borders pressed against one contestant and its seashore facing the other, the Netherlands had to step softly to retain neutrality. Contact with the far empire could be maintained only by sea (late in the war the Dutch finally succeeded in establishing wireless contact with Java) and as a consequence the Dutch colonial relationship became highly dependent upon the whims of the British Mistress of the Seas. The pressures of war forced the British to curtail and restrict neutral shipping, and as a result the links between the Netherlands and the East Indies became exceedingly tenuous.

The most immediate, though not altogether permanent, effect of the war upon the East Indies was a growing independence from the motherland. This was most strongly felt in administration and in economic life. The lack of regular communication gave the governor general greater freedom in determining measures and policies, and shifted many of the higher level decisions from the motherland to the colony. On the other hand a tendency for many proposals and improvements to stagnate under the handicap which the war had placed upon normal activity was also present. The colonial budget was so severely curtailed by armament expenditures that money was often lacking to execute much of the colonial program. The East Indian government could do little more than carry on existing developments and trends while awaiting the return of more stable world conditions. The presence of an extra-parliamentary cabinet in the motherland during the war years also affected colonial affairs. No radical shift or innovation could be expected at such a time. Colonial Minister Pleyte's most daring measure, the formation of a People's Council (*Volksraad*) in the Indies, was a long considered measure which was generally agreed upon by all political parties (see below, p. 141).

The war had brought to fruition the dreams of those who had desired greater economic and entrepreneurial independence from the boards of directors and financial interests of the motherland. Managers of established enterprises had to continue on their own initiative when the controlling hand was made more distant. Far more significant, however, was the stimulation provided by reduced imports and exports. There was a marked trend toward producing the commodities for local consumption which had previously been imported. As a result numerous small industries sprang up. Many of these were founded on such shaky ground that when the war ended they were swept away by the influx of European products.[2] One economic change not erased, however, was the increasing share that non-European nations contributed to the economic life of the archipelago.[3] During and after the war the exports of the Indies to the United States of America increased from two to fourteen percent of the total exports. Imports from Japan increased from two to more than eight percent of the Indies' imports. These relationships never returned to their pre-war basis.[4]

The leaders of the Ethical Colonial Policy had long hoped to awaken a sense of enterprise and commerce among the Indonesian people. The lack of an Indonesian 'middle class' comparable to that in Western society had been one of the most serious handicaps in the creation of a politically independent and socially resilient East Indies. Much of the effort of the Ethici had been directed toward strengthening the economic fiber of the Indonesian people. It seemed in vain. The desa banks were used for little more than consumptive credit and soon lost their cooperative framework; the district banks were used mostly by non-Indonesians and a few members of the prijaji class; indigenous agricultural export products remained inferior to plantation products; and Indonesian enterprise showed only slight signs of advancement. The war years might have stimulated Indonesian enterprise — and to an extent they did — but by far the greatest participation in the burgeoning entrepreneurial development was by the Chinese and Arabs.

It is difficult to assess the reluctance of the Indonesians to engage in money-making activity. Some have claimed that the Dutch colonial system destroyed the Indonesian's sense of enterprise and industry, leaving him economically ignorant and devoid of initiative. Others have taken the view that the Indonesian has never had a sense of economic endeavour and simply does not possess the strength of character required to conduct business operations. Others have found still other explanations for the failure of an Indonesian 'middle class' to develop readily. There is probably some truth in each of these. The colonial situation certainly had untoward effects upon Indonesian economic life. The economic power of non-Indonesian groups in the archipelago made it difficult, if not impossible, for Indonesians to gain a toe-hold in the higher economic brackets. On the other hand, there is little indication that Indonesians are socially tuned to modernized economic life. Wealth and economic prowess have not in themselves carried prestige and status. It is neither possible nor necessary in this study to evaluate conclusively the state of indigenous economic life; it is, for present purposes, sufficient to note the small extent of Indonesian entrepreneurial activity during the first quarter of this century.[5]

In Indonesian society the term 'middle class' can only aptly be used to describe the middle income groups which would include administrators, land holders, teachers, doctors and other professionals. In no way is the term related to the bourgeois, entrepreneurial classes of Western society. To make this relationship leads only to confusion.

Beyond the administrative and economic effects of the First World War upon the colony, there were political and psycho-

logical influences. Turkish participation had drawn the sentiments of many Indonesians to the side of Germany.[6] Particularly
large numbers of Sarekat Islam members allowed their religious
convictions to determine their loyalty. The European community
never countered such sympathies, though it feared their pan-
Islamic implications, for although many were Anglophile, there
was widespread fear of Britain's ally, Japan. Japanese aggres-
siveness was plainly evident, particularly toward China; and Japanese 'over-population' was an accepted fact. Many Europeans
in the East Indies viewed Japan as the greatest single threat to
the archipelago.[7] Politically, therefore, the Netherlands Indian
government followed a course as circumspectly neutral as the
exigencies of daily life permitted.

The psychological effects of the war cannot be readily evaluated.
The war was undoubtedly one of the greatest blows suffered by
19th century Western civilization — never had West European
man dreamed such a cataclysm possible. Much of the stability
and even more of the optimism was erased from the Western
cultural pattern. But how did this affect the colonial relationship? One cannot say with certainty. Perhaps in a myriad of
slight occurrences which pointed up the insecurity and lack of
certainty in Western man. Perhaps in a compensative severity
on the part of some Europeans. Perhaps in a weakness and con-
cessiveness on the part of others. Whatever the form, the influence was subtle and not immediate, but almost certainly present, and bound to be felt by the bearers of a culture as keenly
tuned to human feeling and decorum as the Javanese. To blame
the war for all alterations of Western character would, of course,
be nonsensical. The growing influence of Marxist ideals, the
startling revelations of psychoanalysis, the obvious maldistribu-
tion of the fruits of industry, the 'extra-cultural' thinking stimulated by the youthful science of anthropology, the growing dominance of pragmatist philosophy, the impact of the Darwinian
concepts, the loss of religious ideals, the questioning of the
economic worth of imperialism which Hobson started and Lenin
furthered: all these and many more factors were at work to alter

Western life. Yet it was the war and its concomitant destruction of faith which raised each of these problems and innovations to the status of a cultural dilemma.[8] Only with the war could people of the West return seriously to the writings of Nietzsche; only the impact of war could bestow popularity on Spengler's note of cultural doom. Ford Madox Ford, Vera Brittain, Marcel Proust, John Galsworthy, Eric M. Remarque, and many others could write of a life and a world that had been. Something vital had happened to Western life: Western optimism had been severely shaken.

Indonesian life was neither as directly nor as deeply influenced by the World War as was Western life. Indonesian life flowed on. It was only in the later years of the war that some of the stirrings in the Western World began to influence parts of Indonesian society. The Russian Revolution and President Wilson's Fourteen Points, found a certain response in Indonesian society. More of this later.

Outwardly the most active manifestation of Indonesian desires and ambitions in the years preceding, during, and following the World War is to be found in the Sarekat Islam. Following its rapid growth after its establishment in 1912 (see above, p. 91 ff.), the Sarekat Islam continued to expand. Soon the organization claimed a membership of over two million. Small wonder that the Sarekat Islam is generally regarded the first mass movement in Indonesia. The leaders of the Sarekat Islam are an interesting segment of the Indonesian elite. Their problems and the problems of their organization serve to illuminate the development of an Indonesian elite in the early twentieth century.

The Sarekat Islam is intimately associated with the personality of Raden Umar Sayed Tjokroaminoto, who very soon assumed the leading position in the organization. He was a captivating and moving speaker. He won the heart of the masses and became a symbol of hope for those who felt themselves suppressed or disillusioned. He became the medium through which real and imagined grievances found expression. He was looked upon by many as the embodiment of future good and happiness. Small wonder that by 1914 he had come to be regarded as the *ratu adil*, the righteous prince, who would lead the way to the proverbial paradise. People — particularly the village people — flocked to hear him speak, to touch his garments, to kiss his feet. Word of his grandeur sprang from mouth to mouth. He came in the name of Islam, and it was Islam that held promises of a messiah. Could he not be the long awaited Prabu Heru Tjokro, the traditional *ratu adil?* He came, and was accepted in the name of 'Tjokro'. In a world permeated with mystical relationships and beliefs, this was no mere coincidence of names.⁹ His fame grew. Even among the intellectuals, who were dubious of the mystical associations, his courage and his oratorical skill made him popular. Along with his popularity the strength and mission of the Sarekat Islam grew. Full use was made of modern means of mass communication in order to swell the ranks of the organization.

Actually, Tjokroaminoto, the ideal of the masses, was, although most certainly well-intentioned, not a very strong or resolute character. No one can blame him for being startled at the amazing popularity of the Sarekat Islam; he was not alone in this regard. The circumstances which made his appeal timely and vital were less obvious at that time than at the present. Thus he can hardly be expected to have had a long range program of operation prepared. And he should be applauded for attempting to surround himself with the best available Indonesian intellectuals who would join his organization. But the constant failure to display constructive leadership, the perpetual reduction of policy to short-range considerations, the chronic inability to grasp the future scope of the organization, and finally the unending inconsistency of plans and policy in the face of conflicting advice and pressure by friends and associates, do not serve to build up a picture of him as a strong leader. His one desire was to retain unity in the organization — in order to do this he could, and did, agree with all men. The men about him, who continued to function as a *de facto* central body for the Sarekat Islam even after legal status had been refused, realized the strength of his mass appeal, and knew that without him the organization would disintegrate. It would be a few years yet before the question arose in many minds whether there could be any organization *with* him.

The men of the central body of the Sarekat Islam were, for the most part, well-intentioned, with a strong desire to advance the interests of the Indonesian people. That this ambition should be couched in terms of, and fall within the scope of, the Ethical Colonial Policy should arouse no surprise. The most progressive thing they knew was that the West — in whatever form it had reached them — and the Ethical Policy had both stimulated and offered solutions for their desires. As a group they had no aversion to advancing their own interests, and showed a normal amount of concern with heightening their own status and prestige through the organization which supported them.[10]

Raden Goenawan early found a place in the central Sarekat Islam as the chairman of the West Java branch. A native of Madiun, Goenawan had completed the Administrators' School (OSVIA), and had briefly held one of the lower civil service posts. This work had appealed to him so little that he tried his hand at journalism. In this pursuit he became associated with Tirtoadisoerjo and the Batavia branch of the Sarekat Dagang Islam. But the relationship was short-lived, and Goenawan left journalism to become manager of a hotel in Batavia. He was noted for his vast knowledge of Javanese history and his active participation in the local chapter of the Budi Utomo. His hotel served as an assembly place for like-minded persons. When the Sarekat Islam desired to organize a Batavian branch they recognized Goenawan's potential, for he had wide contacts among Indonesian urban groups. He was asked to serve as organizer. He met with success in his new work — particularly the cooperative and mutual benefit appeal netted good results among the urban Indonesians — and he soon became leader for West Java.

In Bandung the Sarekat Islam was established by a triumvirate: Soewardi Soerjaningrat, Abdoel Moeis, and A. Widiadisastra (Wignjadisastra?). The Bandung organization, *Darmo Lumakso*, founded earlier by Samanhoedi's brother, was bypassed in favor of centering an organization about the above named triumvirate whose popular appeal would assure wider support. Soewardi, as previously indicated, was a member of Douwes Dekker's Indische Partij, and was engaged in journalistic work on *De Expres*, published in Bandung, when he was asked to help found a Sarekat Islam branch in that city. His efforts were short-lived, for when his article 'If I Were a Netherlander' appeared in *De Expres* he was imprisoned and eventually exiled to Holland (see above, p. 65).

A. Widiadisastra and Abdoel Moeis were both associated with the newspaper *Kaum Muda* (Young Society) which they, together with Mohammed Djunas, had started in 1912. Djunas, an Arab from Palembang, provided financial backing for the enterprise. Widiadisastra, from Bantem (West Java), inspired the newspaper with his fiery zeal. He had come to Bandung as a journalist and worked with Tirtoadisoerjo on the *Medan Priayi*. Before Tirto and his paper had fallen from grace, he had dissociated himself from this journal. In Bandung he married the daughter of the head *penghulu* (mosque official) and fell closely into line with his father-in-law's strong religious convictions. Teaching in an Indonesian school, he burned to stimulate the consciousness of the Indonesian people and was thus a natural choice to be drawn into the creation of the *Kaum Muda*. He never was taken into the central body of the Sarekat Islam, but remained active on the local level of the organization until about 1919.

Abdoel Moeis, already mentioned in other connections (see above, p. 53), was brought into the leadership of the *Kaum Muda* to handle details of editing, publishing, and distributing the newspaper. He had gained experience while working for the Dutch-language paper, *Preangerbode*. Moeis, also a journalist in his own right, seems to have been motivated by a sincere desire to improve the welfare of the Indonesian people, but had only the vaguest notions of what this involved. He was inspired more by grievances and annoyances with conditions in government service as he had found them when employed there, than by positive social aims.[11] He was soon taken into the central body of the Sarekat Islam and there rose to be vice-chairman. The *Kaum Muda* rapidly became one of the leading Indonesian-language newspapers.

When Soewardi was arrested and tried for journalistic excesses in an article which questioned the appropriateness of a celebration in the East Indies (which had not yet been liberated from Dutch rule) of the hundredth anniversary of the Netherlands' liberation from Napoleonic rule, both Widiadisastra and Moeis were completely exonerated from any share in the offense.[12] Their failure to be implicated lost to them permanently the trust of the revolutionary movement which was just being born (ca. 1913).

One of the founders of the Semarang branch also found his way up into the central body of the Sarekat Islam — Raden Mohammed Joesoep, a clerk in one of the tramway companies. Together with Raden Soedjono, secretary to the Regent, he had founded the Semarang organization. But Semarang in these years was a volatile city — rapid urbanization and proletarianization had made it fertile ground for discord, and it became the focal point for European and Indonesian left wing and revolutionary activity. When in 1914 and 1915 some of the Dutch civil servants began to use unofficial pressures to keep the native civil servants out of the Sarekat Islam, Soedjono, and a few others who like him held governmental posts dropped out of the organization. Joesoep, perhaps to quiet the already evident separatist tendencies of the Semarang group which stood at odds with the feudalistic, traditional orientation of the Surakarta group, was taken into the central body of the Sarekat Islam. However, it soon appeared he was losing power within his home branch in Semarang where radical groups, whose source of strength lay in the newly organized labor unions, were gaining control. Little is known of what exactly happened to Joesoep, but he rapidly faded from view as the young radical Semaoen gained control of the Semarang branch and within a few years was taken into the central body of the Sarekat Islam.

The princely lands of Central Java were the birthplace of the Sarekat Islam organization. Samanhoedi, the original instigator, was still affiliated with the central body, but his influence was decidedly waning. The organization no longer served his purposes and he had lost usefulness in the eyes of the young intellectuals. A much stronger influence in the Central Javanese lands came to be exercised by Raden Mas Soerjopranoto, member of the House of Paku Alam and brother of Soewardi. Soerjopranoto, a graduate of the Agricultural School in Buitenzorg (Bogor), had participated actively in the creation of the Budi Utomo. Due to certain slightly unethical practices and a desire to engage in more extensive action than the scope of the Budi Utomo permitted, he had thrown in his lot with the Sarekat Islam and was quickly taken up in the intellectual coterie surrounding Tjokroaminoto.

Another important voice from the Central Javanese lands was that of A. Dachlan of Jogjakarta, the founder of Muhammadijah. He remained in close contact with the Sarekat Islam but devoted most of his attention to the Muhammadijah, which carefully refrained from all political activity. Through his efforts there was close liaison between these two organizations which complemented each other; the Muhammadijah working in the cultural field, the Sarekat Islam in the political. One interesting aspect of Sarekat Islam activity in the princely lands was the rapid retrogression of the Sarekat Islam in Surakarta, its birthplace, and the shift of leadership to the other princely center of Jogjakarta.

In Surabaya, the focal point for the East Java activities, Tjokroaminoto retained the leadership. In this area his appeal was greatest and the largest number of people flocked to the Sarekat Islam. The actual operation of the Surabaya organization was in the hands of Mas Tondokoesoema and Raden Adiwidjojo, two young men of whom little is known, but who may be assumed to have been friends of Tjokro's from his earlier days.

Such, in general, was the character of the people who took leading roles in the early Sarekat Islam. Either directly or indirectly affiliated with the organization's central body, they comprised the nuclear leadership for the entire organization. Undoubtedly they reflected to an extent the feelings of the organization's members, and many grievances which they voiced were undoubtedly felt by the Indonesian masses. Yet it must not be forgotten they were leaders, and, as such, had to formulate and to guide vague sentiments into some form of understandable complaint. Most of them were not too skillful at this. Although the Sarekat Islam was supposed to have closer touch with the pulse beat of Indonesian life than any of the other organizations, and even though this contact was closest in the early years of the organization, one must not seek too intimate a relationship between the feeling of the populace and the expression of the Sarekat Islam leaders. The leaders expressed sentiments and grievances which, through their training and contacts in the Western world, had to them appeared justified. They came to feel that all Indonesians would, if sufficiently enlightened, view these sentiments as they did (see below, p. 115). This in itself is not unusual. In fact, it is rather the expected; but in viewing a culture that is rather far removed from that of the West, there is oftentimes a tendency to overlook this basic reality and to assume that ethnic traits remain tied inseparably to cultural traits, or, to turn the phrase, that an Indonesian by birth necessarily speaks from the heart of his people.

On the periphery of this central group of the Sarekat Islam, and at times impinging upon its prerogatives and roles, were a number of men who filled either local functions, or were in one or another capacity, tied to the central body. Since the Sarekat Islam was an economic organization at the outset there were representatives of commercial interests at hand. Mas Hadji Abdoelpatah, of Solo, became treasurer of the central group, Hadji Achmad Hasan Saeni and Raden Dipa Mertana both of Solo also represented commercial interests. Some civil servants joined the organization and a number of these, like A. M. Sangadja, an Ambonese of high birth, who had been employed in judicial work in Jogjakarta, and Tirtodanoedjo, a school teacher, resigned their government posts rather than undergo the unofficial pressures that were often applied. Such sacrifice indicated a strong faith in, and great expectations from, the Sarekat Islam, and it is not surprising that such men became among the organization's staunchest workers.

Other young men were associated with the organization on more questionable grounds. Raden Tjokrosoedarmo, of Surabaya, employee of the legal offices of B. ter Kuile, offered his services and that of his office (for the usual fee) to all sorts of indigenous and Arabic organizations for drawing up statutes, requests for recognized legal status, and the like. Raden Ng. Djajamargasa, of Solo, was employed by the Indonesian civil administration while also belonging to the Sarekat Islam, and seems, to have been an obstreperous and troublesome character. Raden Boerhan Kartadiredja, a wandering turbulent journalist, who had tried his hand at government and private employ, now seemed drawn to the Sarekat Islam in his capacity of writer. Soema Asmara, an aged man who had sampled virtually all walks of life and who tended to cut a ridiculous figure in the organizations' meetings, seems to have been privately employed by Samanhoedi to keep him posted on the activities of the more Western oriented leaders. This is but a sampling of persons who filled roles of minor importance, but stood above the general level of members. The above selection, like the Sarekat Islam membership generally, varies from serious and inspired devotion at the one extreme, to complete pampering of individual idiosyncrasies and frustrations at the other.

Another group, instrumental in founding the Sarekat Islam but marginal to its growth, was the Arabs. Their effort in energizing Indonesian commercial life has already been sufficiently emphasized. Now that the Sarekat Islam began to flourish their influence did not cease. Despite the resolution of 1913 to keep non-Indonesians out, numerous Arabs retained membership in, or actively worked with, the Sarekat Islam. Sayed Ali al Habsji, widely known orthodox religious teacher of Batavia, sought to intensify the spiritual tone of the organization. A similar goal stirred Sayed Abdullah bin Husein al Aydroes, chairman of the organization Jam Yat Chair, who sat at the director's table of the Batavia meetings of the Sarekat Islam. As a religious duty he warmly pleaded for advancement of education as the key to progress. Sayed Achmad bin Mohammed al Moesawa of Sura-

baya wanted to use religion as a unifying factor and was much influenced by pan-Islamic thought. The actual power behind the
smooth-functioning Surabaya branch was the commercially astute
Hasan Ali Soerati who played an active behind-the-scenes part
in the entire Sarekat Islam. He was head of the Setya Usaha
Company which published the *Utusan Hindia* (Indies' Courier)
organ of the Sarekat Islam. He was also responsible for the
success of some of the small cooperative stores which the Sarekat
Islam had established in the Surabaya area. These stores, incidentally, were among the few of their type to succeed, making
the organization's attempts to engage in direct economic activity
somewhat less than a total failure. Personally remaining out of
the public eye, Soerati was instrumental in getting his colleague
Hasan bin Semit seated on the board of the Sarekat Islam to
represent Arab interests.

Certainly not all of the important figures of the early Sarekat
Islam have been mentioned here, but the majority have been
touched upon. Enough has been said to arrive at tentative conclusions about the group. Intellectually most of them stood above
the general level of Indonesians, but almost none of them
belonged to the best educated segment of Indonesian society.
Culturally they had had more than average contact with the
West, and framed their goals and demands in a Westernized
pattern of thought. Economically they came from the middle
income brackets of Indonesian society (this excepts, of course, the
Arabs and commercial members). Socially most were from lesser
prijaji families with an occasional representative of a merchant
family. Although most manifested religious sentiments, none
was descended from active *santri*, or religious, families.

It is possible to divide the leadership of the Sarekat Islam into
three, by no means exclusive, groups. The original commercial
group is the least significant part of this leadership, and begins to
decline almost from the beginning. The most powerful part of
the leadership consisted of Western educated intellectuals and
semi-intellectuals who had found little satisfaction within the
colonial government structure. The third group, originally power-

ful only at the local level, was the religious group. This group grew more powerful when given leadership, and combined with some of the intellectuals when the organization's secular leaders followed too radical a path. This third group was probably more representative of the organization's mass membership than either of the others.

The rapid spread and tremendous popularity of the Sarekat Islam among the Indonesian masses cannot be explained in terms of an intellectual appeal. Certainly the intellectual group of the leaders did bring in a number of members, for their very bearing and attire awed many a villager, but they do not account for the tremendous spread of the organization. Nor can mystical and *ratu adil* attractions account in full for the continued adherence of members. Commercial factors had only a limited appeal. The magnet that drew members was the appeal of Islam, and within Islam it seems particularly to have been the hope of closer communal and brotherly ties that exercised the greatest attraction: i.e., factors of life which Ethical-inspired changes had not been able to fill.[13] There is no evidence to indicate that Reformist or Orthodox religious appeal played the greatest role in forming the Sarekat Islam. Each seems to have had its following, and each was, in turn, used as it seemed best to fit the local situation.[14]

As word of the Sarekat Islam spread to the small villages, it was usually the local religious teacher or religious authority who took it upon himself to lay the groundwork for a chapter. Often he would be visited by one of the young propagandists attached to the central organization who would suggest procedures to be followed. Then, with all the authority vested in him by his religious office, the Sarekat Islam organizer would form a local chapter. The process was usually accompanied by secret oaths, pledges and rituals of a religious nature, and by semi-religious mystical practices such as the selling of *djimat* (tokens) for invulnerability or some special favor. In brief, each locality set out to form an 'in' group, and made the process almost socially irresistible to groups of persons seeking renewed inner solidarity.[15]

In how far the local religious leader sought to use the wider authority of the Sarekat Islam to advance his own stature in the face of local secular authority cannot be judged, but there must have been a fair amount of local wrangling involved in the spread of the organization. Once the local chapter was formed, one of the leading Sarekat Islam figures, preferably Tjokroaminoto himself, would be invited to come and speak. People flocked to see and hear this fearless man of their own race who dared criticize constituted authority, who sat in equal position with princes of the blood, and who had been seated on a chair while speaking with the governor general.

The reasons for joining local chapters of the Sarekat Islam varied. Many felt that it was best not to defy religious authority; others, although perhaps doubting the power of the *djimat* and messianic predictions which often accompanied them, found it wisest to take no risk at being left out of the future good. After all, membership was very reasonable — from ten to fifty cents — and one never knew what power might result from this. Others may have been intrigued by the secret oaths and practices accompanying membership. Many more joined because it seemed the socially acceptable thing to do and because it was wisest to follow the prevailing trend. Whatever the immediate cause for joining, membership was principally prized for the secure sense of belonging which it provided: people once again felt themselves part of a group which cared for them.[16] In large measure the Dutch colonial policies — particularly those which tended to convert the village into an instrument of welfare — had created the necessary moods and sentiments which led to the burgeoning membership of the Sarekat Islam.[17] Without these effects on village life, there would still have been a Sarekat Islam, but it is doubtful if it would have had such success or wide support.

To the villagers the Sarekat Islam provided a sense of security, but they in turn provided the organization's leadership with a large following which gave extra weight to its demands. Once the structure was built the leaders had continually to justify their position. Not constituted for either cultural or political activity,

nd exceeding all economic or commercial goals, the Sarekat
slam could outwardly do little more than proclaim itself concerned with the general welfare and improvement of the Indonesian people. With this objective lying easily at hand, it took but
a short step for the leaders to view their mission as expressive of
the popular will. With conscious effort they set out to uncover and
publicly expose grievances, and, what was usually most painful,
lay the blame at someone's doorstep. Actually little effort was
involved for many people were already restive under the pressures
of the Ethical Policy and were easily persuaded that their ills
were ascribable to a particular tax or regulation. As concerns
the delegation of blame, the entire process was very superficial with no attempt to penetrate the heart of problems; a
particular office, station, or status was the most usual recipient
of blame. In culling grievances, which became a major occupation
of the Sarekat Islam, the organization interjected itself between
the people and the administrator.[18] The people were not long in
recognizing the role of the new organization and began to un-
burden themselves to the Sarekat Islam rather than to the local
administrator who was oftentimes unable to take effective action.

The Netherlands Indian government stood quite ready to meet
and ameliorate the complaints which the Sarekat Islam presented.
In this manner the government advanced one of the aims of the
Ethical Policy, which was to assist and further any movement
that seemed to emanate from the Indonesian people. To some
of the Europeans, especially the most ardent Ethici, the Sarekat
Islam spoke for all the people, and they rushed to get ahead of
the organization and clear the path of its progress. In the Sarekat Islam they saw the glorious, long-awaited awakening of the
East. On the other hand, a growing number of persons in the
East Indies began to question this concessionary position and
felt that the sources of the grievances should be evaluated as well
as their content. Not everyone was convinced of the wisdom of
sweeping away the institutions of the past for the sake of change
— a change naturally directed toward the progress embodied in
the world of the West. In this growing variance of opinions lay

the seeds which were ultimately to destroy both the Ethical Policy and the Sarekat Islam.

By late 1915 it was obvious that the war might continue for some time. Because of the world turmoil Governor General Idenburg had been in office well over the usual five year period. His co-operation with Minister Pleyte had been excellent, for although men of widely separated political views they were as one in their desire to meet and further the wishes of the newly developing Indonesian elite. However, the governor generalship was an arduous post and it was time for Minister Pleyte to appoint a successor. Everyone had expected that the choice would fall upon Van Deventer, but his untimely death in September 1915, precluded this possibility. The paucity of men liberal enough to suit the Minister and with sufficient stature to fill the office made the choice exceedingly difficult. Pleyte finally turned away from the Indies' experts and sought his man from the diplomatic service, a shift made easier by the need for careful guidance in a world full of belligerent powers. His choice fell upon Count J. P. van Limburg Stirum, descendant of a fine old aristocratic family, an artful diplomat, a novice in East Indian affairs, a non-party man, and the type of liberal who considered all men entitled to equal duties, rights, and justice. Somewhat haughty, unfettered by bourgeois values and ideals, and convinced of the good for all peoples inherent in true democratic government, Van Limburg Stirum took over his new function in 1916.[19]

Idenburg was happy to leave. His period as governor general had been a trying one — he had had to be more severe than he wished. Any man faced with his problems would have felt harassed. As one of his final acts in office, Idenburg did what had been on his mind for some time: he recognized the legal status of the Central Sarekat Islam.[20]

With recognized legal status the stature of the Sarekat Islam rose in Indonesian society. Since the central body had been functioning on a *de facto* basis since the very beginning (for purposes of recognition the central body was formally constituted in Surabaya in 1915) the new recognition had small effect upon the actual functioning of the organization. It would now be easier to hold public meetings, particularly at a national level, but there would be added responsibility for the actions of all branch organizations. The chief benefit lay in the membership increases among those groups of people who had previously hesitated to affiliate themselves with an unrecognized group, but in this membership also lay concealed certain disadvantages of a degree of sophistication alien to the early membership.

Slightly before the Sarekat Islam's central body was granted legal status, its membership was augmented by one man who soon became renowned as one of the organization's leading figures: Hadji Agus Salim. Agus Salim came from an upper class family from the Minangkabau region of West Sumatra. After graduation from a Dutch secondary school, he obtained employment with the Netherlands' government which sent him to work in the Netherlands' Consulate in Jeddah. The chief business of the Jeddah consulate was the registration, protection and control of Indonesians participating in the pilgrimage (*Hadj*) to Mecca. Through this work Agus Salim became interested in the religious life of Indonesia, and devoted his free moments to studying Islamic religious writings and teachings. He fell strongly under the influence of Reformist concepts which were at that time a growing force in the Near East. He was certainly not the first Indonesian to see the value of the Reformist teachings for Indonesian Islam. But over and above this he felt a strong sympathy toward those aspects of Reformism which sought to make Islam compatible with modern scientific thinking emanating from Europe, which can best be termed Modernism.[21] Agus Salim became one of the first Indonesian Islamic Modernists. In this capacity he came to play a unique role in Indonesian life.

Upon his return from Jeddah in 1913, Agus Salim taught in his home town of Kota Gedang for two years. In 1915 he went to work for the Netherlands Indian government as a secret police investigator. Rumors had reached the government that a pan-Islamic plot was afoot to start an armed uprising against the government with arms that would be smuggled into the

country on a German ship. Agus Salim was sent to the Sarekat Islam headquarters to discover if these rumors had any
basis in fact. They did not. It was not long, however, before
Agus Salim fell under the spell of the sincerity and good intentions
of Tjokroaminoto, renounced his connections with the Netherlands Indian government, and joined the Sarekat Islam.[22] Tjokroaminoto was happy to have him, for in Agus Salim he had one
of the best educated and most intelligent men who had thus far
joined the Sarekat Islam. Agus Salim combined staunch Islamic
principles with a progressive point of view on social and economic
affairs, and was moreover a realist with regard to the future
goals and potentials of the Indonesian people. Almost from the
moment he joined the organization in 1915, Agus Salim became
a leading influence upon the policies and tactics of the Sarekat
Islam. In the first few years of his membership, however, his
influence was covert and he did not aspire to the wide popularity
of such men as Abdoel Moeis and Soeriopranoto.

One of the first positive measures resulting from Agus Salim's influence was the removal from the Sarekat Islam of all dependence
on messianic *ratu adil* appeals. To a Western trained, rational mind
the *ratu adil* undertone was exceedingly dangerous, for it remained
a force outside and beyond control. No one doubted the strength
inherent in the *ratu adil* concept, but it was felt it must be kept
outside an organization that purported to be seeking a rational
improvement of welfare and that was hoping for legal status with
its concomitant responsibility for actions. Furthermore, to Agus
Salim, and to many other religious men of Reformist inclination,
the *ratu adil* concept was a survival of animistic and mystical
ideas which should be suppressed in Indonesian Islam. The *ratu
adil* sentiments which had arisen were, after 1915, very consciously
quashed. With Agus Salim and Sangadja propagandizing ex-
tensively, the Islamic nature of the Sarekat Islam was emphasized
instead.[23] A new basis was almost found in a purer more vigorous
Islam. Almost, but not quite, for at the same moment that a
more positive religious appeal was made to the rural masses,
other forces were entering the Sarekat Islam and winning strength

among the intellectual group of the central leadership. These were stimulated by Marxist social theory. To an extent the theories of Marx and Mohammed could be made to run parallel, but ultimately the choice would have to be made between the two masters which the Sarekat Islam set out to serve.

Upon gaining recognized legal status the Sarekat Islam was, as in years previous and in years to follow, in difficult financial straits. Despite its claim in 1916 of over two million members, the organization stood on the verge of bankruptcy. The *Utusan Hindia*, the party organ, was able to function only because of support from outside the organization. This had originally come from the Arab groups, but many of them had already withdrawn their support because of the policy, or lack of policy, of the organization, and most of the remainder were soon to shift their interests elsewhere.[24]

As the Arab support waned, the *Utusan Hindia* came to rely upon support from paid advertisements, and these were mostly placed by Chinese merchants. By 1914 it was primarily Chinese money that was keeping the organ of the Sarekat Islam alive. As a consequence the Sarekat Islam rapidly dropped all anti-Chinese principles from its program, and barring an occasional outburst against Chinese such as in Rembang in 1915 (which occurred without the knowledge of the Central S.I.), the Sarekat Islam lost its original anti-Chinese nature.[25] Even as virtually all of the attempts by the Sarekat Islam to establish consumer cooperatives failed — in large measure because they could not stand up against Chinese competition — there was not a word directed against the Chinese by any responsible party member. Economically, of course, the Chinese stood outside the Sarekat Islam; they merely used its newspaper as a convenient advertising medium.

The withdrawal of Arab and commercial support also meant that the religious and intellectual leaders had to carry on as best they could. These leaders found their financial position increasingly precarious. The reason for this was simple: the vast membership was not continuing to pay its dues. In fact, many of the peasants who had joined so readily never paid more than was needed for the membership card. Once this protective card was theirs to use in case the promised paradise ever came, they no longer took an active interest in the Sarekat Islam — not even the religious interest could arouse them, for they were content to let their traditional indifference guide their thinking. The party leaders felt they could not base their strength on such unstable support which, in addition to being reluctant about paying dues, was apt at any moment to engage in local disturbances (even though such disturbances did become less frequent after 1915).[26] The obvious course for the intellectual leadership was to direct the appeal of the Sarekat Islam more toward the urban elements, particularly the working class, while continuing to hold what rural elements they could through the religious appeal. This is actually what happened in the years following 1916. In this manner the urban elements and the organized plantation workers — groups more readily subject to central control — rose in significance within the Sarekat Islam. The leaders of these groups were often imbued with Marxist ideals, and as a consequence Marxism began to make itself felt within the organization.

Marxism, with its anti-imperialistic edge carefully sharpened, came to the East Indies from the West, carried by men of the West, and guided by them for a number of years (at least up to 1920). Among the large numbers of Europeans who came to the East Indies shortly after 1900 there were a number whose Marxist principles were already highly developed. There was no attempt on the part of the home or colonial government to screen out such persons, and soon they came to be found in the administrative corps, in teaching positions, in technical services, and in private enterprise.[27] It was the romantic period of Socialism: concepts were not all clearly formed, the benefits of socialist society seemed destined to come almost automatically, class warfare and historical materialism pointed the way to a better society in which all men would have more equal opportunity. For some reason, a sizable number of these European Socialists came to be located in the city of Semarang. There, with a number of Radical Democrats, they formed a large left wing group of Europeans.

In the years before the revolutionary and evolutionary disciples of Socialism had clearly differentiated themselves, the Socialist elements in the European part of East Indian society worked toward the formation of labor unions. Their earliest efforts were among government employees. Usually the Indonesians followed the example of Europeans in labor organization.

In 1905 the Government Railways Union (s.s.b.) was founded by European transportation employees of the government. It attempted to represent all government railway employees regardless of race. As such, it was a remarkable practical application of the association principle — the practical application stumbled upon the realities of the situation much sooner than did the theory. The top positions in the railways and tramways of the East Indies were held by Europeans who had had experience in the motherland in such enterprises, and by Indo-Europeans whose fathers had in many instances been active in the transportation service. The lower positions were held by Indonesians who, after 1917, could advance to second class clerk, crew foreman, or petty administrator, but before that date saw little future beyond a proletarian existence. To expect an associated labor union to succeed under these circumstances seems unrealistic today, but it was all part of the spirit of that time. The union leadership simply did not speak for the Indonesian members. Very shortly (1909) the lower ranking employees withdrew from the Government Railways Union and joined the Union of Tram and Railway Personnel (v.s.t.p.), formed in Semarang in 1908,[28] which through force of circumstances became, as all later Indonesian unions, delineated by racial boundaries. It was quite logical that the entire Indonesian labor movement should assume strong racial characteristics, characteristics which little troubled the vast Indonesian rural population, but which became most significant to those Indonesians torn loose from their traditional society and placed in juxtaposition to Western society where racial concepts had long enjoyed a certain vogue.

The labor union movement burgeoned rapidly among Indonesians in government service. In 1911 a Customs Officers Union

(P.B.P.) was formed,[29] in 1912 a Teachers' Union (P.G.H.B.),[30] in 1916 a Pawn Shop Employees Union (P.P.P.B.)[31] and a Netherlands Indian Opium Regime Union,[32] and in 1917 a Union of Indonesian Employees of the Department of Public Works (V.I.P.B.O.W.)[33] and a Union of Employees of the Government Treasury.[34]

Influenced by the Western style organizations which began to appear in Indonesian life, unions were also formed in nongovernmental enterprises. About 1915 local organizations of wage earners and agricultural workers began to appear. In 1917 a Union of Factory Personnel (P.F.B.) was created among the employees in the sugar industry. In 1918 a Union of Workers and Farmers (P.K.B.T.) was founded by the revolutionary socialist, A. Baars.

The split between revolutionary and evolutionary socialists had occurred in the Netherlands in 1912 when the revolutionary Wijnkoop formed the Socialist Workers Party (S.D.P.), while the evolutionary Troelstra continued the Social Democratic Workers Party (S.D.A.P.). The socialists in the East Indies led by H. J. F. M. Sneevliet formed the Indies Social Democratic Organization (I.S.D.V.) in 1914. This organization contained socialists of all inclinations until 1917 when the more moderate socialists formed the Indies Social Democratic Party (I.S.D.P.) and left the I.S.D.V. to the more revolutionary elements led by Sneevliet. In the East Indies both groups of Socialists took a strong stand against the dualistic nature of the colonial relationship, and in this they were joined by progressive and radical liberals (the Ethici), members of the Indische Partij (which after 1913 continued to function under the name of Insulinde), and an assortment of individuals from other parties. These groups varied more in procedure than in aim. Through their resolute stand against dualism, the left wing parties won a sizable following among those Indonesians with a certain amount of Westernized education who were moving into the elite positions of Indonesian society.

The I.S.D.V. of Sneevliet with its resolute program of action gained a strong hold over the Semarang Union of Tram and

Railway Employees (v.s.t.p.). Almost immediately some of its agents also began working their way into the Semarang branch of the Sarekat Islam. Their activity was facilitated by the acceptability of left wing thinking in Semarang. Within a few years (probably by 1916) a few key men were controlling all three organizations.

The Semarang branch became a difficult group for the central leadership of the Sarekat Islam to control. Although following the general aim of the Sarekat Islam to raise the standards of the Indonesian people, the Semarang group rejected the Islamic appeal, clamored for revolutionary action, and upon the slightest provocation dubbed the more moderate Sarekat Islam members as bourgeois. This label of 'bourgeois' has generally been used by Socialist writers down to the present-day when referring to the Sarekat Islam.

Sneevliet and his cohorts realized that control of their cherished revolutionary movement would in last instance have to be borne by Indonesians. They began cultivating protégés to carry their gospel. Foremost among the young Indonesians indoctrinated by Sneevliet was Semaoen, a young man from a lesser prijaji family. Semaoen had a receptive mind and proved an apt pupil: soon he was one of the leaders of the i.s.d.v., while retaining his key position in the Railways Union where he had originally been discovered. By 1916 he was forcing his way upward in the Semarang Sarekat Islam and by 1918 had pried open the door to membership in the central body of the organization (see below, p. 142).[35]

After gaining recognized legal status in 1916, the events in and about the Sarekat Islam can most easily be viewed through an analysis of the annual National Congresses which the organization held. These Congresses, made up of representatives from many local chapters, heard and discussed various problems and plans of the current year. In itself this was a democratic enough process, but the decisions on the course to be followed were usually made by a handful of leaders. Through the records of these meetings one can today determine the conflicts of ideals and ambitions within the organization, and in this manner view the struggles within this segment of the newly developing elite.

From June 17–24, 1916, the First National Congress of the Sarekat Islam was held in Bandung.[36] The directional meeting, preceding the congress, was held at the home of the Regent of Tjiandjur, R. A. A. Wiranatakusumah.[37] That a Regent would play host to the Sarekat Islam leaders was already an indication of change. Prior to 1916 the higher native administrators had kept aloof from the Sarekat Islam. Now, however, some of the more progressive Regents, of whom Wiranatakusumah was certainly one, saw that the movement had a value. They, in the tradition of good Ethici, might do well to place themselves at the head of it, rather than tag along ignominiously in its wake. The new legal status relieved them from the subtle pressures which had been exerted on many government employees, and made the risk of offending lesser civil servants of the European corps worth taking since their new role met with the approval of the highest government authorities.

The Sarekat Islam for its part had long forgotten its 1913 resolution to exclude all civil servants and was prepared to welcome such powerful and influential persons. Particularly in West Java where some of the Regents had been selected for Westernized training and where the Regent families had retained strong positions in the social order, close associations between the Indonesian administration and the Sarekat Islam developed. That such associations were not penalized by the Netherlands Indian government is evidenced by the fact that when the government set out to remove European guardianship from the indigenous administration, it began with the Regent of Tjiandjur (see below, p. 181).

Another West Java family to participate in Sarekat Islam activities was that of the Regent of Serang (Bantèm), Achmad Djajadiningrat, whose brother Hasan became the leader and organizer of the Serang Chapter. Needless to say, the Sarekat Islam in this area came to function in large measure as an extension of the policies envisioned by the enlightened Regents.[38] Yet it served a useful function and the desire to improve welfare was sincere. The untimely death of Hasan Djajadiningrat in 1920 robbed the Sarekat Islam of one of its finest leaders.

Koesoemo Oetoyo was another of these progressive Regents who did much to improve conditions in Japara; he worked with the Sarekat Islam, for he felt that many of the grievances it expressed were truly felt by the people as a result of the government's zealous policy for improvement in the villages. That enlightened Regents did not always cooperate with the Sarekat Islam is shown by the case of Koesoemo Joedo of Ponorogo, who adopted an attitude of armed neutrality toward the Sarekat Islam in his Regency.[39] Much seems to have depended upon local circumstances and personalities involved.

At the directional meeting in Tjiandjur it was decided not to recognize Mas Marco, the representative of Raden Goenawan of the Batavia Sarekat Islam.[40] It is not possible to determine exactly what lay behind this move, but it is certain that Hadji Samanhoedi, the original *formateur* of the Sarekat Islam, was involved. Samanhoedi must have been ever more provoked by the direction the Sarekat Islam was taking, for it had completely lost sight of the economic-commercial purposes for which it had been established. Once before Samanhoedi had called upon new leadership when the organization seemed to be slipping, now (1915–16) he seems again to have sought someone to bring the organization back on the commercial path. His choice fell upon Raden Goenawan, the Batavia and West Java leader. He seems to have convinced Goenawan to withdraw from the organization with his chapter and its funds. The move was not too successful; the other Sarekat Islam leaders held firm against Samanhoedi, and Goenawan returned to the fold. Samanhoedi was present at the directional meeting but attended no further meetings of the Sarekat Islam. Soon he withdrew from the organization, and faded from view. Goenawan, who had fallen from grace, was sent off to Sumatra as a propagandist, his power in West Java falling to Hasan Djajadiningrat, and his position in the Central Sarekat Islam falling to Abdoel Moeis.[41] It is noteworthy that any claim to leadership by either Goenawan or Samanhoedi seems inextricably entwined with the organization of the Sarekat Islam. Once dissociated from the organization, they drop as rapidly from view as they first arose. With a few exceptions, the other Sarekat Islam leaders were in similar positions.

At the very beginning of the very first day of the First National Congress (1916), the Sarekat Islam Chairman, Tjokroaminoto gave the keynote address. First he took special care to point out that he had no *ratu adil* intentions.[42] Then he went on to applaud the new spirit of the government which had granted legal status to the Sarekat Islam and which was advancing the association principle. The purpose of the Sarekat Islam was viewed as the improvement of Indonesian welfare and one of the means chosen to achieve this was criticism of government policies. He went on to say that this government was a protective government and much loved by the Sarekat Islam; it was to be hoped that there would soon be a colonial council and that natives might soon join in administration and law making. He expressed the hope that the goal of self-administration would be achieved in ten years. "Our motto should be: together with the government and in support of the government to steer in the proper direction," he said.[43] He continued by stating that it was unfortunate that the training grounds for political life, the city and district councils, were largely closed to natives, but added that as the government was working to improve this situation we must be patient. It was hoped that the evolution toward democracy resulting from education and the spirit of Islam would proceed in the proper direction under Dutch guidance.[44] The election of desa heads was felt to be the basis of Indonesian democracy, but here much could be improved; the desa head should have at least a Second Class Native School education, the desa council should be superior to the desa head, and the desa head should be freed from police duties. The lot of the desa man should be of utmost importance to the Sarekat Islam and general welfare should be improved at this level.[45]

Other speakers carried on in much the same trend as Tjokroaminoto. Rather than list all their comments, it seems more appropriate to analyze the tone and content of what Tjokroaminoto said. The tone of the entire speech speaks of a desire for cooperation with the government. Recognition had raised the hope for further advances and ameliorations, and before this First National Congress had ended, Tjokroaminoto could point with pride to a concession from the government with regard to suffrage rights in elections for city and district councils. Everyone with an income above 600 guilders a year could now vote. This, of course, gave only a small number of Indonesians the right to vote, but it was regarded as a step in the right direction.

More remarkable, however, are Tjokroaminoto's views on desa reform. His comments, which are phrased in terms of Westernized local democracy, are about as far removed from the realities of desa life as one can get. Yet his ideas continued to be advanced. In the years after 1916 it is Hasan Djajadiningrat who was the strongest advocate of desa reform. These proposed reforms fit in nicely with the plans of the ardent Ethici of the Dutch community and also with the aims of the Sarekat Islam leaders, both groups being interested in pushing the villager into more active participation in the new life of Indonesian society. Village changes, when they came, were to go in quite a different direction than envisioned by these advocates of a Europeanized form of communal life (see below, Chapter IV, p. 249).

Tjokroaminoto's mention of the government's association principle was little more than a sop to the liberal Ethici who still conceived the future of East Indian life on that basis. It is doubtful, however, that his association utterances were in any sense deceitful, for a great many of the Indonesian elite were closely tied to the Ethici, and thought in terms of association. In reality, however, association was by 1916 a failing cause. A few individual successes and well-intentioned laws of the government could not compensate for the failures in practical application.[46] The dualistic nature of the colonial relationship was gaining in strength throughout the entire first quarter of the 20th century. This duality was a natural result of the contact of two cultural patterns, each of which recognized its own range of values and goals. For the most part a barrier existed between European and Indonesian society, and this barrier was not eradicated by some Indonesians receiving Western style education. In fact many of these better educated Indonesians were often the very ones who strengthened the barrier from their side.

All Indonesian organizations (with the exception of the Indische Partij which was not really indigenous) set up exclusive barriers to membership. The association idea was furthest advanced — and perhaps most removed from reality — in the Theosophical Society which envisioned a brotherhood of man encompassing all beliefs and races; but even here there were, by 1916, indications that association would not work. Association did not die a rapid death, however. It lived as an ideal in the hearts of many Europeans and some Indonesians. It was a grand ideal, fully worthy of being perpetuated, but it was sowed in an environment so unfavorable that it was never really given a fair chance to succeed. It could at most achieve fruition in some distant future when conditions of life had somewhat altered.

The colonial council about which Tjokroaminoto spoke was soon to materialize. The plan to do something of this sort had long been under consideration, for it was regarded as a logical progression in the decentralization process started in 1903. Decentralization was not in practice proving to be very successful; by 1914 it was obvious that the process was too limited in scope, and failed to provide suitable outlets for the capacities of East Indian society. Too many persons had viewed decentralization and the future welfare of the East Indies as exclusively a matter of administrative reform. Minister Pleyte was not among these. He conceived of the colonial council, which he had created by the law of December 1916[47] and named *Volksraad* (People's Council), as quite distinct from the administrative arrangement in the colony. He chose instead to tie it closely to the colony's financial independence.

In practice not the creation but the form of the Volksraad was deplorable. It was given great powers in determining the East

Indian budget, but was given no executive powers which would, of course, have been impossible without fundamental administrative and political changes. The government intended eventually to make some of the necessary changes through the establishment of lower echelon representative councils to which the Indonesian administration would be subordinated, but these were decentralization plans of the future (see below, pp. 205–6 and 250). All that appeared in 1916 were plans of the colonial government to withdraw the European control over affairs in those areas which seemed capable of independent control by the indigenous administration (see below, pp. 181–2). This, however, had no connection with building up popular support for the Volksraad. The Volksraad was premature in that it preceded any local representative structure in Indonesian society, and was in this sense also unrealistic. The Volksraad did have meaning within the European social group in the East Indies, for within this group the process of decentralizing authority had had remarkable success. Here the Volksraad was regarded as a great step forward in loosening the ties that bound the colonists to the legislature of the Netherlands; as such it was part of the process of gaining autonomy.

The Volksraad was not an immediate failure, however. At the time of its creation it was regarded as a remarkable concession; and there was a moment when it appeared as if it might become something really functional (see below, pp. 190–1). Moreover, it became a podium for the expression of grievances in which it had perhaps its greatest value. It was, of course, also a training ground in political awareness and procedures for certain Indonesians, but on a very limited scale. Indonesians in general, and some Europeans in particular, continued to regard the Volksraad as something that *should* be representative of the Indonesian peoples and that *should* be a forum in which they might express their legislative desires. The Volksraad never fulfilled this need despite the fact that it was granted legislative powers and that Indonesians came to form one-half of its membership (see below, p. 251), for it remained far distant from the main stream of Indonesian life and representative of only one particular type of thought.

Returning to the First National Sarekat Islam Congress, many speakers spoke on matters near their hearts, but all were characterized by moderation of tone. The plan to combine Socialism with Islam was raised by the Arab capitalist Hasan Ali Soerati. This obviously had no relation to Marxian socialism, but rather conceived of socialism as a general welfare doctrine.[48] Raden Mohammed Joesoep suggested that other chapters engage in the formation of labor unions as had been done in his city of Semarang — a suggestion that was ultimately followed to a limited extent.[49] Semaoen, representing the i.s.d.v., suggested that the Sarekat Islam strive toward more radical goals, but he was cut short and not encouraged to develop his ideas.[50]

Between the time that the First National Sarekat Islam Congress was held (June 1916) and the Second National Congress met in October 1917, an event occurred which greatly affected sentiments and which tended to lead the Sarekat Islam as well as other Indonesian organizations more directly toward political action. This event was a direct result of the World War and flowed from concern over the defense of the archipelago. Before 1914 it had been generally felt that the navy should be the first and strongest line of East Indian defense. As a consequence little was done toward materially increasing the military power in the archipelago. About 1915–1916 voices began to be raised for strengthening the land defenses. The fact that the ex-Governor General J. B. van Heutsz actively backed this move made it a matter of high political concern.[51] In the East Indies those persons interested in stronger defense had formed the Comité 'Indië Weerbaar' (Committee for the Defense of the Indies). The threat, real or imaginary, was Japan.[52] Once the defense of the Indies became a matter of open discussion in the motherland, it was decided that any extension of the military forces in the colony could only be accomplished within the framework of an indigenous militia with some system of compulsory military service for Indonesians. This was somewhat more than the original members of the Comité had bargained for, but the ball was out of their hands.[53] When Governor General Idenburg suggested that the delegation which they were preparing to send to the Netherlands be supplemented by representatives of the Indonesian people, they could only acquiesce. Early in 1917 the Comité made up of Europeans and Indonesians sailed for the Netherlands.

The delegation which arrived in The Hague in March 1917 contained representatives of the Sarekat Islam, Budi Utomo, Regents' Union and the Princes' Union. The decision to join the Comité had not always been easy; particularly the Sarekat Islam had had to weigh the strong objections of the Semarang chapter toward the Comité before deciding to delegate Abdoel Moeis as its representative. Moeis was not without restrictions, however, for the leaders of the Sarekat Islam felt that the desire of the Dutch to draft Indonesians into the armed forces was a tool with which concessions toward granting them a stronger position in the newly developing social hierarchy could be pried.[54] The Sarekat Islam would only lend its support to the conscription of Indonesians, if some form of representative body were established in the East Indies, and if Indonesians were given greater opportunities toward administering and improving themselves.[55] The Budi Utomo had attached similar stipulations to its participation in the Comité.

At the time the Comité arrived in the Netherlands the question of the Indies' defenses was rapidly becoming a political football within the States General. The members of the Comité were everywhere feted and cordially received; even a royal reception was arranged.[56] Through the wide range of contacts which they made in the Netherlands the Indonesian members of the Comité felt reassured in the ultimate goal toward which the motherland was guiding them, but each found his particular sentiments most gratified by one or another of the Dutch political parties. The Budi Utomo found its closest ties with the Radical Democrats and moderate Socialists. The representatives of the upper prijaji and upper Indonesian administration, Regents and Princes, found their closest affiliation with the Liberal and right wing religious parties which seemed prepared to grant them the greatest privileges with the least interference in their pattern of life and thought. Abdoel Moeis received confirmation of what had been a strong suspicion: namely, that the desire of the Sarekat Islam leaders for a heightened status within the scope of an East Indian government structure would be best advanced by the Social Democratic Workers Party and other moderate left wing elements. The Dutch revolutionary Socialists had missed out completely. Failing to reckon with the all-too-human personal ambitions of the aspiring elite, they had applied cold dialectics with an intensity that had frightened even Abdoel Moeis.[57] They were to learn more tactful procedures in dealing with Indonesians.

The defense question died in the States General. The left wing parties refused their support on grounds that the defense plans were inspired by self-interested groups, while the enthusiastic support of the Liberals, who had hailed the measure as the will of the people, was not sufficient. Indonesian conscription became a chronic problem, but agreement never seemed possible; the Japanese invasion of 1942 put a final period to this much discussed issue.

The Indies' Defense Movement was, from an Indonesian point of view, not without value. For one thing it drew the Sarekat Islam, and the other organizations, into the realm of actual political demands and gave some stimulus to the definite formation of aims and principles which formerly had remained exceedingly vague and unregimented.[58] Furthermore, it gave members of the Indonesian elite group who envisioned their future in the context of a better position within the colonial relationship (and this included almost the entire elite at this time) a somewhat more definite idea of which groups in the Netherlands were prepared to help them attain their goals. Other factors were at work, and any heightened self-awareness among Indonesians was a gradual, not a sudden process. The defense question is simply one of a multitude of experiences which influenced the sentiments and life of the Indonesian elite — their reaction to all these issues was so conditioned by a myriad of considerations that the directional impulse remained diffuse.

By the time the Second National Congress of the Sarekat Islam met in Batavia (October 20–27, 1917),[59] a more strident tone was noticeable. This was partly due to the concessions the government had made to Indonesian self-consciousness. The opening of government jobs to all qualified persons regardless of race, the removal of the head tax which had replaced feudal services, the unification of the criminal law code, the final abolition of the Forced Cultivation System, the establishment of a People's Council, the expansion of education, and the uniform regulation of cooperative societies gave the Sarekat Islam leaders cause to feel that some of their demands were being met. But they were not satisfied. They personally had many more demands for what they considered necessary to promote Indonesian welfare. But they were also experiencing more pressure from the tightly organized urban chapters of the organization. These chapters were increasingly influenced by Socialist theories which in one way or another envisioned total social revision; thus they had an unbounded supply of demands which their leaders were expected to meet. It was a grand game: no one knew who stimulated whom, but everyone soon began demanding bigger and better concessions. In many urban centers the man with the greatest promises had the greatest popularity.[60]

Tjokroaminoto's keynote speech was calm and undemanding. He pointedly spoke of self-administration in the future and saw the People's Council as a step in this direction.[61] Somewhat otherwise, however, was the tone of two other men high in the Sarekat Islam hierarchy — Agus Salim and Abdoel Moeis. Salim, either from the Koran or from some of his Dutch friends, had acquired evolutionary Socialistic theories and took the occasion of the National Congress to advance the drainage theory of capitalistic exploitation.[62] The high rate of wartime profits of certain enterprises, particularly sugar, with a concomitant general rise of prices accompanied by a retention of wage scales, tended to lend support to the belief that the wealth and resources of the archipelago were being drained away by European enterprises. Actually such a supposition is difficult to support with facts.

Agus Salim in addition to his activities in the Sarekat Islam was now also editor of a newspaper, *Neratja* (The Balance). *Neratja* had come into existence to meet the government's desire to present the social and political issues of the day to the readers of Malayan language journals in a more favorable light then was the case in the private and organizational newspapers.[63] These latter, such as *Kaum Muda, Utusan Hindia, Sinar Hindia, Nasional* and a number of others which found a sales appeal among the growing number of literate persons, directed continuous abuse at every shortcoming of the government. The government began to feel that it had a poor press within the Indonesian social group and that its efforts toward change were little appreciated. A number of untoward incidents after 1916 convinced the government that a positive improvement in press relations was necessary. *Neratja* was consequently subsidized. It was the brainchild of the Adviser for Native Affairs, Dr. G. A. J. Hazeu. The editorship was placed in the hands of Agus Salim, who was regarded as one of the most perceptive and far-sighted of the newer Indonesian elite.

At the time the Second National Congress was in session there appeared in *Neratja* a basic platform for the Sarekat Islam, illustrating rather clearly the Socialist bent to the thinking of the organization's leaders. It was briefly and cogently stated:

> The goal of the Central Sarekat Islam is to achieve an increasing influence of the peoples and ethnic groups of the Netherlands Indies in the administration and government, with self-administration as the end in view.
>
> The Central Sarekat Islam denies the right of any people or group of people to rule another people or group of people.
>
> In consideration of the fact that the majority of the native people exist in miserable living conditions, the c.s.i. will continuously oppose any domination by sinful capitalism.
>
> In order to properly exercise civil rights, the c.s.i. regards moral as well as intellectual development a necessity. For this development she regards religion as the best means.
>
> With due respect to all other religions, ...the c.s.i. regards Islam as the most suitable religion for the moral development of the people.

The State should remain outside religious affairs and handle all religions on an equal basis.

The c.s.i. seeks cooperation with all organizations and persons who are in accord with this platform.[64]

Obviously a new note had been introduced and a new emphasis indicated from the time of the original Sarekat Islam platform in 1912 (see above, pp. 92-3). In fact there was even a decided change of tone from the Sarekat Islam platform drawn up only two months earlier by Hasan Djajadiningrat.[65] This most recent change was brought about by the insertion of the second and third paragraphs (quoted above) into the program of Hasan Djajadiningrat, which otherwise remained unchanged. The added sections are the ones which question the justice of colonialism and capitalism; they clearly show the direction in which the Sarekat Islam was moving: namely, toward the precipitation of a conflict in which basic economic and social realities of the East Indian colonial relationship would be challenged.

In this 1917 platform of the Sarekat Islam the term 'sinful capitalism' stands out as an interesting expression of a growing Indonesian sentiment. The term implies that there must be a form of capitalism which was 'non-sinful'. The distinction is never finely drawn, but in general what is meant is that all foreign or non-Indonesian capital is sinful — probably because it drained wealth from the archipelago. But then Indonesian capital would not be sinful — an interesting manifestation of group solidarity. The revolutionary Socialists objected to this and logically considered all capitalism sinful, but their opinion was a minority. The majority of the Sarekat Islam leaders were inspired by the ideals of the Ethical Policy to raise the welfare of the people. For the most part they showed little awareness how this was to be accomplished other than by governmental action. This reliance upon state action did not mean they were Marxists, and consequently there was no need for an unequivocal attitude on capitalism. Most of these leaders continued to use Marxist arguments without clearly realizing their incompatibility with the realities of the existing government, which they expected to advance their welfare. Because they were not good Marxists does not necessarily mean they were bourgeois either.

Abdoel Moeis, recently back from his Holland trip, reflected somewhat different sentiments from Agus Salim. Moeis seems to have been greatly influenced by the Nationalist ideas of the Indische Partij. He was a friend of Mas Darnakoesoema, Western educated son of a Bantem administrative family, who had tried his hand at Western business life and journalism but was now continuing Douwes Dekker's organization under the name Insulinde while the leader was in exile. These Nationalist concepts, plus the favorable disposition of the government toward the demands of Indonesian organizations, prompted Moeis to make a statement concerning the realities of life. "If one looks behind the outer purposes of all native organizations which propose to improve the condition of the native, one indisputably sees that they have only one goal, namely, freedom (*kemerdikaan*) of the Indies." Nothing, according to Moeis, could stand in the way of this inherent aim of all native organizations.[66]

Here was the open assertion of eventual freedom. The Netherlands Indian government heard it along with everyone else, but made no move. Why, after all, should they? This was in last analysis one of the aims of the Ethical Policy, or had at least become one of the aims. The Indonesians were to be guided to eventual freedom: it was not to be an immediate process, it was to occur under a Westernized plan of development (one spoke still of association, but acted on an assimilation basis — egalitarian laws and plans were always Western in concept), and it was to produce a democratic Indonesian society.[67] Moeis, himself, seems not to have regarded the statement as particularly threatening, for the next day he strongly opposed Semaoen's proposal of non-cooperation with the Volksraad which was then in the final formative stages, and went on to ask that the government use its appointive powers to assure the presence of Sarekat Islam representatives on this Council.[68] This was what the Ethical government sought: an expression of desire on the part of Indonesians. Then the government would move to meet such expressions which were regarded as the true expression of living and vital desires of the people, and would move ahead with the emerging Indonesian consciousness toward a better Indonesian life.[69] It was a noble desire, a desire to move with the spirit of the time, a desire to allow the unrestricted deployment of Indonesian energies toward modernization and improvement under the protective blessings of the government.[70]

In the European part of East Indian society the attitude of the government toward Indonesian expressions of complaints left much to be desired. Here, below the hierarchy of the central government, were men who stood in daily contact with the problems of colonial life and who were faced with the practical problem of keeping an administrative district or a business enterprise running. They were not simple, heartless brutes devoid of all noble inspiration, but they found it ever more difficult to see the wisdom of the Ethical Policy which was, in their eyes, becoming senseless, weak, diffuse, and ill-advised. If one was to guide toward a better life for the people of the East Indies, one should keep the reins tightly in hand, and not give free play to a movement whipped up by the inflammatory demagoguery of a few Indonesians. The advancement that had occurred to date was the result of foreign energies (mostly European) and these energies must not be ignored in the future processes of modernizing the state. Such sentiments were unfortunately on occasion supplemented by the somewhat more base thoughts stemming from feelings of racial superiority and general insecurity. The result of all this was that beneath the official concessionary policy, Europeans evinced a certain fear of and hostility toward the native movements. The Indonesian organizations came to operate in an atmosphere brightened by high flown ideals of the government, but electrified with tensions from the local, daily realities of East Indian life.[71]

This very existence of a discrepancy between announced government aims and the personal attitudes of lower government personnel and private individuals may serve as a partial explanation of the tortuous tactical path of the Sarekat Islam and other Indonesian organizations. During the period covered in this chapter this path led toward ever more radical proposals of action. The Indonesian leaders during this period had gone far in accepting the ideals of the Ethical Policy even though these ideals were admittedly not inspired by Indonesians. These ideals served the leaders as keys for operation in the Western sphere of life. They were sorely annoyed, therefore, in following their Westernized course, to encounter inconveniences laid in their paths by men of the West (lower civil servants, journalists, entrepreneurs, etc.) upon whose sentiments they had evidently trod heavily while pursuing a policy sanctioned by the government.[72] Their annoyance was even greater when the source of their inconvenience was an Indonesian administrator or civil servant. The incidents of daily life which annoyed the politically conscious group of Indonesians were not easily forgotten or forgiven, as an overactive sense of inferiority and incompetence lay close to the surface. At first their wrath was directed against individuals who seemed to be treating them incorrectly, but later (who can say when the change occurred? perhaps about 1920) they came to feel that the government and the system were at fault and were dealing with them in an unfair manner. The Indonesian cosmos out of which they had sprung was based upon a firm enough autocratic hierarchy to disallow breaches of coordination. Discrepancy between word and deed meant either intentional duplicity or decay of the organ of government. The Indonesian political leaders soon came to choose one or the other of these explanations and adapted their tactics to the situation.

The Ethically inspired East Indian government, meanwhile, was in difficult straits. It was not unaware that only a small segment of the European population stood favorably disposed toward its actions. It could rely only on a handful of administrators and a few journalists and professional men for active support — the remainder were either passive or hostile. In the motherland there was more support, but war had increased the distance home. Nothing came even close to revolt, but criticism ran high. It became harder and harder to fill openings in the higher administrative positions. Leading Ethici, wearied by long years of service and growing adversity fell from the service. They were irreplaceable. Governor General Van Limburg Stirum could only watch the drama unfold about him. For as long as possible he stood behind a progressive liberal program, but events bore heavily upon him and he was forced to yield (see below, p. 190).

Returning to the Second National Convention of the Sarekat Islam (October 1917), it is to be observed that one of the leading speakers on the agenda was Raden Mas Soerjopranoto, brother of Soewardi.[73] This member of the House of Paku Alam had received his education in the Dutch Secondary Agricultural School, where he had actively furthered the cause of Budi Utomo in the early years of that organization. After graduation he spent some time as foreman on a sugar plantation and had observed first-hand the impotence of the individual worker against the strength of Western enterprises. He also noted that the Regents helped the sugar planter rather than the worker, and came to feel (or was led to believe by Socialist thinkers) that the prosperity of the sugar areas was more illusory than real. In order to correct these abuses he formed an organization not far removed from the Indonesian pattern of life but reflecting Westernized concepts of social justice and progress.[74]

The Adhi Dharmo founded in Jogjakarta about 1915 was a workers' organization which through cooperative effort created schools for laborers' children and sought to assist and expedite the interests of plantation workers. This organization remained officially unrecognized and proved to be not too effective. In 1917 the Adhi Dharmo was refurbished as a Western style labor organization to represent the interests of field and factory workers associated with plantations. This union became known as *Personeel Fabriek Bond* (P.F.B.). Soerjopranoto became its leader and consequently the leading Indonesian labor organizer outside the revolutionary Socialist fold. His labor activities and his utopian socialist principles helped the Sarekat Islam along the road toward a growing support on organized urban and labor elements and away from the large mass support of the rural population. As the Semarang group, representative of left wing labor elements, gained influence in the Sarekat Islam, Soerjopranoto was forced to keep pace with its propaganda and moved closer to a revolutionary standpoint than he had originally anticipated.

In May 1918 the Volksraad (People's Council) was officially opened. Both Tjokroaminoto and Abdoel Moeis received seats, the former appointed, the latter elected. Governor General Van Limburg Stirum had used his appointive powers to assure an assembly of persons who were sincerely interested in advancing the welfare of the Indonesian people. The government for its part showed a readiness to heed positive suggestions from the Volksraad — the number of such suggestions as well as the amount of destructive criticism was rather overwhelming and a source of surprise to many persons. The revolutionary Socialists who, by their own choice, were not represented on the Council condemned the entire experiment as a capitalist trick and branded all the Indonesian members as imperialist tools. It was not long before differences arose among members of the Sarekat Islam — vitriolic attacks were levied against Abdoel Moeis, whose name was associated with the Committee for the Defense of the Indies. His foremost attacker was the second most powerful Indonesian member of the Semarang group, Raden Darsono.

Darsono was another of those young men who had become disillusioned with conditions under the colonial government. Born into a lesser prijaji family, he received his education at a school which trained foremen for plantations. While at school he came into contact with the writings of the men of the Indische Partij: Douwes Dekker, Dr. Tjipto, and Soewardi. Upon graduation (1916) he became a soils expert with the Department of Agriculture, but in less than two years left this job and returned to his family in Semarang without definite purposes. In Semarang he read widely, particularly in Marxist works, and became a free lance journalist for the *Sinar Hindia* (Light of the Indies), a leftist Semarang daily. His definite shift to revolutionary Socialism came in 1917 when Sneevliet was brought to trial for journalistic excesses in the Socialist organ *Het Vrije Woord* (The Free Word).[75] Darsono, puzzled as to why a Hollander would struggle for Indonesian rights, attended the trials regularly and fell under the spell of Sneevliet's arguments of defense. Here he also met Semaoen, who found in him a kindred spirit. Soon Darsono was sent to Surabaya (Semaoen had just come from that city — the shift probably being made for tactical purposes of keeping men out of their home environments) to edit the revolutionary Socialist newspaper *Suwara Raja* (The Great Voice) and to pilot revolutionary propaganda among the workers there. Before leaving Semarang he had joined the Sarekat Islam chapter there, and began his attacks upon the moderate leaders from Surabaya.[76]

When the Third National Congress of the Sarekat Islam met in Surabaya from September 29 through October 6, 1918, the leaders held closed sessions to smooth out the controversy between Moeis and Darsono. Semaoen and Darsono immediately played their trump card: they threatened to withdraw the Semarang organization from the Central Sarekat Islam. Nothing could have been better calculated to terrorize Tjokroaminoto — his entire life was directed toward preserving the unity of the Sarekat Islam.[77] Conflict of ideologies and the consequences of irresponsible methods meant less to him than keeping the organization intact. To hold the Semarang group Semaoen was brought into the central steering committee and Darsono was made an official propagandist.[78] The public learned that Darsono would in the future first try to settle internal differences within the central body before bringing them into the open.[79] What had been threatening for some years finally became an accomplished fact. The revolutionary Semarang group with its firmly developed program was seated in the innermost councils of the Sarekat Islam.

There was a more excited tone at the open sessions of the Third National Sarekat Islam Congress than there had been at earlier meetings. On the first day Hasan Djajadiningrat gave his annual speech on village reform which showed a humanitarian concern to readjust village life along much the same lines as the Ethici had followed for some years. He warmly supported the draft considerations of Minister Pleyte which were designed to limit the power of the desa head through the creation of desa councils — a proposal which was placed before the Volksraad the following year but never become law.[80] When Hasan Djajadiningrat had finished his speech, Semaoen asked if the Sarekat Islam planned to do nothing more than talk about this matter. This was enough to challenge Tjokroaminoto, who retorted, "If they (the government) don't hurry and meet our demands, demands which live in the hearts of all the people of the Indies, then we will in five years time establish our own local councils, regency councils, district councils, and a Central People's Council (*Landvolksraad*)."[81]

This set the mood for the remainder of the convention. The following day Hasan Djajadiningrat was asking the government to remember the French Revolution.[82] And the day thereafter A. Baars, a Dutch engineer and key member of the I.S.D.V., who was a guest at the Congress, joined in the discussion to call for the freedom of the Indies from capitalist exploitation.[83] Tjokroaminoto threatened revolution again on the issue of private estates (those privately owned and governed areas whose owners possessed far-reaching public authority) which he wanted to see the government buy back[84] (shortly thereafter a law was passed with this aim in view), and finally Semaoen made his position clear by branding the Ethical Colonial Policy as a divide and rule tactic.[85]

With amazing indulgence the government overlooked all this. It listened with interest to reasonable suggestions, particularly those about village reform and taxes, which were raised at the National Congress. The government also took measures to alleviate conditions which had led to disturbances on Sumatra.[86] These unpleasant experiences — in 1916 in Djambi (Southeast Sumatra) and in 1917 in Tapanuli (Northwest Sumatra) — had been investigated and found attributable to overzealousness for material advancements and improvements, and a desire of local administrators to show a balanced tax return.[87]

The civil administration, which had been made the scapegoat, was furious, for it claimed to be doing no more than was expected by custom and by the written and unwritten tenets of the Ethical Policy.[88] Small wonder that they felt that the government was working against them; the government, for its part, felt it once again had to deal with the usual sort of reactionary elements, and continued to listen with interest to what the Sarekat Islam had to say.

Between the Third National Convention and the Fourth which also met in Surabaya, from October 26–November 2, 1919, several events occurred which catalyzed tendencies inherent in the Sarekat Islam. In November 1918 the Social Democrats in the Netherlands had shown an inclination to follow the pattern of the German upheaval which had sent the Kaiser packing. For a few weeks the threat seemed very grave. Advance communications allowed these sentiments to be almost immediately felt in the East Indies. The Dutch Social Democrats took the lead in forming a combination of parties within the Volksraad. This Radical Concentration, as it was called, contained most of the Indonesian parties including the Sarekat Islam, along with the progressive Dutch groups. They demanded further concessions on the road to self-government and a liberalizing of the administrative process, i.e., self-government. Tjokroaminoto took this occasion to point out that the Sarekat Islam was working with the Socialists of the Semarang group because it had discovered that in its struggle for improvement of conditions it had found it necessary to combat 'sinful capitalism'. The Governor General, impervious to the anxieties of the European community, was not opposed in principle to the demands of the Radical Concentration. Forced to act quickly and unable to get advice from The Hague, he promised the creation of a commission to investigate and consider changes in the political structure of the Netherlands Indies (see below, p. 183 ff.). On December 17, 1918 this Reform Commission was brought into life. Its work forms an interesting facet of the colonial relationship and will be discussed in greater detail below (see pp. 190–193). The revolutionary threat in the motherland subsided in a few weeks while the matter never really became a threat in the East Indies. However, the concessions brought on by such slight stirrings led some persons to think along even more radical lines than they had previously.

Part of this growing radicalism came to be closely tied to the Sarekat Islam and had serious effects upon it. In June 1919 there was an outburst of violence in (Toli Toli) Middle Celebes in which a number of native officials and one European lost their lives. This outburst had followed a propaganda visit to that district by the Sarekat Islam Vice-President, Abdoel Moeis. It is difficult to fix the cause and effect relationship in these events. The Sarekat Islam had been meddling in troubled waters in Celebes. For some time there had been a contest for power between some of the old adat chiefs, a question of hereditary rights being involved. When the Sarekat Islam entered the scene, one local group immediately joined it en masse in the hope of gaining wider support for its cause. There is little doubt that the leaders of the Sarekat Islam knew the situation in Celebes was very delicate. The statements Moeis made on his propaganda trip were probably no more incendiary than what he and others had been saying on Java for some years. Yet in the disturbed environment of Celebes his statements might have been all that were needed to precipitate violence. One must take care, however, not to draw the causal relationship here too closely. There were many factors in Toli Toli which might have lain behind the outburst.

Then in July 1919, just after the trouble in Celebes, the Garut Incident occurred. The actual events are fairly well established, but the underlying causes and motives have been subject to many interpretations. In the village of Leles in the Regency of Garut which lies in the Southeastern part of West Java, an area inhabited by Sundanese people, there was resistance by one Hadji Hasan to the forced delivery of rice to the government. The general disruption of normal transportation following the close of the First World War had created such a depleted rice stock in the East Indies that the central government had found it necessary to requisition rice, against equitable payment, in order to avert a possible food crisis. The Sarekat Islam took this occasion to demand that the sugar estates give up lands for the planting of rice. Much abuse, some probably justified, was directed against the sugar industry. The government investigated the possibilities, but found the use of sugar land for the immediate relief of a food shortage to be impracticable.[89] The Sarekat Islam suffered a defeat on this issue — a defeat not well accepted by many of its leaders. No doubt the government purchases of rice gave certain bases for grievance, particularly since the entire production of rice was closely linked with customs and beliefs of the people.[90] At any rate Hadji Hasan, a fairly wealthy landowner of Leles in Garut, refused delivery of a part of his rice to the government on grounds that it would deprive his own family of their needs. The matter was not pressed, but Hadji Hasan seems to have called his family together, started the purchase of white cloth (which was worn in battle), and began assembling weapons. Three days later some of the local civil administrators with the Resident at their head, accompanied by a body of troops, came to bring matters under control. Hadji Hasan with his entire family barricaded themselves in their house, refused to discuss anything with the authorities present, and seemed prepared for forceful resistance. The troops opened fire: first, one volley through the roof, and when this proved ineffectual, one through the house. Hadji Hasan and several members of his family were killed and the resistance immediately ended. This, in brief, comprised the outward events of the Garut Incident.[91]

From the side of the civil administration there seems little doubt that the affair was badly bungled. Criticism from moderate and radical elements of the Indonesian population[92] as well as from many Europeans was not long absent.[93] Various investigations were immediately begun, and as the investigators began to probe more deeply into the affair, it soon became apparent that more was involved than had been originally suspected, or at least outwardly clear from a knowledge of the immediate events.

In the three days between the time that Hadji Hasan had first refused rice delivery and the time that the shooting incident occurred, the Sarekat Islam, or at least certain members of the Sarekat Islam, seems to have been engaged in some devious plotting.[94] These individuals came to be associated with a group known as the Section B of the Sarekat Islam. Their plans were aided by the unscrupulous practices of one Hadji Ismael who had for some time been selling *djimat* (religious tokens of invulnerability) to the local population.[95] Ismael's aims were purely monetary and his actions were in no sense unusual within the Indonesian context, but he did play a part in crystallizing in Hadji Hasan the hope of successful resistance. The link between the militant sentiments within the stubborn old farmer and the Section B organization was Hadji Hasan's son-in-law, Hadji Godjali.[96] Godjali was a member of the Section B, a secret group, apparently not known even to regular Sarekat Islam members, which sought an immediate and forceful overthrow of the government.[96]

The investigations following upon the shooting incident uncovered evidences of the intentions and nature of this group. It appeared that certain members of the Central Sarekat Islam were implicated — most specifically Sosrokardono, Secretary of the c.s.i., founder of the Pawnshop Employees Union (p.p.p.b.), and closely linked to the Semarang group.[98] There also was some evidence pointing to Tjokroaminoto's tacitly approving the organization, although not actively encouraging it.[99] The Section B was revolutionary in the most direct and simple sense of the word; they seemed to think in terms of murdering all Europeans and Chinese and in this manner taking control of the government.[100] Various degrees of religious mysticism were certainly involved but there seems to be no manner of measuring their intensity. The fact that such an organization could find a foothold in the rather prosperous Garut area where there were no European plantations to provoke resentment was a decidedly unpleasant surprise to many persons in the archipelago.

There has always been some question as to the reality of the

Section B which the investigation discovered. Investigations often turn up evidence that someone wishes to find. To an extent this is probably the case with the Section B of the Sarekat Islam. The manner in which the government took action against Hadji Hasan suggests that they suspected more than a family incident. There was in all probability something known as the Section B or some other revolutionary group in the Garut area — these things had sprung up in Indonesian life under various guises since time immemorial — and the government, or at least the local administration, which usually kept close watch and was well informed on such activities, probably knew about it. The group in itself was probably quite insignificant, but once there arose the possibility of its being tied to a national organization such as the Sarekat Islam, it assumed a new significance. The Sarekat Islam was becoming more radical and it is well known that many local administrators (both Dutch and Indonesian) were growing annoyed and frightened by the privileges and power which the organization was gaining. Speculating for a moment, it might be possible that the local administrators of Garut, in defiance of the Ethici-controlled central government in Batavia, decided to make so strong a case against the Sarekat Islam that it could not be ignored, thus forcing the hand of the government against the organization. The resistance of Hadji Hasan, with his family-ties in the so-called Section B, was perhaps a most opportune occurrence for forcing just such an issue. There is no positive proof of this, of course. If, however, one considers the rather summary dismissal of Resident De Stuers by Governor General Van Limburg Stirum a short time after the Garut Incident, then there is no doubt that there were matters involved which vexed the government.

The repercussions of the Garut Incident were most keenly felt within the Sarekat Islam itself. The great bulk of its membership, which at this time was claimed to be over three million, had joined for the religious or associational aspects of the organization. They had not subscribed to a radical or revolutionary political organization. The fact that the central nucleus of leaders had

taken it upon themselves to advance radical social and political ideals had either not been made known or had passed
beyond their comprehension and interest. Now, however, that
the movement had, in the eyes of the government, obtained a
revolutionary tinge (news of the Garut Incident spread rapidly)
they cared for none of the struggle involved. Once again their
local administrators, European and Indonesian, who had to an
extent been supplanted by the Sarekat Islam, began to grow in
stature. With the exposure of the revolutionary nature of the
Sarekat Islam, its membership began to melt away like the
proverbial snow before the sun.

The first group to defect on a wholesale basis after the exposure of the Section B was the Arab merchants who had been
among the original stimulators and founders.[101] Most of them
had been inactive for some years, but now they severed all ties.
The Djamiatul-Hasanah, affiliated with the Politiek Economische
Bond (P.E.B.) — recently founded to further the non-revolutionary
development of the East Indies — and the Al Irshad, an Arabic
religious organization which had split from the early Jam Yat
Khair under the leadership of the Reformist Soorkati, picked up
the bulk of these Arab members. The Budi Utomo filled its ranks
with many of the more moderate Indonesian elements who now
left the Sarekat Islam.[102] However, the greatest loss of popularity
was among the small peasant membership who had for some
years been inactive and indifferent toward the Sarekat Islam (but
had always been counted as members) and who now drifted
completely away from the organization. These people for the
most part joined no other organization.

Another organization that began to expand from local to national
dimensions at the same time that the Sarekat Islam was losing its
appeal was the Muhammadijah, which had been founded in
Jogjakarta in 1912 by A. Dachlan (see above, p. 85). In 1920
this organization began to establish religious schools throughout
the islands.[103] It had never opposed cooperation with the Sarekat Islam, particularly on an individual basis, but had circumspectly refrained from any political activity. Muhammadijah,

however, had a definite religious program which is something that the Sarekat Islam never had. The latter fully employed religious sentiments, but would make use of whatever Islamic current seemed to be the strongest in a particular area. The Muhammadijah, on the other hand, followed the pattern of Islamic Reformism and was opposed to, and opposed by, the Orthodox religious elements. When Muhammadijah began to expand over the East Indies, some Sarekat Islam members, while still retaining their position in the Sarekat Islam, joined in close liaison with the movement. Some of the religious elements who were disgruntled with the politics of the Sarekat Islam were probably channeled off into the Muhammadijah about this time, but the great strength for Muhammadijah came from those Moslems who were beginning to partake of a fuller economic life (see below, pp. 166–7).

The unpleasant incidents in 1919, linked closely to the Sarekat Islam, served to fortify and intensify sentiments in the larger part of the European community in the East Indies. The European press, with a few exceptions, had been fulminating against the Sarekat Islam in greater or lesser degree since the earliest days of the organization.[104] Speaking for and exerting influence upon the growing Dutch and Indo-European community, the press also criticized the attitude of the East Indian government so that by 1918 Van Limburg Stirum could well complain of the lack of understanding and sympathy he received in the East Indian press.[105] It is quite understandable, however, that to the average European in the East Indies, who felt himself closely tied to the capitalist economic system, the growing shouts of 'class struggle' and 'dictatorship of the proletariat' were not only frightening, but had of necessity to be taken seriously. The Europeans were, in last analysis, in the East Indies to make money; there was no doubt where they stood, and they quite rightly regarded revolutionary socialism as a threat to their existence.[106] For the most part, not caring to reason too deeply in such matters, the Europeans came to see every threat to the established order as Communistic or revolutionary. Thus many radicals and liberals found their ideas labelled 'Communistic' by the European press.

The petty bourgeois attitude so prevalent among Europeans in the East Indies built up the spectre of Communism in Indonesia into something far exceeding its actual strength and influence. The picture which has been passed on to us, and which is still perpetuated today, can only be flattering in the utmost to the Communists. The Communist movement was spectacular and makes dramatic reading, but it was not very large, nor did it form an essential part of the development of leadership in the Indonesian social order. Its greatest threat perhaps lay in its ostentation, for there was always the possibility that some Indonesians might seek an outlet for their frustrations by joining an organization whose aims and outbursts made it a consistent opponent of the established colonial order. This did not occur to a great degree (see below, Chapter IV, p. 232 ff.), and the movement remained in essence that of a small group which was more or less successful in exploiting discontents that arose in a changing social order, but which never succeeded in indoctrinating large numbers of people with its revolutionary doctrines.

The incidents of 1919 seem to have had startlingly little effect upon the leaders of the Sarekat Islam, as shown by the discussions at the Fourth National Congress in Surabaya (October–November 1919). The loss of a large part of the peasant support and practically all of what remained of the economic groups, seemed only to intensify the desire of many of the leaders to turn toward the better organized urban and worker groups. On the first day of the Congress, Tjokroaminoto complained of the futility of directing requests and suggestions to the government (he probably had the question of rice production on sugar lands in mind) and expressed the intention of exerting other pressures. "For this purpose it is necessary to have an organization with more amalgamation and unity of concept, than the Sarekat Islam with its $2^{1}/_{4}$ million members, has shown itself to possess. The first step toward reaching this goal must be sought in a central labor union."[107]

The concept of a revolutionary central labor organization which would include unions of industrial and agricultural workers (Persatuan Perhimpunan Kaum Buruh — PPKB)[108] had been advanced by Sosrokardono in May 1919. Shortly thereafter he had been placed in custody because of implication in the Garut incident. The central union concept was raised at the Fourth Sarekat Islam Congress by R. M. Soerjopranoto, head of the plantation and factory workers union (P.F.B.).[109] Soerjopranoto now proposed an amazing plan that hinged on a coordinated operation of all groups which had participated in the Radical Concentration in the People's Council in November 1918 (see above, p. 144). This bore many of the outer aspects of syndicalism. Operating directly under the Central Sarekat Islam was to be a Central Union (*Vakcentrale* — the term 'Revolutionary' had been dropped) which was to operate on a threefold set of principles: (1) the class struggle, (2) political action toward a social democratic goal, and (3) cooperative effort.[110] The Central Union would form a framework for workers' councils which would be represented in one chamber of an envisioned government of the future. The other chamber would consist of the parties of the Radical Concentration. Together these chambers would conduct the struggle against capitalism and foreign domination. Tjokroaminoto went along with this program and called for a future meeting in Jogjakarta (December 25–26, 1919) to lay the groundwork for this plan. But at the Fourth National Congress something had struck deeply into his consciousness — when Soerjopranoto had advanced his concept, he had been widely proclaimed as "the coming man of the Sarekat Islam." This piqued Tjokroaminoto, as he had neither intention nor desire to lose his stature in the Sarekat Islam.[111]

All was far from unity at the Congress and there was no indication that all the leaders of the organization, or for that matter even all the radical leaders, were prepared to go along with Soerjopranoto. Soerjopranoto's chief support at this time came from the Semarang group which strongly favored proletarian action and minimized the role of Islam as an agent of progress. Shortly before the National Congress there had been a proposal to transform the Sarekat Islam into the Sarekat India (United Indies) and to push the Central Labor Union effort.[112] This proposal had come from Alimin Prawirodirdjo, a young Javanese who had received much encouragement from the Adviser for Native Affairs, Dr. G. A. J. Hazeu. Now that Hazeu had returned to the Netherlands strongly criticized and broken in spirit, Alimin began to reveal himself as an advocate of a program which lay between that of the Semarang group, who envisioned close connections with Moscow, and the Douwes Dekker group, which still held to its all-encompassing nationalism.

Douwes Dekker, incidentally, had had his exile commuted by Governor General Van Limburg Stirum and had returned to the East Indies in 1918 to begin again actively campaigning for his ideas. One of his main desires was to win the Sarekat Islam to his viewpoint (see below, p. 159 ff.). On November 1, 1919 he addressed the Fourth Sarekat Islam Congress and warned the members against too much emphasis on the economic class struggle. The Indies are not yet prepared for a class struggle against capitalism — Indies nationalism, which is at heart a movement for economic expansion, will have to find powerful allies he explained. He went on to point out that these allies could be found in American and Japanese capitalism.[113] A remarkable idea, but not one that found wide favor in Sarekat Islam circles.

The most powerful antidote to the revolutionary tendencies within the Sarekat Islam came from a group which withheld itself from active participation at the Fourth National Congress. This group, led by Agus Salim, sought to bring the Sarekat Islam back into the scope of religious concepts. This movement now became closely associated with the problem of the Turkish Caliphate in the Near East. Although not plaguing the government with revolutionary-socialistic tendencies, it held the threat of an equally strong pan-Islamism which also espoused socialistic principles, though not of a revolutionary nature.[114] The Sarekat Islam was sailing through heavy seas; Tjokroaminoto was experiencing great difficulty in keeping the organization on any course. And to complicate matters, voices within the Sarekat Islam were beginning to ask just what the course was, and what good was coming of all this wrangling.[115] The Sarekat Islam had already lost the great power of numbers and now it seemed as if the remaining nucleus would be scattered.

At the December 1919 meeting in Jogjakarta of the labor groups who wished to form a central union, the formation of a Union of the Labor Movement (Persatuan Pergerakan Kaum Buruh-P.P.K.B.) was effected. Chairman of the new organization was Semaoen; vice-chairman, Soerjopranoto; and secretary, Agus Salim. An internal struggle within the central labor union now began between the revolutionary elements (Semaoen, Bergsma, Alimin) of the Semarang group, and the radical elements (Salim, Moeis, Soerjo-pranoto), known as the Jogja group, for control of the labor movement with a membership of 72,000. The fact that the labor organization's headquarters came to be located in the chairman's home town, Semarang, gave the revolutionary group an initial advantage.

The first congress of the newly-formed central labor organization (P.P.K.B.) was held in Semarang in August 1920. Earlier the same year (May) the Semarang-centered revolutionary socialist organization (I.S.D.V.) under the leadership of Darsono — Sneevliet had been exiled and Semaoen was in Moscow — proclaimed itself the Communist Party of Indonesia (P.K.I.). This added a certain tension to the atmosphere in which the first central labor congress was held. The tension was augmented by the actions of the union organizer Soerjopranoto during most of the year 1920.

Since March of that year the plantation and factory workers union (P.F.B.) under Soerjopranoto (nicknamed *Radja Mogok*, the strike king) had been threatening the sugar planters with a strike because wages had not kept pace with the increased cost of living.[116] It was no secret that the rising cost of living was hitting laborers hard. In September 1919 the government had requested a labor commission to investigate the possibility of a minimum wage act.[117] In March, when the strike action threatened, the government, through its representative in the Volksraad, clarified its policy on labor strikes. If it were a question of improving working conditions — a strike for economic ends — then the government would assume a neutral position and at most offer mediation; however, if the strike was being used as a political weapon, then the government would have to take measures to curb such excesses. Clear enough, except, of course, it was not said who would have the final word on the economic or political nature of a particular strike. At the Union Congress in August the Semarang group chided Soerjopranoto for failing to consult the Central Labor Organization before issuing his threats. The Communists wanted to use the strike as a political weapon in order to gain the power of government and did not hesitate to say so.

A split in the labor movement almost occurred. On July 29, Sutan Mohammed Zain, president of the teachers' union (P.G.-H.B.) and himself a Western trained and oriented teacher, wanted to have Communists expelled from the central union so that employers would grant recognition. Calmed by Abdoel Moeis at the first congress, he decided to hold off on his demands.[118] Tjokroaminoto now went further than ever in his zeal to maintain unity: he now declared himself to be a Communist in principle.[119] The split did not occur. It was decided to move the Central Union Headquarters to Jogjakarta — thus removing the initial advantage which the revolutionary group had won, and placing future congresses under the somewhat more moderating influence of the Jogja group.

The feelings within the entire labor union movement were so aroused, however, that both the Semarang and Jogja groups began to push for strike actions. On August 9, 1920 the P.F.B. decided to invoke the long threatened strike against the sugar planters, but the government stood prepared and declared the move political; among the workers there was little fervor to engage in a strike, and the strike effort fizzled. A proposed general strike never materialized, for the Semarang group, after an unhappy experience with a local railway strike, decided not to push for a general strike.[120] Soerjopranoto's plantation and factory workers' union (P.F.B.) went rapidly downhill after the abortive strike effort and broke apart when the sugar planters failed to give it any recognition. The remaining months of 1920 saw numerous small local strikes in Deli (East Sumatra) and Surabaya, but these were not of much significance, for the desire to further such activity remained limited to the small group of extremist leaders.

The Sarekat Islam had planned to hold a Fifth National Congress in October 1920, but it had to be postponed until the next year. Alimin,[121] Moeso,[121] Sosrokardono,[122] Sanoesi,[123] Najoan,[121] Bratanata,[124] Tirtodanoedjo,[124] and Hadisoebroto[124] were all in jail. Tjokroaminoto had to appear as a witness in Tjiamis. Abdoel Moeis had to attend Volksraad meetings. Only Soerjopranoto and Agus Salim remained to guide the organization. They held an organizational meeting early in October 1920. Semaoen, still in Moscow, had sent Darsono to represent him, but Soerjo and Salim refused him admittance to their inner council. They now considered pushing through the matter of party discipline at the National Congress which was scheduled to start on the 16th of October.[125]

On October 6, 7, and 9, 1920, however, Darsono took his revenge in a series of articles in *Sinar Hindia* (organ of the P.K.I.), in which he attacked the Sarekat Islam and its leaders. The information he published had long been a public secret, but seeing it in print made a great impression among Sarekat Islam members throughout the islands. His critique was directed against the slight influence which the Sarekat Islam, due to its vacillating policies, had had upon affairs in the Indonesian world. Tjokroaminoto was labeled a fair-weather Communist, and attack was levied on the financial position of the Sarekat Islam which despite the large membership claimed by the organization remained on the verge of bankruptcy.[126] Finally he called attention to Tjokroaminoto's automobile and to the commercial enterprise which one Brotosoehardjo ran with Tjokro's wife, with the implication that Sarekat Islam funds supported these ventures. The Darsono articles, and the subsequent attempt to patch the breach, lessened the prestige of the Sarekat Islam leaders in the eyes of those semi-intellectuals who had continued to lend their support.[127] It was decided to postpone the National Congres until a more auspicious time. The Sarekat Islam stood at low ebb. Although its stability would gradually improve, it never again became the movement with mass appeal which it had once been.

The preceding pages which have discussed developments in the Sarekat Islam in the years before, during and after the First World War — years which saw the rise and decline of the organization — have raised many points concerning Indonesian organizational life. A few of these points can be elaborated further to clarify the position of the Sarekat Islam.

Many historical accounts designate the Sarekat Islam as 'a popular movement'. This term has gained a certain vogue among the Indonesian nationalists of the present day. If one understands by 'popular movement' a large following among the masses, then the Sarekat Islam prior to 1920 certainly applies, and could well be considered the only 'popular' aspect of the Indonesian freedom movement before the Second World War. However, if the term is meant to imply participation by, or approval from, the mass membership in the policies of the organization, then the 'popular' aspects of the Sarekat Islam are open to serious questioning. Popular support had been won on a mystical, superstitious, socially pressured, religious basis.[128] This support had little or nothing to do with the policies and demands advanced by the central Sarekat Islam leaders, particularly in the years following the First World War. The Sarekat Islam leaders could claim, of course, that their far-reaching socialistic programs and policies were designed for the ultimate benefit and advancement of the masses whom they represented. No doubt many of the leaders were sincere in this belief, many others unfortunately used it only to cover a lust for personal prestige and gain. Whatever the motivation, the advancement of a welfare policy placed the Sarekat Islam leaders on a par with the leaders of the Ethical Policy, and here they could not compete. The theories of the Sarekat Islam leaders were, like those of the Ethici, conceived outside the cosmos of Indonesian life, and, like those of the Ethici, had to be applied from outside, envisioning the improvement of Indonesian society toward ill-defined welfare goals. One cannot help but be struck by the similarities of aim and purpose between the Ethici and the Sarekat Islam leaders — there is no conclusive evidence that either group touched a basic chord in the Indonesian masses with its welfare and improvement programs.[129] The fact that they expired simultaneously may well be more than coincidence.

From the time of its creation in 1913 until 1920, the Sarekat Islam was certainly the outstanding example of Western style Indonesian organizational life. Its leaders became important figures in Indonesian society and must certainly be classed as a part of the newly forming elite of that society at that time. They were, with a few exceptions, moving into elite positions from lesser status; and with these same exceptions, they lost much of their prestige — certainly their top elite role — as the Sarekat Islam began to disintegrate and lose popularity. Tjokroaminoto remained an impressive personality, though certainly stripped of much of his luster and reduced in stature; his sons and brothers came to clothe positions of more than average prominence. Agus Salim remained a guiding light behind the religious activities of the Sarekat Islam and is still a widely known personality. His realization that force and violence would only provide excuses for suppression of the limited Indonesian movement remaining after 1920 made him one of the most acceptable 'nationalist' Indonesians to the Dutch government. He managed to find favor among both Dutch and Indonesian groups and did much to make Islam a vital and dynamic force in Indonesia. A few others gained brief prominence in the Communist movement (see below, Chapter IV, p. 210 ff.), and enjoyed a short-lived career which some were able to continue after 1945. But the remainder and bulk of the Sarekat Islam leaders either became lesser forces within Indonesian society, or faded completely from view — sometimes by choice, sometimes by pressure.

The Sarekat Islam will always retain a place in Indonesian

history. However, from the position of retrospect permitted the historian, it cannot be said that the Sarekat Islam leaders became permanently an essential part of the newly emerging Indonesian elite. This negative fact is as important as a positive fact in understanding the new elite. The Sarekat Islam was the largest Indonesian movement of its time. It unquestionably influenced vast numbers of Indonesians — especially those who were to be among the Indonesian leaders of the future.

Other Indonesian Organizations

Another organization operating actively during this period (1914–1920), which influenced the developing elite, but which did little to supply top leaders for Indonesian society, was the Indische Partij. It will be recalled that its policy of revolutionary nationalism had provoked the government into exiling its top leadership (see above, p. 65). After the exile of Douwes Dekker, Dr. Tjipto, and Soewardi in 1913, the party had moved its headquarters to Semarang and continued operation under the name Insulinde. The party lost none of its ideals, but close surveillance of its leaders and press by the government made revolutionary activity somewhat unfeasible. Under Governor General Van Limburg Stirum the exiles were permitted to return[130], and in 1918 Dr. Tjipto was made a member of the first Volksraad. With the return of Douwes Dekker and the freedom of movement granted Dr. Tjipto as a member of the Volksraad, Insulinde began to show new life and zest.[131] Local chapters became more active and the party organs began condemning government policies and personnel. The strictly nationalist concept, which differed from that of the revolutionary and evolutionary socialists in not being anti-capitalist and in wanting to consider social, economic and other problems only after national independence was won, continued to be promoted.[132] But now it stood prepared to employ the tactics of Communism which Douwes Dekker and Dr. Tjipto had had good opportunity to learn from their contacts in the Netherlands.[133]

Douwes Dekker had hoped to find in the Sarekat Islam a medium for transmitting his nationalist concepts. However, he conflicted with the strong revolutionary concepts of the left wing Sarekat Islam leaders, who sought to arouse the urban proletariat, a move which Douwes Dekker wisely enough regarded as impracticable for the time. He also came into conflict with the zealous Moslem members who were somewhat dubious about Insulinde's theosophical affiliations, and with many of the leaders who were not convinced of the open association principles underlying much of Douwes Dekker's thinking. Insulinde's consequent rejection by the Sarekat Islam served to throw its activities into ever more radical lines. Making full use of disillusioned semi-intellectuals (a tactic perfected by the Communists), and offering fantastic and irresponsible promises, Insulinde played a part in exciting local disturbances which erupted in 1919. This was the year of the Toli Toli Incident and the Garut Affair. It was also the year of many small disruptions, in Tjileungsi, Tangerang, Tjipari and Telok Putjung, to limit the list to only West Java.[134] It was also the year of the army disturbances in Surabaya which resulted in exile for the Dutch Communist Brandsteder. Most of these incidents were not attributed to Insulinde; not so, however, the Solo Affair of May 1919 which was directly instigated by Insulinde's top leaders.

While Douwes Dekker was engrossed with trying to win over the Sarekat Islam, Dr. Tjipto was throwing sparks at a decidedly explosive situation in Solo (Surakarta). Here the local Insulinde chapter, nominally headed by one Miss Vogel, but in reality controlled by a certain Hadji Misbach, was gaining many members. Hadji Misbach, a man of some religious stature, had managed to overcome the Marx-Mohammed controversy which was at this time splitting the Sarekat Islam. He was able to make the Koran read like the Communist Manifesto and effectively won a certain following which he drew into Insulinde.

General conditions in the Solo area, which was part of the princely lands and only indirectly controlled by the Netherlands Indian government, were not satisfactory.[135] Feudal services,

which years before had been replaced in the remaining parts of
Java by a head tax, were still in force in the princely lands, and
in addition the standard of living was lower than in most other
parts of Java. The Netherlands Indian government was aware
of these shortcomings, but due to the delicate power relationship with the princes it had to move with great caution. Finally
in 1918 the beginnings of reform were instituted and the situation showed prospects of improvement. Then in 1919, in the
same areas of Solo where the government reforms were being
tried, resistance against taxes and feudal services occurred.

Behind the peasant resistance stood Dr. Tjipto, Hadji Misbach,
and the local Insulinde chapter. Dr. Tjipto, famed for his outspokenness, had upon occasion condemned feudal services in
open statements within the walls of the Soesoehoenan of Solo's
palace — for this he can only be admired. Now, however, he
and Misbach, for reasons that appear quite irresponsible, began
promising the peasantry protection and succor if they would
resist their feudal services and taxes. Misbach bolstered these
promises with mystical religious tokens and symbols. This campaign was knowingly conducted in an area where government
reforms were just beginning to bring alleviation from the very
conditions that the Insulinde leaders sought to combat. On the
one hand this consideration heightens the irresponsibility of the
resistance action, but on the other, supports the contention that
reforms and changes, no matter how well-intentioned, serve to
dislocate old patterns of life, creating disorientations which make
a community receptive to the appeals of revolutionary elements.

As regards the actual resistance, it was minimal and bloodless.
Support by Insulinde was more verbal than actual, and the arguments used to create resistance could easily be countered. In
an attempt to keep the fire burning, Douwes Dekker himself
came to the area, and heaping fuel upon the still glowing embers
caused a second brief outburst, but to little avail — there was
too little fuel to start a major conflagration.

At the Eighth Insulinde Congress held in Semarang (June 1919)
shortly after the Solo Incident, the organization disclaimed any

association with the affair. A vote of praise to the valiant Hadji Misbach, who had drawn the immediate consequences attached to stirring up the population and had temporarily been deprived of freedom of movement, was passed, however.[136] At this congress a proposal to change the organization's name from Insulinde to Nationale Indische Partij was defeated. Shortly thereafter Douwes Dekker withdrew from Insulinde and established a separate Nationale Indische Partij in Bandung.[137]

This split in the movement is indicative of new sentiments operative in the Indo-European social group in the post war years. Many Indo-Europeans began to deplore the radical course of their organization Insulinde. When Douwes Dekker withdrew from Insulinde, the remaining members also abandoned the organization and formed an entirely new organization called the Indo-Europeesch Verbond. In part, this was a reaction against the revolutionary tactics of Insulinde, but of greater importance is the positive aspect of the new group which sought quite consciously to affiliate the destiny of the Indo-European with that of the full-blood European; i.e., to place the Indo-European community behind the policies of the Netherlands Indian government.[138]

The change within the Indo-European community which made this type of organization possible had been gradual. Since the beginning of the century, but particularly since 1913 when equal pay was granted in government positions regardless of race or place of training, the lot of the Indo had improved. This improvement had been accompanied by an amelioration in the relationships between the Indos and Totoks (full bloods)[139] which had led an increasing number of Indos to view their future welfare within the framework of the established colonial governmental authority. During the 1920's and 1930's the Indo-Europeesch Verbond continued to grow, and partly due to its own strength and partly due to a reticence on the part of other groups, it came to dominate activities in the Volksraad during these later years.[140] From the first it began to draw Indo-European members from Douwes Dekker's newly formed Nationale

Indische Partij which declined rapidly into complete ineffec-
tiveness.[141]

The collapse of the Nationale Indische Partij resulted in a
dispersion of the revolutionary nationalist group. Douwes Dekker
and Soewardi went into other lines of endeavor, while Dr. Tjipto
continued to devote much of his energy to furthering any movement directed against the government.[142] Many followed the
pattern of Mas Darnakoesoema, who made use of his Westernized
education to enter the civil service of the decontrolled Regency of
Bandung.[143] A handful gravitated into the newly established
Communist Party, foremost among these being Hadji Misbach.
The political party of Douwes Dekker had been most effective in
stimulating others and in supplying them with courage to act. Its
real purpose, however, had been to provide persons native to the
East Indies, particularly Indo-Europeans, with leading positions
in the management of affairs. By 1920 the social realities of East
Indian life had altered to such an extent that this latter goal had
been in large part actualized. The continuing radicalism of
Douwes Dekker served only to embarrass the bulk of his Indo
support while it failed to win any new adherents. Credit must be
given Douwes Dekker for his rapid withdrawal from active
political life and his shift in emphasis to other lines of endeavor
without losing sight of his ultimate goal of an independent Indonesia.

If the Sarekat Islam and the Indische Partij failed to push their
leaders permanently upward into the nucleus of the newly developing elite, the Regent's Union and the various princely groups[144]
failed to participate in this development because they held their
members above the operative level of the new elite. Small wonder that these organizations soon devolved into little more than
honorific clubs which were not taken too seriously either by their
members or by outsiders. It was natural for both Regents and
Princes to wish to protect and retain their traditional status and
prestige, but this was made extremely difficult in the face of the
policy of the Dutch government. In so far as this policy was
concerned, most of the Regents and nobles moved along with

it, acceding to the wishes of the government in local policies and assuring their children the best Westernized education available. But there is no question that the prestige of their official position was affected, even though many of them made a personal adjustment for themselves and their family. The loss of prestige attached to the official positions of top Indonesian administrators and nobles seemed to be most keenly sensed among the growing group of western trained intellectuals and semi-intellectuals. These were the elements eager to assume the power positions which the Dutch colonial government was forcing the upper elite to vacate. There is some doubt that the little people of Indonesia were ever clearly aware of the declining prestige of their chiefs despite the fulminations of the Sarekat Islam and the Indische Partij. Within the Indonesian cosmos which continued to prevail in most villages, a Regent or a Prince remained a great figure who, if he was ever seen, was treated with utmost respect and deference.

In so far as individual Princes or Regents sought either to guide or move with the Indonesian organizations springing up at this time, their efforts bore no relationship to the princely groups or the Regents' Union. The affiliation of some Regent families with the early Sarekat Islam has been mentioned (see above, p. 125), but this occurred almost exclusively in West Java. More, as would be expected, joined the early Budi Utomo, for among its leading members were found representatives of the Houses of Paku Alam and Mangkoenegoro and an occasional Regent such as R. A. A. Koesoemo Oetoyo. Other Regents found their ideas better represented by some of the Europeanized parties based on the association principle. Thus Achmad Dja-jadiningrat and Wiranatakusuma joined the *Nederlandsch Indische Vrijzinnige Bond* (Radical Democratic Union) and Koesoemo Joedo joined the *Politiek Economische Bond* (Political-Economic Union).

The Regents and high Indonesian administrators performed their greatest service for the newly developing elite by setting the example of behavior and service for the younger civil serv-

ants. In this regard their influence was great.[145] The Regents had
for the most part lived longest in close proximity to European
culture here; they had developed a life pattern of living next
to, but dissociated from, the Europeans. This became the
accepted pattern for the Westernized Indonesian elite. Their
official positions also made them orientation points within the
structure of the colonial government for the younger elite. They
were instrumental in helping the colonial government function
smoothly, and in permitting a constantly greater integration
of Westernized Indonesians into that government. They set the
example of devotion to duty which came to characterize most
Indonesian civil servants, and they placed this devotion above
any particular group or ideology which controlled the political
institutions of the country. Here, within a broadening Westernized base, came to be found those persons who held Indonesian
society together and kept it functioning in its modernized fashion.
The real social leaders, as opposed to the purely political leaders,
were found in this group. Within this important segment of the
elite the example of life set by the Regents remained important.

Those Indonesians with Western style educations, entering
the civil service or administration and devoting themselves to
their new duties, form the great bulk of the new elite. Their
lives are not as eventful as those of the political and organizational
leaders, but they performed an equal, or even greater, role in elite
development than the latter. Unfortunately there are no biographies, or memoirs, or diaries to quote from here, and if there
were they might make dull reading, for these people lived a
quiet life devoted to their personal and family problems and to the
fulfillment and perfection of their assigned duties. They were not
unaware of Indonesian organizational life, and many of their
ideals would be formulated through these organizations, but
they viewed their personal advancement within the confines of the
colonial relationship. Most of them did not join an Indonesian
organization of any sort. They formed that great stratum of personnel so essential to any group which seeks to control and maintain a modern administrative state.

Realizing that the bulk of Indonesian elite development occurred outside any of the organizations, it is nonetheless necessary to turn to organizational life to determine attitudes and sentiments. The feelings of the wide elite were expressed in daily doings and thoughts which have been lost to the student studying the past. Therefore, despite the recognized inadequacy and incompleteness of the method, it is necessary to return to a consideration of organizations in order to determine some of the problems and aims that influenced some, one never knows how many, of the elite.

The two organizations that had the most actual influence upon elite development during this period were probably the Muhammadijah and the Budi Utomo. By adopting the tactics of the European missionary groups, and by applying the Reformist ideas of Islam, Dachlan's Muhammadijah became a local success. His personal abilities and the efforts of his co-workers, Mas Djojosoegito, Hadji Abdoellah Sirat, Hadji Agus Salim, Hadji Fachroedin, and a number of students at the Teachers' Training School in Jogjakarta were in large measure responsible for the success of the organization. Muhammadijah remained circumspectly outside politics, although its members might belong to other organizations active in the political field. Dachlan saw that any political activity is necessarily meaningless without a large number of participants. He proposed to form such a group through establishing schools: schools which would uphold the teachings of Islam while meeting the requirements and standards of Westernized education. This was the basis of the Jogja experiment and it was eminently successful — the government stood prepared to subsidize all schools that met its requirements, and just as Christian schools had received subsidy, so now too (1915) the Muhammadijah school was subsidized.[145a] This was a great step forward for the organization and gave it a stability which attracted many of the religious members from the Sarekat Islam.

The success of the Muhammadijah school drew it to the attention of those Indonesians who favored a good education for their children because of the better chances for higher status it offered, but who were reluctant to send them to a Christian or even to a religiously neutral school. This group contained the local religious leaders who might or might not have had connections with the Sarekat Islam, but who as a group were economically above the generally low level of Indonesian life. If one can speak of any organization displaying a bourgeois or middle class character, it would be Muhammadijah rather than the Sarekat Islam, for it came to speak for those Indonesians whose economic status left little to be desired, but who were nonetheless seeking constant betterment. There was always close liaison between the Sarekat Islam and the Muhammadijah, but the well situated members of the latter organization never needed to have the Sarekat Islam speak for them politically; their interests were not impeded by the Netherlands Indian government. The years following upon the First World War were years of a lowering purchasing power for the general masses, but a time of prosperity for this rising Indonesian entrepreneurial and landowner group (which cannot be considered a class until about a decade later).[146] Their support permitted Muhammadijah to spread from its local base after 1920 to various cities in Java and Sumatra. Success never altered the primary aim of the organization, and it remained devoted to educational, charitable, and religious work.

What cannot help but be a source of frustration to the historian is the lack of documentary material, either primary or secondary, about the organization Muhammadijah. This is particularly irritating because Muhammadijah has produced a fair number of local leaders of contemporary Indonesia and also a few of the top leaders. Unfortunate as this lack of evidence is, it is not too startling, for in the first place the gradual and quiet nature of the movement made it far less obtrusive than the theatricals of politically inclined organizations; and in the second place, neither Indonesian nor European writers who were expressing public opinion were inclined to take this Islamic Reformist movement seriously since it lay outside their secular view of the changes in Indonesian society. The net result was that in the colonial period of 20th century Indonesian history, few writers took serious notice of this very essential facet of elite development — yet in cooperation and in harmony with the Netherlands Indian government this formation went forward. As a movement, Islamic Reformism seems to have had a strengthening effect upon Islam in Indonesia, but this cannot be measured for lack of evidence on both the past and present state of the religion. It can be stated with some certainty, however, that through the work of the Muhammadijah and the *Jong Islamieten Bond* (Young Islamic Union), which was formed in 1925 as a joint effort of the Sarekat Islam and Muhammadijah, a group of young leaders emerged, who through a deep religious conviction stood in close contact with a large number of the Indonesian people and who wielded great influence among broad segments of the Indonesian population. More than any other group they came to interject themselves between the people and the group of Westernized administrative leaders. During the colonial period they remained passive toward the outside government and viewed their task in terms of winning influence within their own society, but in later years they were to form one of the most active elements in the creation of the new Indonesian state.

The organization that was generally thought by contemporaries to reflect most clearly the aims and desires of those Indonesians who came to lead the development of the elite was the Budi Utomo. It had been born out of a mingling of various sentiments and reactions alive in the upper strata of Javanese society. By 1914 it had thrown off some of the extremes within its original composition, but it still remained far from a homogeneous endeavor. No single set of principles or line of action emerged in the Budi Utomo to which one can point as the attitude of the new elite. But the Budi Utomo did represent the social classes who assumed critical positions in the new elite, and within the diversity of sentiments of the organization, there always remained a certain common ground of unity. It would probably not be incorrect to seek this unifying factor in the common consciousness of the elitist role and in the shared concept of leadership. This leadership and this elitist role were to be exercised in the cultural, social and economic realm as well as in political fields of endeavor. In general the organization sought to draw strength from the Javanese culture and cosmos in synthesis with the West. Probably no other group did so much to mold the Westernization of the new Indonesian elite into a synthesis with Javanese concepts and ultimately to strengthen the cultural awareness throughout the archipelago.

In 1915 Budi Utomo departed from its social-cultural principles when it took part in the Committee for Defense of the Indies (Comité 'Indië Weerbaar'). In the hope that participation in this movement would result in an improvement of the position of the Indonesian people within the colonial relationship the Budi Utomo sent the Western trained teacher, Mas Dwidjosewojo, as its representative. The committee did not gain positive results, but the way was opened for the Budi Utomo to take part in further political activity. With the formation of the Volksraad, Budi Utomo decided to take part in the elections for that body and was able to send Dwidjosewojo as its representative to the first session.

Meanwhile in 1915 Budi Utomo sponsored the first Indonesian youth organization, *Tri Koro Dharmo* (Three Noble Goals). The impetus in forming this organization came from Dr. Raden Satiman Wirjosandjojo, whose brother Soekiman, also a graduate of the medical training school (STOVIA) and later to be active in Islamic organizations, had already gone to the Netherlands to complete his medical training. They were sons of a Javanese merchant. The ostensible purpose of the youth organization was to promote social activities among Javanese students enrolled in secondary schools away from their home environment. The organization sought to stimulate a Great Java cultural concept among the student youth — a concept that would encompass the culture of the Madurese and Sundanese as well as the Javanese people. In the interest of this cause the name of the youth organization was changed to *Jong Java* (Young Java) in 1918. But the Great Javanese culture concept had little appeal and by 1920 the Sundanese and Madurese students had withdrawn from active participation in the organization. They now set up their own

youth organizations, following the example of the Sumatran students who in 1917 established the *Jong Sumatranen Bond* (Young
Sumatran Union), and of other ethnic groups such as the Mina-
hassans and Ambonese who also established their own separate
organizations. The time was not yet ripe for a unitary concept,
but the day was not far off. When it arrived, however, it would
be more wisely couched in terms of Greater Indonesia rather than
of Greater Java.[147] It was among the young men who were students at the time of the formation of these youth organizations
that this Greater Indonesia concept would come to fruition —
their common experiences and their contacts at Westernized institutions of learning was in no small measure responsible for
cultivating this idea which would later be refined for them by
European scholars.

Young Java, although claiming to be non-political, served as a
recruiting ground for future members of Budi Utomo and, as such,
it planted the seeds of political and social awareness among its
youthful members.[148] The concept underlying the thought of
Satiman, a concept which found realization in the development
of the new Indonesian elite, was that the traditional Indonesian
elite based upon hereditary principles must make way for, or at
least be expanded to include, Indonesian intellectuals, and the
basis for entry into the leadership group of Indonesian society
must be education rather than birth. This was to be accompanied
by an ever wider participation by the leader group in the handling of its own affairs. This in no way altered the fact that students
should only participate in active politics after the completion of
their schooling, but it did prepare them for assuming leading
roles within the Indonesian social order. Actually this was, in
rather more direct terms, the educational aim of the Ethical
Policy.

Naturally many of the more conservative members of the Budi
Utomo who constructed their life exclusively about Javanese
hierarchical and cosmological concepts were not in immediate
accord with this idea, nor were many of the regents who placed
rather high value on their hereditary rights. It was not exactly

the guiding concept of the Sarekat Islam either, for its leaders had in large measure rejected or been rejected by the practical application of their Westernization experience; or of Muhammadijah, which founded its appeal upon religion and could have little sympathy with the theosophical and agnostic tints of Budi Utomo and Young Java.[149] Nor did the revolutionary groups wish to accede to the idea of the intellectuals moving into leadership positions.

So it was that the young intellectuals who were coming to assume the important positions in the changing social structure were not completely represented by any one of the existing organizations.[150] In general, however, it was Budi Utomo which won the membership of those who wished to engage in organizational activity, for this organization offered them the greatest scope for action. Because the young intellectuals who joined the Budi Utomo were already those who desired to take an active hand in changing existing conditions, and since the intellectual elite concept found favor among those educated youth from the lesser prijaji or merchant milieus who had no stake in the existing order,[151] there was a tendency in the post war years for the Budi Utomo to take on a more radical nature. In general it can be said that the organization fluctuated between radicalism and moderation until late in the 1920's when it finally found a degree of stability (see below, p. 216).

Since the formation of the Peoples' Council (1918) some members of the Budi Utomo had been becoming ever more involved in politics. In the Volksraad the Budi Utomo placed itself behind a program calling for "the creation of a parliamentary form of government with a national spirit and an electoral law to bring this about; furthermore, equality and uniformity of law." This was to be achieved by "national legislation directed toward the removal of social causes which create or strengthen inequalities of conditions of development between various members of the population."[152] This latter was in large part directed toward the desire to remove the remaining restrictions on Westernized education which gave advantage to the upper classes and leading families of Indonesian society, and to permit capabilities to be a more deciding factor in the selection of future students and (as would naturally follow) *formateurs* of the new elite. In this endeavor the young intellectuals received assistance from various private foundations sponsored by Hollanders who were desirous of assisting young Indonesians through scholarships and study grants to acquire a good education.

In November 1918, when the Social Democratic disturbances in the Netherlands found their repercussions in the East Indies in the form of a Radical Concentration in the Volksraad, the Budi Utomo joined the concentration with a wait-and-see attitude. This tenuous alliance endured for more than a year, but the Budi Utomo was never a very active member of the concentration.

Radical and nationalist doctrines which were affecting other Indonesian organizations did not spare the Budi Utomo as is shown by the organization's Tenth Anniversary Book which appeared in 1918.[153] Goenawan Mangoenkoesoemo speaks of the influence which Douwes Dekker had in leading the Budi Utomo into political lines[154] and clearly indicates the dissatisfactions that gripped the young intellectuals with regard to the restrictions imposed by the colonial government upon Westernized education.[155] Soewardi Soerjaningrat, close follower of Douwes Dekker's nationalist theory, wrote from out of exile on the similarity of Javanese and Indonesian nationalism. Javanese nationalism, he feels, cannot be exclusive, for the domination of the Indonesian peoples by the people of the Netherlands has laid close ties between all peoples of the Netherlands Indies.[156] Although Javanese culture has much to offer, the struggle must not become exclusive, for in the remaining Indonesians the Javanese find their 'allies by necessity'.[157] Such sentiments were to change in form as years went on, but the general content of the intellectuals' program would remain much the same — a program which found its essential stimulation and refinement from European or Europeanized intellectuals. These sentiments tended to lead the Budi Utomo ever deeper into political activity. Meanwhile, most of the Budi Utomo's members seemed chiefly concerned with cultural problems. Most of the organization's meetings were taken up with problems of education, development of a viable Javanese language, and the retention of Javanese culture within a rapidly changing life. Much of this element's active participation in Budi Utomo was siphoned off through the creation of the *Java Instituut* in 1920 which attracted persons predominantly interested in Javanese culture.

An undetermined (but probably great) influence on the gradual drift of Budi Utomo into more active political participation is to be found in the daily experiences and contacts of the young Indonesian students and intellectuals. In the atmosphere of the Westernized school these young Javanese found a life that differed from what they had known in their home environment. Not only was the difference one of physical environment, but what was far more important, one of mental environment: perhaps only slightly inaccurately generalized as the difference between a scientific-rational attitude and a mystical-animistic attitude. In many instances the individual student could neither completely accept nor completely reject either the Western or the Javanese thought pattern: many remained uncertain.[158] In this state of uncertainty they came into contact with European teachers — particularty as they entered the secondary schools. In so doing they came into contact with varying shades of Western opinion, with a variety of European concepts regarding the Indonesian and his future, and with a multitude of personality types.[159] European school teachers rank high on the list of individuals who shaped the personalities of the new elite, yet very little is known about them: only through a random comment on the part of an old student is it possible to gain some slight insight into the real nature of the daily relationships in the schools. One thing seems certain: the Dutch government had no easy time recruiting teachers for service in the Indies and was inclined not to examine the qualities of its hirelings too closely.[160]

Over and above the relationship of student and teacher was the nature of the subject matter taught. In an attempt not to rouse sentiments the controversial aspects and glories of Indonesian history were, logically enough, played down in the classrooms. But many an Indonesian, living in a country ruled by another race and another people, wondered about the lessons to be learned from the Dutch struggle for independence against Spain, or the French Revolution, or the unification of Germany under Bismarck. Applying these concepts in an environment typified by a rapidly changing colonial relationship which clashed in obvious, unconcealed measure with the liberal spirit of the time, it is small wonder that the Budi Utomo was carried ever further by its younger men into the turmoil of East Indian politics.

In 1919, the Budi Utomo, concerned by the gains in membership of Insulinde in the Surakarta area which should have been a Budi Utomo stronghold, voted by a very narrow margin to seek to advance itself among the masses of the people. The difficulties that beset the Sarekat Islam at this time permitted Budi Utomo to increase its membership. Guiding this new move was one Raden Soetopo, who as editor of the party organ, *Boedi Oetomo*, was able to exert great influence on many of the indecisive members.[161] But matters moved too far. Radical tendencies had created too much disturbance in Indonesian life; this was not what the Budi Utomo desired. In 1920 the majority of the organization's members rejected the new entanglements, broke with the ever more leftist measures of the Radical Concentration, and expressed loyalty to the government. At the same time, however, the organization expressed the wish that the liberal policies of the Netherlands Indian government be continued. In view of the recently released report of the Reform Commission of 1918 this desire was to become of paramount importance in future developments.

Government Policy and Attitude

The Dutch Ethical Colonial Policy in the years during and after the First World War practically defies analysis. In fact there are those who would conclude the Ethical Policy in 1913 and term the period thereafter something else.[162] Others again view the Ethical Period as extending to 1942. In this essay the year 1920 will be used as a closing date for the Ethical Movement. These differences reflect the variety of opinions as to just what the Ethical Policy was and what it meant to do. For our purposes the feature of the Ethical Policy which should be most emphasized is its dynamic character which sought to change and remodel (usually in a Western manner) with a view toward improving welfare and living standards of the great mass of people of the East Indies. Whatever time seems most suitable for terminating this policy, there must be no misapprehension about the abruptness of the change. The selection of the year 1920 here is made because the dynamic element of the Ethical Policy seems to end *about* that time,[163] not because there is a sudden reversal in the welfare attitude or in the avowed desire of eventually instituting self-government. The year 1913, on the other hand, could well be termed the end of the 'policy' part of the Ethical Movement, for 'policy' implies a certain guidance and control, and there is little indication of direct governmental control after 1913[164] — at least not until about 1921, and then it was control in another direction.

Whenever one decides to date the Ethical Policy, there is little doubt that the period from about 1914 to about 1920 is difficult to appraise. The reason for this has already been implied. It stems from the fact that if the Netherlands Indian government had any policy, it was to have no policy. This, of course, is an exaggeration, but it is the only means available for explaining the many paradoxes which arose in these years. Although there is no positive evidence for this, it was almost as though the Netherlands Indian government felt that it would allow all the changing relationships and interrelationships in the Indonesian, European, and Chinese parts of East Indian society to seek their own levels as based upon the forces of some natural law. The supreme authority would act as referee to see that no one stepped out of bounds and that the entire process ran peaceably and without violence.[165]

The many paradoxes arising naturally out of the reaction of self interests within the changing colonial relationship made the government's task of maintenance of peace and order ever more difficult and subject to criticism. Of these paradoxes, the one that lay at the core of the relationship was touched upon by the Marxist writer D. M. G. Koch.[166] In brief, his analysis points out the logical fallacy in raising the welfare, education and hopes of a people while at the same time permitting foreign elements to enjoy social, legal, and economic advantages in the country of that people. From this one basic paradox many lesser ones follow. It is largely within the scope of the problems arising from this basic issue that the conflicts which ultimately lead to severe questioning of the colonial relationship are found.

Fundamental to an understanding of the changes occurring within the upper spheres of Indonesian society is a general view of the educational policy of the Netherlands Indian government and the problems that arose from it. The educational design of Snouck Hurgronje, which envisioned the transformation of the traditional indigenous aristocracy into a Western educated elite, was for many years followed in theory. In practice, however, certain encroachments were made upon this theory. It was easy enough to restrict the Administrators' Schools (o.s.v.i.a.) to the sons of the higher prijaji, but with the creation of medical training facilities, secondary law school, and other institutions of more than primary Western calibre, it became necessary to draw students from a somewhat less than high prijaji status. These students, once their education was completed, began to oppose the existing educational restrictions (as well as social restrictions inherent in the colonial relationship). They demanded that the birth requirements be removed from Western type education, and their demands grew particularly loud when the government sought to limit the Dutch-Native Schools (1914) to children "whose parents either through office, descent, prestige, or training were in leading positions in indigenous society." These intellectuals found their most receptive organ of expression in the Budi Utomo, and this organization became the leader in championing the extension of Western education to all who wished it.

The government was inclined to heed the demands of these Indonesian organizations, but it could not in one move cut away the ground upon which its administration and authority was built. Therefore, the process continued to move slowly forward — more rapidly than before, but still too slowly to satisfy those leaders of the Indonesian organizations who came largely from the lesser prijaji class and most keenly felt every inequality between their positions and those of their hereditary superiors. In a circular of November 29, 1913, no. 2744, the Netherlands Indian government reaffirmed the hereditary rights of the Regents, but established certain qualifications of training and education which they would have to meet in order to fill their positions.[167] In 1914 when the *Bestuursschool* (Advanced administrators' school) was opened, there were no restrictions as to birth or social status placed upon the students. The restrictions upon entry into the Dutch-Native Schools, which had caused such a furor among the young intellectuals of the Budi Utomo, proved unretainable in practice — particularly when non-government organizations such as Christian missions and Muhammadijah formed private Dutch-Native Schools, equal in all respects to the government's schools, but without social restrictions. Furthermore, the nominal cost to the family of sending a son to these schools placed them within range of virtually the entire prijaji class. This trend of lowering the upper prijaji and raising the lesser prijaji was continued throughout the first quarter of the 20th century.[168]

In practice the process was gradual and evolutionary, and did not, in final analysis, lead to a complete turnover of the social order. The desire to partake of a Westernized education and the will to make the financial sacrifice of supporting a son through the necessary years of schooling, remained limited almost entirely to the prijaji class. Some sons of technicians, merchants, or better situated villagers and an occasional commoner who was aided by a Dutch family managed to find their way into the Westernized educational system, but this was decidedly an exception. The general rule was for persons out of the prijaji class to send their children to the Westernized schools, and this class was large enough and expanding rapidly enough to fill the Westernized institutions of learning as rapidly as they were provided. Within the scope of Westernized economic life and within the confines of the civil and technical administration (highest offices excepted) there came to be a rather free social mobility for members of this educated group, a mobility which was largely divorced from traditional status and which was based on training and ability. Here was formed the new elite of Indonesian society — not really a new elite, but rather an expansion and extension of the old.

The desa school had in practice provided more education than most villagers at this time found needful. Not infrequently a passive hostility to this bulwark of popular education existed and it was not uncommon for school attendance to be regarded as a curse of Allah, or as just another means of exacting tribute.[169] None of the Indonesian organizations made a strong issue of furthering or improving village education and their attempts to establish non-governmental village schools met in general with little success.[170] In the course of years the desa school became more accepted, but, its success remained restricted. Perhaps some of the doubt in the villagers' minds as to the value of schooling stemmed from some of the results they had seen in those youths who had wanted more than the village could offer and had made their way to the Second Class Native School, or, as it came to be called, Standard School.

The Standard School did not expand so rapidly as the desa schools or more decidedly Western types of schools, but it continued to exist and to function as a minimum educational base for many of the urbanized Indonesians and for those villagers who desired advancement into the urban sphere (this latter being stimulated by population pressure in some areas).[171] Many semi-skilled and lesser clerical positions were filled by students of the Standard Schools, but their education was not sufficient to win them entry into even the lower ranks of the much vaunted civil administration. For those who wished to pursue their education further the Standard School proved to be a blind alley (see above, p. 70). Most who completed the Standard School were satisfied to seek a position for which their training had qualified them, but some wished to gain further entry into the world of the West with which they had had some experience. Unfortunately this was not possible for them so that they became among the most dissatisfied elements in Indonesian society.[172]

Returning now to the relationship of this Westernized education to some of the basic paradoxes of colonial life, it is to be noted that the Dutch-Native Schools were almost immediately equated to European schools. Consequently they provided entry to all advanced educational training normally available to Europeans. In order to cope with the influx in enrollment the secondary school system was expanded. By 1919 the pressure on college preparatory work had become so great that a special secondary academic course for university work was instituted for Indonesians. In 1920, the first college, an engineering school, was started in Bandung and opened its doors to all qualified applicants. The quality of education offered in the Westernized schools was comparable to the same level of education in Europe — this standard had to be maintained for the European families in the East Indies who might wish to continue their children's education in Europe and who would expect them to enter European schools at the same level as East Indian schools. The quantity of this education seems to have fallen somewhat short. The school shortage was to grow worse as the years went on, becoming an ever graver problem, but at the time of the First World War it had not yet reached major proportions.

The founding of the Dutch-Native Schools created a demand for trained teachers. Part of this need was filled by recruitment in Europe of Dutch teachers, but part also had to be met by the establishment in 1914 of an advanced teachers' training school in Purworedjo (Java). Even earlier the government had encouraged native teachers to seek advanced certificates comparable to European teaching certificates, but few had done so. Now with the need and the possibility open to Indonesians to gain advanced teaching certificates, the government was faced with the problem of compensation.

In 1913 the government had in principle opened all official positions to members of all races: qualifications of education and experience would in theory be the only determinants. This principle soon came into conflict with the matter of compensation.[173] In most services Europeans held the top positions and were paid on a scale based upon the European standard of living. Indonesians for the most part held the lower positions and were paid in accordance with the native living standard in the East Indies. In the teaching profession, which was in most instances a government service, Indonesians with the same qualifications as Europeans first began to appear in some number. Here the test case on the practicability of equal compensation for equal rank and position regardless of race would be conducted. It was decided to pay these Indonesians the full European salary, which would, of course, raise them to a disproportionately high level in comparison with their fellow Indonesians. The government decided that in the 'mixed' positions, where less than half the personnel were Indonesian, the European salary scale would be retained until more Indonesians could be trained.[174]

This was satisfactory as a temporary expedient, but soon would lead to difficulties. Not only did the expanding government services become unbearably expensive with the growing number of persons on a European pay scale, but the question of what to do about Europeans in those positions which came to be filled in the major part by Indonesians had to be faced. It was not possible to obtain or retain Europeans at a native level of compensation, and the government could not seriously consider this possibility. Nor was it possible to retain the European pay scale throughout, for the economy which was founded upon the encouragement of capital through low tax rates did not permit such a move. To return to a differentiated pay scale along racial lines would contravene principles upon which practically the entire Indonesian elite had strongly formed convictions. By 1920 this matter of compensation had become one of the problems confronting the colonial government and formed one aspect of the great paradox of the colonial policy. This particular problem found no immediate or happy solution though many of its sharpest aspects were somewhat smoothed over through a system of 'tropical bonuses' for European employees.

As the government laid the groundwork for extending education and training to Indonesians, it also laid the foundations for local autonomy of Indonesians. The decentralization process, started officially in 1903, was regarded by some as the vehicle for extending participation in government to all population groups of the East Indies. By 1914, however, it was fairly evident that decentralization had proved to be only a limited success.[175] The city councils in the European dominated urban communities functioned with some success, but the district councils proved to be unnatural creations which had no basis in reality. Meanwhile the actual influence of Indonesians in the administration of the country remained severely limited by the well-meaning interference of the European administrative corps. The eventual aim of turning the administrative machinery over to well-educated Indonesians was also far from its mark. The government was not unaware of this. In order to begin placing control of internal affairs in the hands of the Indonesian administrators and civil servants, the government started a program of removing European tutelage in certain areas (*ontvoogding*). The process was started in 1918 in Tjiandjur and was soon thereafter applied in several other regencies. It consisted of turning over certain administrative matters to the Regent, thus permitting him to regulate certain segments of the civil service corps. Careful control characterized the entire *ontvoogding* process — even with select Regents in select areas, only the less important services and responsibilities were turned over by the Dutch administration.[177]

The *ontvoogding* process was not favorably regarded by the newer members of the expanding elite group. Particularly those in the Indonesian organizations protested against a measure which seemed to strengthen the power in the hands of traditional authority. The creation of a People's Council (Volksraad) at about the same time did not quiet these protests for what this newer part of the elite really wanted was a hand in the operation of all affairs. The Volksraad did ease some of the pressure, but only the creation of Regency Councils and the extension of wider autonomy after 1925 began to meet the demands of the new elite.[178]

The Peoples' Council (Volksraad) was regarded by most Hollanders as a great step forward in the struggle for East Indian autonomy, but, as already indicated above (see pp. 129–30), it was not based on a representative political structure in Indonesian society. The Volksraad had been conceived as an advisory body to the Netherlands Indian government; it was not meant to be a parliament with responsibility for providing laws for the state. Yet, many persons, both Indonesian and European, associated with the Volksraad, began from the first to view their responsibility in broader terms than the design of this institution permitted. They viewed their function as one of preparing the way for complete autonomy of the East Indies. The Indonesian members of the early Volksraad seemed especially intent upon achieving broad measures of autonomy and self-government for Indonesians.

When the Volksraad was opened in May 1918 the functions and operations of the new body had not yet, of course, been tested in practice, so that there was no immediate dissatisfaction. Only the revolutionary socialists regarded it as a sham and would have no dealings with it. To almost all educated Indonesians it seemed to offer the possibility of further political participation in the future. Persons from almost all of the Indonesian organizations were seated in the first Volksraad, and it was quite natural for them to feel that they came to represent not only their organization but all the Indonesian people.[179]

Passions and hopes exceeded the realities of the situation. The first few months of the Volksraad made many of its members feel that they were too confined by the government. The government, for its part, was inclined to view the future of the Volksraad in rather expansive terms, but was somewhat surprised by the almost instantaneous desire of the Volksraad for more power. It was not in the nature of the Van Limburg Stirum government to hold tight rein on affairs, however,[180] so that when the occasion presented itself later in 1918, the government went in the direction of extending authority of the Volksraad.

Nineteen hundred and eighteen was an election year in the Netherlands, and the business cabinet of Cort van der Linden was terminated. A combination of right wing and center parties formed a government which left a strong block of Social Democrats in opposition.[181] A. W. F. Idenburg, long associated with East Indian affairs as Governor General and Minister of Colonies, now came again to be Minister of Colonies in the new government.

The events of November 1918 in Germany surrounding the end of the war, the overthrow of the monarchy and the establishment of a republic with largely Socialist support, had repercussions in the Netherlands. In early November 1918, the Dutch Social Democrats made a bid to seize the government. For some days there was confusion, but when the air cleared the moderate elements had rallied and had firm control of the situation.[182] The Socialists recanted.[183] When the first confused reports of events in the Netherlands reached the East Indies a Radical Concentration was created in the Volksraad under the guidance of European Socialists. Almost all Indonesian groups who had representatives in the Volksraad joined this concentration, for it espoused the extension of Volksraad power and wider participation in government by all the peoples of the East Indies.

Meanwhile the Governor General Van Limburg Stirum had been receiving rather alarming reports from Minister of Colonies Idenburg on the extent of the November 1918 difficulties.[184] As a staunch advocate of democratic principles in the East Indies, he had exhibited great tolerance toward the developments in Indonesian society and strongly favored the obliteration of racial inequalities in governmental, judicial, and economic life. Yet, as almost all liberals of his day, he was convinced that the economic foundations of a strong East Indian colony must be laid by capital investment from abroad. When confronted with the demands of the Radical Concentration, he was personally not adverse to making far reaching concessions of authority, but he felt that all changes should occur in an orderly manner so as not to disrupt the functioning of the state or the economy. He had no instructions from the Minister in The Hague; many of his advisers were panicky; no one was certain how widespread the desire for these changes in the East Indies was; it seemed clear something had to be done.[185] Acting on his own initiative, Van Limburg Stirum promised the creation of a Reform Commission which would investigate possible extensions and revisions in the nature and power of the Volksraad, and also in the structure of the Netherlands Indian administration. The Commission came into being in December 1918 and represented all phases of political thought. The very *raison d'être* of the commission, however, inclined it toward change and reform of the existing order.[186]

From much of the European community in the Indies, as represented by its press, and from much of the civil administration who once again felt negated and disregarded in a situation which they felt to have under control, the Governor General was subject to criticism.[187] The strongest abuse, however, came from the politicians in the homeland who regarded Van Limburg Stirum's acts as irresponsible concessions to revolutionary fright. Fock, one of the early supporters of the Ethical Policy, now president of the second chamber of the Netherlands Parliament, vacated the chair in order to raise his voice in protest against the Governor General's action. Seldom had such passions been aroused.[188] But the aging A. W. F. Idenburg, since the elections Minister of Colonies, firmly supported the actions of the Governor General and refused either to censor him or to veto the Reform Commission.[189] Idenburg explained the Governor General's move as the only possible concession to the forces of the time and insisted that the reluctant Dutch government accept it as a postponing tactic which would allow further considerations at a later date. Privately the Minister was not in complete agreement with the

Governor General's rather far reaching concessions;[190] he rightly saw that only a change in the nature of the Volksraad which would make it into a responsible governing body would satisfy the advocates of reform.[191] This type of change he was not prepared to support, for he felt that the political leadership of East Indian society would then fall into the hands of a small group of educated and egocentric persons who would lose sight of the larger developments of the area.[192] The correctness of this attitude cannot be tested; suffice it to say, it prevailed. When the Reform Commission was installed in December 1918, its sphere of operation was limited to reform of the Volksraad within the existing political structure and to reform of the administrative system. Meanwhile, both Minister of Colonies Idenburg and Governor General Van Limburg Stirum were convinced that constructive measures toward creating a politically viable society should be started. They began to implement this aim through the creation of lesser political bodies, such as Regency and local councils, which would then form a basis for a higher political body.[193] Before this could be advanced very far, however, Idenburg's failing health forced him to resign his cabinet post.[194]

Idenburg's successor in the post of Minister of Colonies was Simon de Graaff. Conservative, friend of capitalism, believer in administrative rather than political decentralization,[195] convinced of Indonesian immaturity,[196] he typified as did no other single person the new spirit which was to dominate the political aspects of Dutch colonial policy. To his opponents, and they were many, his mind seemed as twisted as his body, and he was commonly known as 'Simon the Liar'. Even to some of the leading conservative politicians his deviousness must have been trying, but he was kept on year after year and cabinet after cabinet because he fitted into the policies of the right wing and because no one else had such a phenomenal storehouse of facts and information about the detailed operations and personnel of the colonial administration.[197] That his influence was not more disastrous than it was, was due, in the first place, to the increasing separation of East Indian affairs from control in the motherland,

and, in the second place, to the fact that the most significant aspects of the newly developing colonial policy did not operate directly through politics and politicians but rather through professional administrators and intellectuals in direct contact with the Indonesian elite.

The relationship between the Governor General and the new Minister of Colonies became one of veiled hostility.[198] They were completely antithetical. The Minister openly advocated continuation of the Ethical Policy and could not therefore force an issue for the immediate replacement of one of the most obviously Ethical Governor Generals whose term in office had slightly more than a year to run. The Governor General, for his part, was not the man to give up his station. The result was a battle of attrition — a battle in which time was against the Governor General; here was most clearly fought the last battle of a dynamic Ethical Policy.

Van Limburg Stirum had, during his years as Governor General (1916–21), to face great problems in pushing his policy of equal rights and justice for all peoples of the East Indies.[199] He very soon alienated a large portion of the European community who had definite ideas about racial inequality and the 'place' of the Indonesian.[200] He had no strong press. All groups knew they could expect justice and equal treatment from him, but he held himself aristocratically aloof and had a personal rather than a mass appeal. In this already difficult situation he found himself handicapped by the encumbrances of an administrative state; he needed strong, resolute persons capable of implementing his ideas and programs. Men who believed with him, but could act without him. Instead he found himself surrounded by civil servant mentalities quite incapable of the necessary breadth of action. Men who had been pressed into a bureaucratic mold and who could not be expected to run risks of independent action which would affect their careers and advancement.[201] This problem was not new to the East Indies, but under a policy which attempted to referee, not guide, events, the strong bureaucratic nature of the East Indian administration appeared in its worst light. The

European civil servants, in large measure further removed from Indonesian society than had been the case a generation earlier, quite naturally sought their approbation from the European community, and were reluctant to act against the oftentimes limited and shortsighted interests of the European group.[202] Everyone had the notion of working for the best interests of the Indonesians, but the unpleasant occurrences of early 1919 convinced a growing number of persons that the present government was leading the country to ruin and anarchy rather than to constructive welfare. The Governor General found the circle of his friends and supporters decreasing. In 1918 his irreplaceable friend and colleague, A. C. D. de Graeff, vice-president of the Council of the Indies, returned to the Netherlands. One of the last persons to share the Governor General's feelings on native affairs, Dr. G. A. J. Hazeu was so maligned by his fellow Europeans when he tried to present the Indonesian side of the Garut Affair that he left his post and the colony (January 1920) broken in spirit.[203] There was a growing reaction both at home and in the colony against the free unfurling of native political movements. Slowly the Governor General was forced to retreat from his advanced Ethical position.

The increasingly radical nature of the Indonesian parties at this time helped to make the Governor General's position completely untenable. In July 1919 he had his representative in the Volksraad, W. Muurling, remind that body that the government was favorably disposed toward the native movement and was preparing the ground for representative councils at the lower levels of society.[204] It was his last completely optimistic statement. Overt acts against the government soon thereafter became more flagrant than ever before. When forced to choose between maintenance of the government and submission to the radical demands of the Indonesian and Dutch left wing politicians, the Governor General could make only one choice. On September 1, 1919, he spoke of the government's favorable attitude toward the native movement but expressed his disillusionment at the recent disturbances of order. In hard certain tones he reminded all that "whoever wished to leave the path of legality, bites on iron", for the government would maintain the existing legal system and resist all threats to it.[205] The Governor General was tightening the reins. He was caught in the dilemma created by advancing Indonesian self-consciousness on the one hand, and the retention of existing relationships, particularly economic, on the other. He envisioned far-reaching, progressive action, but his field of action was being ever more limited. After November 1919 when S. de Graaff became Minister of Colonies, the progressive solution lost ground to another method of coping with the problem of the colonial relationship.[206]

During the twentieth century the Netherlands Indian government had been able to promote many changes in Indonesia, but it had not dared to tamper with the economic realities of the colonial relationship. The private economic interests of the Netherlands were quick to condemn any alteration of their favored position or any desire to change the private capitalistic nature of the colonial tie. These interests were able to make their desires felt. Yet during the twentieth century the colonial economic ties had an increasing tendency to drag the Indonesian out of his native economic environment and into the world market place. As the European concerns operating in Indonesia sought to supply world markets with raw materials and products of the East Indies, the involvement of Indonesians became ever greater.[207] Most Indonesians involved in the production for world markets were common laborers, though many were also employed in supervisory posts. These people, though often paid as little as possible, were none the less intimately tied to the fluctuations inherent in the free-functioning capitalist world economy.

The years 1914 to 1920 saw numerous price fluctuations of East Indian products on the world market. The war years tied produce up in warehouses and cut plantation production to a minimum, with the result that many Indonesians were advised to turn their attention back to production of their own food stuffs. The end of the war saw about two years of great prosperity for the Western exporters. The world needed and wanted products of the East Indies — the Western economy was making great profits.[208] Some Indonesians, particularly agriculturalists, shared in this general prosperity, but the majority of the laborers associated with Western economy found any slight benefits they gained swallowed up by the rising cost of living. In 1920 exports began to assume normal proportions and prices on the world market began to decline from their high point.[209] This resulted in great losses in the Westernized East Indian economy which resulted in numerous bankruptcies. The Indonesians were again affected by having their wages cut faster than the standard of living was declining. Enough has been said to show the difficulties experienced by Indonesians in the colonial economic relationship. Some Indonesians could find a way out of this fluctuating life by devoting their attention more exclusively to the cultivation of their own land, but this was no longer possible for all of them. A number of these displaced Indonesians would form the base of future revolutionary movements against the colonial government.

The economic realities of East Indian life turned most of the politically conscious Indonesian leaders against the existing system. They looked for some degree of state or social control of the economy in the hope that the benefits from the archipelago's resources would accrue to the inhabitants of the islands. In a word they favored some type of Socialism. This by no means indicates, however, that any significant portion of the Indonesian elite were political revolutionaries. Some of the organizational leaders might have been swept along by revolutionary doctrines, but when the revolutionary events of 1919 and 1920 drew the strong disfavor of the government, most of them pulled back. In 1920 the Budi Utomo withdrew from the Radical Concentration. In the same year many of the members of the Sarekat Islam began to feel that party discipline would be necessary to rid the organization of its revolutionary left wing. These Indonesians were not turning against Socialist doctrines, they were simply not convinced that revolution qua revolution was the answer to the problem that faced Indonesian society. In general they hoped for a continuation of the Ethical Policy as they had learned to know it during the past decade, for their aims and ambitions had become closely entwined with that policy.[210]

Unfortunately for them the dynamic Ethical Policy was dead — killed by the irresponsible actions of Indonesian organizations and by changing relationships within the governments of the Netherlands and the Netherlands East Indies. Even Van Limburg Stirum could not completely hide his disappointment at the path which Indonesian organizational life had taken, and in May 1920 spoke of the Sarekat Islam as a 'discredited' organization.[211] However, he was not blind to the fact that the essence of the colonial dilemma lay in economic problems and strongly condemned the employers for keeping wages low and for failing to follow the government's suggestion to raise them.[212] The Governor General found himself unable, however, to take forceful action in the economic field, for the home government would not support him here. His heavy spending for public works had not succeeded in smoothing out the impact of the post war economic recession on Indonesian society. The home government condemned him for his excessive government expenditures and urged a balanced economy upon him. Seeing the increasing power of European economic interests, the Governor General during his last year in office noted that the East Indies had been developed by Netherlanders — their task was not ended, there was yet much work to be done: it would have to be done by fresh, earnest workers devoted to the development of the East Indies.[213] Implicit was the hope that a more consciously-responsible economic activity would in the future raise the welfare of the Indonesian people and would draw them into closer association with the Europeans and the Western way of life — a process that would lead to the ultimate betterment of all and to the dissolution of the dualisms of the colonial relationship.

Nowhere is the motivating spirit of the Ethical Movement so clearly shown as in the Report of the Reform Commission instituted in December 1918 to consider reform of the Volksraad and administration of Netherlands India. The Report was completed in June 1920. It is a document impregnated with much of the best of Western liberal and progressive thinking; it speaks of failures and shortcomings in the past, but it looks to the future with optimism, an optimism founded on the faith that a continuation and extension of the Ethical attitude toward developing the Indonesian people will lead to a democratic future for all inhabitants of the East Indies. In a sense it is also a tragic piece, for coming when it did, it could only serve as an epilogue to what had been a glorious epoch in Dutch colonial policy.

Although the Report fell out of tune with the times, it was not without influence. The fact that the Report was supplemented by numerous minority reports almost makes it appear as if there were no common agreement between the members of the commission.[214] Actually the measure of accord was greater than the discord, for only one minority report, signed by three members of a commission of twenty-eight, was in complete and utter disagreement with the tone and content of the final Report.[215] The remaining minority reports were in large measure the airing of personal views or disagreement with details of the plan of action proposed by the Report. The minority reports were, however, practically all in agreement with the main proposals made in the Report, and these general proposals were in essence, if not in spirit, followed by the government in planning for the future.

The Commission had interpreted its task in the widest possible sense, and apparently felt itself little bound merely to make suggestions about the Volksraad and about administrative change. From the Commission's point of view it must be admitted that such suggestions made in a void would be meaningless; what the Commission did was to lay a plan for a completely new political structure of the East Indian government. No one had denied the need for this type of work. Nor had there been much disagreement on the general direction which reform should take: it must steer toward autonomy for the East Indies as a whole and toward autonomy for various subdivisions of the East Indies within the larger framework.[216] That the regulation of internal affairs should occur in the colony, free from the influence of the motherland, was accepted and was really little more than the logical consequence of the decentralization process which had started in 1903. This was in no sense to be regarded as a desire for a complete break — the tie to the crown remained strong and there was no claim made for regulation of external affairs from the archipelago.[217] With the transfer to the Indies of the administrative and legislative powers there was an expressed desire to extend the participation of the population in the governing process.[218] Here grave problems arose due to the varying backgrounds and educational levels of the East Indian population. With some exceptions it was agreed that there should be as wide participation as possible concordant with the maintenance of stable government, and that all energies should be directed toward evolving the colony in the direction of full participation by all inhabitants in affairs of state.[219] This participation should in first instance occur at the local level in organs emanating the people, but this should not preclude the existence or functioning of a central legislative body with real powers.[220] There was no common agreement among the Commission members as to how this local and central autonomy should be arranged and adjusted. Beyond stating that they all envisioned an ever widening participation by the people in government, little can be said.

So far there was rather general agreement, and so far the Report falls within the expected range of the obvious Ethical aims. This much had been generally expected from a Commission appointed by a progressive Governor General with the mission to make changes. Furthermore this was more or less the accepted method of regarding the future — all persons wanted autonomy, and most persons spoke of wider participation in government though they might have meant this in a restricted sense. In this much of the Report one can see much that came to form the goals of the future — goals which were in a sense realized. But the Report went on and aimed beyond what was obvious and generally accepted. In so far as it exceeded the commonly accepted concepts and patterns of Western thought, it met with a rather cool reception. In so far as the Report exceeded the usual limits, it might be said to be expressing the wishes of a politically conscious segment of the Indonesian elite — several of whose members were members of the Commission — and progressive and socialistic European thought.

It is not possible to point to one line or one thought in the Report and say, here it exceeds, and, here it follows, the accepted thought of the day. The dynamism which carried Ethical concepts beyond what they had been in the past is more subtle than that and is formed by numerous lesser thoughts and considerations which give the Report a decidedly progressive tone and carry it beyond the general acceptance which had been hoped for. In part it is the emphasis upon the new consciousness of nationalism which is beginning to develop among the Indonesian people living within the confines of Dutch power.[221] Partly it is the awareness of, and emphasis upon, the racial problem and the proposed solution to this problem by legislating it, along with other dualities of life, out of existence.[222] The clear appeal to association which flowed from the desire to bring all people of the East Indies within the dynamic (Western) way of life added to the tone.[223] The desire to dip into the heart of village life and readjust the traditionally formed inequities of the Indonesian desa, bringing it into line with the Westernized democratic thought which must shape the future, rounds out the background of faith in Western progress which the Report carried.[224] This faith was no longer an accepted axiom of Western life in the East Indies, however. It was small wonder that the Report encountered heavy opposition.

At almost the same moment that the Reform Commission was created in the East Indies (December 1918), a commission had been created in the Netherlands to recommend changes in the Netherlands Constitution, which it was generally felt needed revision on such matters as succession to the throne, people's initiative, referendum, and the composition of the States General in order to bring it into line with modern political and social developments.[225] This Constitutional Commission, which was not greatly concerned with colonial affairs, submitted its report in October

1920, while the Reform Commission's Report was still under consideration by officials of the government. The Minister of Colonies, S. de Graaff, saw an opportunity to incorporate some of the more acceptable aspects of the Reform Commission's Report into the Constitutional change which was being undertaken.[226] Particularly those suggestions for a greater degree of autonomy for the Netherlands Indies met with such wide approval that it seemed expedient to incorporate them in the Netherlands Constitution. The process of constitutional change was not completed until 1922 and will be discussed further below (see Chapter IV, pp. 204–5). Suffice it for the present to note that the greatest influence exerted by the Reform Commission's Report on actual legislation for the colony was through this constitutional change and the laws which resulted therefrom. This influence was due more to the generally acceptable nature of some of its recommendations and to a coincidence of timing than to any wide acceptance by the Western world of its more progressive concepts.

The ideas of Minister of Colonies De Graaff are clearly shown in the Administrative Reform Bill which he had the Governor General present to the Volksraad in September 1920. This bill envisioned a rather far-reaching administrative decentralization, and as such was an extension of one aspect of the earlier decentralization processes of the East Indies. Since, however, the bill ran through the legislative process at the same time that the Reform Commission's Report was being discussed, and since the Report had said something about further decentralization, and since the Administrative Reform Bill became law the same year (1922) that the constitutional changes were approved, there has been a natural tendency to confuse the measures for administrative reform with some of these other affairs. Actually the administrative reform is quite a separate matter; a matter on which the Minister had been working long before the Reform Commission was created. It was the manner of reform in which he placed the greatest reliance for solving the problems of the colonial relationship. Actually it never came to be tested as a sole solution to the problem, but if it had been, it probably would have failed miserably. Its chief significance stemmed from the fact that the extension of autonomy which came after 1922 was administered within the framework provided by Minister de Graaff's administrative reform bill (see below, p. 203 ff.).

Chapter IV

SYNCRETISM AND CONSERVATISM, 1920– CA. 1927

The Government's Changing Attitude

Indonesian sentiments and feelings, and the attitude and policy of the Dutch government toward the East Indies, showed gradual change during the entire 20th century. The year 1920 must not be thought of as delimiting particular attitudes or feelings. Changes were certainly occurring around 1920 that heralded new attitudes, but these moved slowly and appear as changes only when viewed from the historical vantage point. It is doubtful that people in Indonesia during the 1920's were as clearly aware of change as shall here be indicated. If there was a new policy by the Dutch government — and it appears today there was — it was never announced as such. If there were new Indonesian attitudes, they were regarded merely as modifications of earlier thought. Modifications occurred as part of daily life. It is difficult to say exactly where these modifications were leading, for before the new concepts could be stabilized the severe economic depression of 1929 intervened. It disrupted conditions so much in both Indonesian and European societies that endeavors in all directions had to be altered.

The early 1920's are characterized by a retrogression in the political influence of Indonesian organizations. It was a period of re-grouping and re-shuffling accompanied by a great verbal din. Indonesian life, and changes in this life, did not move primarily within political groups — groups which during the 1920's counted their membership in the hundreds and at most in the thousands. Nor can one really speak of the Indonesian elite being formed here. What was formed here was a political elite whose greatest value during the 1920's, much as today, is as a symbol for various attitudes and feelings, a symbol which under proper circumstances might rally normally quiet forces in Indonesian life. This symbolic power is not without significance, and it certainly illustrates more clearly than any other means the range of ideological choices available to the more self-conscious Indonesians. For this reason political groups will be considered here in greater detail than their immediate significance or their small memberships might seem to warrant.

During the 1920's the membership of the Sarekat Islam declined rapidly. In part, as already mentioned, this was due to the difficulties with the government and to the disrepute into which some of the organization's leaders had fallen, but in part it was also due to a general indifference from the mass membership. These factors were augmented by the fact that during the preceding decade the government had gone far toward meeting the desires and grievances which the Sarekat Islam had originally reflected.[1] To form a politically viable group the Sarekat Islam leaders had turned to labor union activity. This placed them in direct competition with the Communist leaders, some of whom retained their membership in the Sarekat Islam. In appealing to dissatisfied elements in Indonesian society, and also in making extensive and oftentimes unrealistic promises to worker groups, the Communists were generally more successful than the more moderate and more religious leaders of the Sarekat Islam. These latter leaders became ever more convinced that the Communists would have to be removed from the organization, but this was not easy, for above all else Tjokroaminoto opposed a split in the organization.

It was in an atmosphere of armed truce between the two factions within the organization that the Sarekat Islam held its postponed Fifth National Congress in Jogjakarta from March 2–6, 1921. Here a pre-meeting agreement was reached which incorporated both Islamic and Communistic concepts in the newly evolved platform. Agus Salim and Semaoen were the formulators of this new plan.[2] Salim declared Islam to be democratic and socialistic, as he had done often in the past. Semaoen was willing to accept a Moslem plank in the platform in order to keep a unified organization through which to work.[3] The acceptance of the Islamic ruling was made even easier when Salim informally suggested that strictly religious issues be settled in the Muhammadijah rather than in the Sarekat Islam.[4] The program which resulted from all this was anti-imperialistic, anti-capitalistic, pro-Islamic, and pro-international. The Communists boasted of victory; rather prematurely, it appears.

The Sixth National Congress of the Sarekat Islam was held later the same year (October 1921). Tjokroaminoto had been taken into custody in August on charges stemming from the Garut Incident. Agus Salim and Abdoel Moeis were in control of the meeting. They considered the time right for forcing the issue of party discipline which would remove the Communists from the organization. The groundwork for a split had been prepared some months earlier. The preceding June the Central Labor Union (P.P.K.B.) had met in Jogjakarta in an effort to patch up differences emanating from previous strike actions and leadership disagreements, but instead of resolving their differences, the Semarang and Jogja groups had split completely.[5] A Revolutionary Union headquarters was set up in Semarang by Semaoen while the Central Labor Union in Jogjakarta continued under Sarekat Islam auspices. The armed truce had erupted into open conflict, and Salim and Moeis were prepared to carry the fight into the heart of the Sarekat Islam. The great issue of party discipline found Salim and Moeis aligned in debate against Semaoen and Ibrahim datuk Tan Malaka, a Minangkabau (West Sumatra), European-educated school teacher. Tan Malaka had been actively advancing Communist schools in the Semarang area since his return from Europe in 1919 and was becoming one of the most brilliant Indonesian exponents of Communist doctrine.[6] The Islamic plank in the March platform of the Sarekat Islam was too firm for the Communists to pry loose. The charge of being irreligious weighed heavy against the Communists, and when Salim countered Marxian social doctrines with Moslem social teachings, the Congress voted overwhelmingly to institute party discipline. The Communists withdrew from the Central Sarekat Islam. They had been outvoted at the Congress, but they were not yet out-maneuvered in the struggle for control of local memberships.

Meanwhile politically conscious Indonesians from various parties had shown growing concern over the failure of the Netherlands and Netherlands Indian governments to implement the progressive proposals of the Reform Commission. In April 1921, the government had laid its proposed constitutional changes before the Volksraad for consideration.[7] These proposed changes received rather general approval, for they embodied many of the generally accepted principles of the Reform Commission. However, they did not convey the same progressive tone as the Report of the Reform Commission, and this was keenly felt by some of the politically minded Indonesians. They felt that the Indonesians had not been granted a share in the autonomy which the constitutional changes would assure the East Indies. In December 1921 they set afoot the 'Autonomy' action, demanding wider governmental acceptance of the proposals of the Reform Commission.[8] For a brief moment it looked as if the 'Autonomy' action might create unity among various of the Indonesian groups, but this did not materialize. Three Regents who had taken a leading role in the action quickly dropped out. It was implied, but never proved, that government pressure had been exerted; it was also implied, but never proved, that the Communists were using the movement to advance their interests.[9] The action disintegrated rapidly under determined governmental opposition and the parties went their separate ways.

The more severe attitude of the Netherlands Indian government, where in 1921 D. Fock had become Governor General, was also shown in the handling of labor disputes. The strike of pawn shop employees in January 1922 made clear this new attitude. The Union of Pawnshop Employees (P.P.P.B.) had remained in the Central Labor Union dominated by the Sarekat Islam; in fact, it had, since the rapid disintegration of the Union of Factory Personnel (P.F.B.),[10] formed the nucleus of the old Central Labor Union. The rising cost of living had for some time been a grievance among many branches of the government's services,[11] but the strike which broke out in the pawnshops of Jogjakarta in January was ostensibly directed against new service regulations which delegated duties, formerly done by lower personnel, to higher personnel. The strike action occurred without the consent or prior knowledge of the union leaders and seems to have been stimulated by a Communist dominated group working within the union in the Jogjakarta area. Abdoel Moeis, who was head of the pawnshop workers' union, felt he could not renounce the strike action of his own union and set out to persuade the member unions of the P.P.P.B. in other cities to join the strike action. In this he was not successful — he had got no farther than Garut when the government arrested him.[12] Meanwhile, support for the striking workers came from the Revolutionary Union headquarters in Semarang which under the direction of Tan Malaka and P. Bergsma planned to issue orders for a general strike. The government quickly arrested these two and exiled them two months later.[13] The general strike never materialized. With the arrest of Moeis, Salim became head of the P.P.P.B. He quickly called a meeting of the entire union which disclosed that only a minority of the pawnshop employees were on strike and favored continuing the strike action. The majority condemned the strike as politically inspired. The strike was rapidly terminated and Salim managed to salvage something of the pawnshop union. During the strike the Netherlands Indian government acted with a degree of ruthlessness unknown in preceding years. The right of assembly in Jogjakarta was suspended,[14] and the city was beleaguered by police and a civilian guard (organized by the infamous Berretti who was later implicated in Japanese espionage activity). As a result of the strike about a thousand of the striking workers were discharged from their jobs.[15] These actions left little doubt in anyone's mind regarding the change in attitude toward Indonesian political and labor union activity exhibited by the new government.

In April 1922 the government released Tjokroaminoto from

jail with no indication of his guilt or innocence. The Sarekat Islam to which Tjokroaminoto now returned was a disintegrating movement. The introduction of party discipline during his absence had driven out the Communists and split the organization. Some chapters went over to the Communists intact, calling themselves *Sarekat Islam merah* (Red Sarekat Islam)[16]; most chapters split.[17] Members dropped out of the organization more rapidly than ever, especially after the failure of the pawnshop workers' strike. Tjokroaminoto returned in low spirits, but with some hope of patching up his organization.

In May 1922 Semaoen had returned from Moscow to find the Communist Party leadership badly decimated by the government. This leadership, at a party conference in Semarang in December 1921, had expressed the desire to work toward a united front effort among the various Indonesian political groups. Semaoen was prepared to follow this general tactic, and, of course, found Tjokroaminoto in a receptive mood.

It was no longer possible to fuse the two parent organizations, but cooperation was advanced by reuniting the labor union movement. This occurred in June 1922 in Madiun with the creation of the Union of Indian Trade Organizations (P.V.H.).

The first action of the new Central Union was to announce its disapproval of Governor General Fock's latest economy measures which proposed removal of the cost of living bonus granted to all government employees since 1920. The union's action had wide support among Indonesian organizations, for the government action directly affected persons of the expanding elite group who either were members, or were good prospective members, of these organizations.

The government of Governor General Fock seems to have been little swayed by all this. For one thing, this new government was not inclined to depend upon the native political movement for anything,[18] but, for another, it had one fundamental aim which it was determined to realize despite the consequences: that was the aim of saving money. Van Limburg Stirum had left an unbalanced budget. This was partly due to his magnanimous spending for large public works which could only pay for themselves over a period of time,[19] and partly to the failure of Ministers Idenburg and De Graaff to speed through higher taxes on entrepreneurial profits during the prosperous years following immediately upon the First World War.[20] Fock had instructions to economize. He envisioned curtailments from low to high, but — and in this he had full support of the home government — capitalist interests must be neither injured nor discouraged. The Council of Entrepreneurs in The Hague and the Sugar Syndicate in Amsterdam strongly pressured the government to favor its selfish interests.[21] Through reduced taxes and lowered import and export tariffs their profits were increased by some millions of guilders — guilders which naturally did not find their way into the government treasury. At lower levels, however, the government was eminently successful in its thrift measures. Cost of living bonuses were removed, some of the lower (and younger) personnel were discharged, and plans for expanding various of the government departments were curtailed.[22] Taxation, which was already heavy, was increased. Particularly the native population suffered, for they were taxed at a different rate from Europeans on the theory that they too should contribute to the expenses of a government which benefited them. During the post war years, when wages and prices were both rising, the income tax for natives became relatively less but was still estimated at eight percent.[23] At the time that wages were declining in the recession of the early 1920's, the Fock government increased income taxes so that in the years following 1922 the average native income of 225 guilders a year paid about ten percent in taxes in Java and Madura: a percentile average, as Koch points out, which was only reached in European incomes above 9,000 guilders per annum.[24] The Fock government also increased land taxes at a time when the prices of agricultural products were beginning to taper off.

The growing complaints from Indonesians and Europeans called for an investigation.[25] Instituted in 1922, this investigation concluded that the native peoples of Java and Madura were over-

taxed.[26] But it was 1926 before this conclusion appeared and by
then economic conditions were improving again. In that same
year (1926) the report on general economic conditions in the
East Indies requested by the Netherlands parliament in 1924 also
was published.[27] This report was somewhat more optimistic. It
had found neither a serious decline in living standards (as compared with 1913) — there was no advancement either — nor
were millions of people living in a deplorable state. It did admit,
however, that when comparing conditions with the abnormal
war years there was a recession to be noted.[28] It seems probable
that the abnormal war years soon came to be felt as quite normal
by a great many people, and it is doubtful if the recession that
followed was viewed as a return to normalcy by the individuals
involved. The economic situation gave ample cause for grievance
in the early 1920's but had gradually levelled off by the mid 1920's
when prices had dropped to meet earnings.[29]

The economics and repressive measures of the Fock administration were the most noticeable manifestations of change in the
Netherlands Indian government and drew the most criticism.
Other changes that also received notice were the Administrative
Reform and the Constitutional changes. The Administrative Reform Bill became law in April 1922.[30] It revived the process of
decentralization through the delegation of authority from higher
echelon to lower echelon units.[31] This concept had lain dormant
during the Van Limburg Stirum period when plans were made
to create indigenous councils which would receive their power
through a popularly based appeal. In 1919 the Volksraad had
been asked to consider Regency Councils which would gain their
authority from the community that produced them. These councils were dropped when Minister de Graaff's new Administrative
Reform Bill was brought forward for consideration the following
year. When this bill passed, it made the functioning of any
Regency Councils which might be formed in the future, dependent upon the higher administrative units for their authority. At
any rate, no Regency Councils would be created for a few years.
The Administrative Reform Law provided for the division of the

East Indies into first, provinces, and second, other districts.[32] It further stipulated that councils might be instituted in these provinces and other districts, and that these councils, subject to certain restrictions which guarded against malpractices, were to regulate internal administration and other local affairs. All this was not too clear, but.what ultimately happened was that the law was applied principally to Java which came to be divided into three provinces, East, Middle, and West Java, while the remainder of the archipelago was treated quite separately. Even less clear was what was meant with 'other districts'. The actual law spoke only of urban communities[33] (the only units that had displayed any vitality under the earlier decentralization procedure), but the practical application of the law brought Regency Councils under this heading. The administrative reform, along with the Regency Councils which were eventually created, served one great purpose: that was the creation of more administrative and civil service posts for educated Indonesians who, with their Western school diplomas and desire of prestige-bearing government posts, were beginning to flood the market.

The Constitutional changes affecting the East Indies had been scrutinized by the Volksraad in April 1921 and made their way through the Netherlands' Parliament with only insignificant changes. In spirit they remained what the Volksraad had approved and what Minister de Graaff had initiated under stimulus of the Reform Commission Report.[34] It was December 27, 1922, before the changes that had been made in the Constitution were publicly known.[35] Those articles which affected the East Indies provided that the governor general would conduct the general administration except for such matters as were specifically delegated to the crown;[36] further that the political structure of the East Indies would be established by law. This latter referred to the widely acknowledged need for a complete revision of the Fundamental Law of 1854 which had been amended six times since its creation[37] and now needed a complete rewriting. It would ultimately emerge in 1925 as the *Wet op de Staatsinrichting* (Law on the Organization of the State), also known as the *Indi-*

sche Staatsregeling. The Constitution went on to say that the representative body of the East Indies would, with exceptions and conditions determined by law, have a voice in matters of state. The much desired autonomy, at least for the European population, was guaranteed through a provision which allowed internal affairs to be regulated by organs of government established in the East Indies.[38] These changes corresponded to the most agreeable proposals of the Reform Commission, but they missed entirely the progressive tone of the Reform Commission, for nothing was said which guaranteed far-reaching changes for groups other than the European.[39]

The actual impact of this shortcoming was heightened by the new tripartite division of the population of the East Indies into European, Native (or Indonesian), and Foreign Asiatic, which was established by law in 1919.[40] This division was applicable to legal and administrative regulations in particular.[41] At the time the law was passed it was regarded as merely a classificatory step on the way to assimilation of all Westernized groups regardless of race, for it was passed in the heyday of legal unification which envisioned all groups being placed under one law.[42] The law of 1919 along with other laws of the time made it easy for an Indonesian to enter the European group or, if he wished, to subject himself to European laws and courts. The three-fold division was established to protect those Indonesians who were not yet 'advanced' enough to fall within the unified legal systems.

With the advent of the Administrative Reform Law and the Constitutional Changes of 1922, however, this tripartite classification assumed new aspects. These laws provided a new position for the Westernized or Europeanized part of the population. The educated Indonesians could partake of this if they wanted, but it would have necessitated withdrawing completely from the Indonesian group. Naturally this aroused feelings among many of the educated Indonesians who were eager to see further autonomy extended to the Indonesian population group as well. Actually, this was being done through the removal of tutelage from many of the Regencies and was further advanced when Regency Councils were created, but this was not what some of the political-minded, educated Indonesians had in mind. They were thinking in other terms, terms in which they would control the operation of affairs of state, terms which could only be realized through complete independence for the Indonesian people. Probably the most profound effect of the changes of 1922 upon the politically conscious Indonesians was to bring the realization to a small group of well-educated Westernized Indonesians that if they were to control the destinies of the Indonesian people they would have to break away completely from the Netherlands Indian government.[43]

Under the provisions of the amended Constitution it was clear that a great part of the political future of the East Indies hinged upon the spirit and content of the new political structure which would have to be established by law. It was 1925 before the new Law on the Organization of the State (Wet op de Staatsinrichting) became law, but from early 1922 on the proposed changes in the old Fundamental Law of 1854 provided politicians and statesmen with subject for debate. Minister de Graaff was among the first to commit himself when in February 1922, thus several months before the Constitutional changes were announced, he stated that he would not consider a complete revamping of the old law but instead only revisions.[44] Governor General Fock presented the Minister's revisions of the old Fundamental Law to the Volksraad in June 1922. De Graaff's and Fock's proposals completely failed to provide for participation by the Indonesian people in the government of the East Indies.[45] If it were not clear before, it was now painfully obvious that the new government was breaking completely with the spirit of the Reform Commission Report.

Protest against the government's position on these matters was almost immediate. The first counterblast in the struggle was sounded by a group of European, liberal-intellectuals who, although not in complete agreement with the Reform Commission Report, still desired to see greater participation by the Indonesian people in their own future. This group drew up an outline for a new 'Structure of State', making this public in May 1922.[46] In

November 1922 the Dutch Socialists in the East Indies took the lead in forming another Radical Concentration which joined together all groups in the Volksraad who were opposed to Governor General Fock's proposals, and who desired to see the proposals of the Reform Commission more closely followed. Both the Sarekat Islam and the Budi Utomo joined this concentration. Despite the protests of the Radical Concentration, however, the Volksraad accepted the changes as proposed by Fock in December 1922. It was clear that the Netherlands Indian government and the majority of Europeans and Indo-Europeans in the East Indies, who controlled the Volksraad were not prepared to extend real and meaningful political authority in general affairs of state to the Indonesian people.

The policy of the Fock government on these political and administrative matters was never too clear. That is to say, it was clear enough what the government was doing, but it was not clear in what larger context, if any, the government viewed this changed attitude which it clearly exhibited. The government continued to speak in Ethical terms and to regard itself as Ethical. Actually its policy was based on a contradiction of terms: namely, a Conservative Ethical Policy. It obviously distrusted the Indonesian organizational movements, opposed any large extension of powers to the Indonesians,[47] and favored the Europeanization of the East Indian government. If this, along with economy measures, was what the government wanted to do, it should have dropped the pretence of being Ethical. The continued employment of this disguise makes the political realities of the early years of Governor General Fock's administration most difficult to uncover. The very fundamentals of Dutch attitude toward Indonesians were changing, but this did not clearly emerge until about 1925.

Indonesian Change and Development

The immediate effect of the government policies in 1922 was to drive the Indonesian organizational movement into more radical lines.[48] The Radical Concentration in the Volksraad was one manifestation of this development. But even more decisive was a general feeling among the better educated Indonesians that the government was indifferent to their aspirations and demands. Especially the politically conscious Indonesians felt this, and they increasingly felt that they could only achieve their aims by opposing the government. This opposition began to take the form of non-cooperation with government plans and institutions. In meetings held in January and February 1923, both the Sarekat Islam and the Budi Utomo showed marked tendencies to embark on a non-cooperative path.[49] This non-cooperation was accompanied and bolstered by a large scale rejection of imperialism and capitalism which it was felt kept the Indonesian in a degraded state and was largely responsible for the economic pressures of 1921 and 1922. Considering the close affinity between European socialists and the Indonesian organizations, and the influence that socialist thought had on the movement through Islamic and Marxist principles from the very first, it should create no surprise that non-cooperation now became intimately tied to socialist thought. At the same time that this radical tendency was becoming apparent, the Indonesian organizations were seeking new bases of support in the hope of recouping the losses they had sustained in the years after 1920. Realizing their weakness at this time (1922/23), none of the organizations were ready to contest matters with the government openly.

The Sarekat Islam reoriented itself about a dual program of action. In the first place there was a reemphasis on Islamic principles, but now, more than ever before, an emphasis on unity and cooperation of all Moslems — a concept usually termed Pan-Islamism. Events in the Middle East had stimulated this wider concern, and although there is always some doubt as to the actual strength inherent in Pan-Islamism there is no question that in the early 1920's it was generally regarded as a real issue. Pan-Islam was a factor against which Snouck Hurgronje had warned the government on numerous occasions in the past, so it was only natural that the government tended to look with some disfavor upon this apparent strengthening of the movement.

From October 31 through November 2, 1922, the First All Islam Congress was held in Cheribon. The Congress sent congratulations to Mustafa Kemal (Ataturk) in Turkey and created an Islamic Council which would handle religious affairs for the Sarekat Islam. An unexpected development of great future significance was the split in the Indonesian Islamic community which occurred at this Congress. It was between the Reformist groups, represented by the Muhammadijah and the Al Irshad (an Arabic organization), on the one hand, and the orthodox religious teachers and scholars on the other. It was certainly not to the advantage of the Sarekat Islam, and a Second All Islam Congress was delayed until May 1924 when it was finally held in Garut.[50] The split became complete there. Only the Reformist elements appeared at the Congress.[51] The Central leadership of the Sarekat Islam now became closely linked with Reformist tendencies in Islam. The Garut Congress raised the Caliphate question which became a matter of discussion and debate for some months.[52] The fate of this question and the entire Pan-Islamic tendency was finally settled by events in the Near East which put an end to the aspirations of the Indonesian movement. When Pan-Islam, as an issue, died, the Sarekat Islam which had now constituted itself into a party,[53] made a natural and easy shift of emphasis to Islamic Reformism and Modernism. The shift was made doubly easy by the fact that the leaders of the Sarekat Islam, the All Islam Congresses, and the Muhammadijah were in many instances one and the same persons.[54]

The second phase of the dual reorientation of the Sarekat Islam was toward the creation of an inter-island, East Indian unity of all the Indonesian people under the aegis of Islam. The Sarekat Islam had long had chapters on many of the islands outside of Java, but most of the organization's activity had centered on Java. With the rapid decline of the Java membership, however, it was decided to concentrate on bringing the outer islands into more active participation. This followed shortly after a burgeoning interest in capital expansion into these outer islands and

also in the midst of a reorientation of government policy toward these islands as a result of investigations into disturbances
there. In 1923 Tjokroaminoto toured Borneo and Celebes
and Abdoel Moeis went to Sumatra in an attempt to advance the concept of an All Indies Congress.[55] They were
met there with general indifference on the part of the people
and, in the case of Moeis, with hostility from the government as
well. Undeterred by his failure to win much support in the
outer islands, Tjokroaminoto called together a preparatory session for an All Indies Congress in January 1924. At this preparatory meeting held in Surabaya, the entire plan collapsed.
Thus the second phase of the reorganized Sarekat Islam was
stillborn. The failure of the All Indies Islamic movement forced
the Sarekat Islam to lean ever more heavily upon its Java membership and upon Islamic Reformist ideas. The Sarekat Islam
Party, much reduced in size from the earlier Sarekat Islam, increasingly became a political action group for Reformist and
Modernist Islamic ideas. It had completely lost its mass following.

The Communist Party, which expected nothing from the government anyway, was interested in government policy only in so far
as it enabled dissident and dissatisfied elements to increase, for
it was here that the Communists sought their support.[56] With
the return of Semaoen from Russia in May 1922 the party began
to rebuild. The government policies aroused enough dissatisfaction to make certain groups more receptive than ever to Communist doctrine, but the Communists' principal support still
came from the revolutionary urban elements in general and the
Semarang-centered Union of Tram and Railway Personnel
(v.s.t.p.) in particular.

Semaoen had received no specific instructions from Communist
headquarters while abroad and consequently depended largely
on his own judgment in determining party policies. This was
now more than ever possible because all the Dutch Communists
who had been operative in the East Indies had been exiled. Semaoen proceeded to rebuild along the same lines the party
had been following during the past few years; namely, direct-

ing major attention toward gaining a hold on the labor union movement[57] while encouraging the extension of those rural-based groups of Red Sarekat Islams affiliated with the main party. The fusion of the labor union movement in June 1922 (see above, p. 201), was largely due to his efforts. The government's thrift measures of 1922 charged the air with tension resulting in increased demands for strike action. These demands were pushed by the Semarang groups and formed the core of the program at the December 1922 meeting of the Union of Indian Trade Organizations (P.V.H.). In January 1923 the Rail and Tramway Union began urging a general strike as rebuttal to the government's measures. These demands were reiterated at local union meetings in February.[58] This pressure from the labor unions came at the same time that the government's political measures were pushing the Sarekat Islam and the Budi Utomo off the path of cooperation.[59]

In this atmosphere a congress of the P.K.I. (Communist Party) and the Red Sarekat Islams was held in Bandung and Sukabumi in March 1923. Darsono had returned from Russia shortly before this congress, but again had brought no specific Comintern policy for guiding the Indonesian Communist movement into channels other than those which Semaoen had chosen. The meeting displayed a high pitched revolutionary fervor; from Semaoen's attacks on capitalism and Darsono's attacks on dualism to Hadji Misbach's espousal of the common aims of Communism and Islam there was a continuous abuse of the government and the forces which stood behind it.[60]

Early in May, after negotiation had failed, the long threatened Rail and Tramway strike occurred. Within a month the strike had ended and Semaoen was confronted with the choice of being interned on Timur or exile — he chose the latter. Any hope of a general strike vanished almost the moment the local strike in Semarang was started; the member unions in other parts of the East Indies were lukewarm and failed to take part in what consequently turned out to be nothing more than a local strike. The Sarekat Islam remained indifferent, Budi Utomo had rejected non-cooperation only a few months earlier and had returned to its moderate course (see below, p. 214), and the government had used swift and severe measures to return the situation to normal.[61] The government restricted the Communist dominated local schools at the same time it suppressed the strike.[62] The failure of the strike was a severe blow to the Labor Movement and the Communist Party.

The leadership of the party now fell to Darsono who was forced to reorganize from the residue remaining after the strike. The weakening of the labor movement caused him to turn his attention to the rural support organized in the Red Sarekat Islams which now came to be called *Sarekat Rakjat* (People's Unions). The *Sarekat Rakjat* were recognized as an integral part of the Communist movement at a party meeting in April 1924,[63] and in June 1924 the P.K.I. adopted a party program giving equal importance to workers and farmers in the creation of the Communist state.[64] At this meeting Darsono spoke of a membership of 1,000 for the actual Communist Party.[65] This figure did not, of course, include members of affiliated organizations, but was limited to party members who might be expected to know something of Marxism and the nature of the Communist revolution.

It was also in June 1924 that Indonesian Communists attended the Pan-Pacific Conference of the Comintern in Canton. Here they were infomed of the recently adopted Comintern policy that emphasized the need for gaining control of the trade union movements as a prerequisite for successful revolution. This new policy was carried back to Indonesia and applied by some of the leaders with such zeal that there was soon talk of Leftist deviation. In September 1924 the Indonesian Communists decided to cease expanding the movement among the rural masses and to concentrate on labor. Finally at the December 1924 Congress it was decided to abolish gradually the Sarekat Rakjat which counted over 30,000 members[66] and to increase the strength of the actual party. During 1925 the Communist movement expanded its hold among labor groups but lost much of its peasant support.[67]

The Communist Party employed tactics used by other organizations in building up its membership. It played upon superstitions, made full use of any existing grievances, and exploited the average Indonesian's awe for a man with some education, or at least a man who exhibited the outward appearance of being educated. All this had been done before. But starting about 1925, when the Communist movement seems to have fallen into the hands of hotheads, the party began to ally itself with social outcasts and terroristic bands which were always to be found on the periphery of Indonesian society. Late in 1923 Hadji Misbach had affiliated himself with such groups in the Solo area, engaging in bomb throwing and anarchistic activities until the Netherlands Indian government interned him in New Guinea.[68] Now the Communist Party began to use these elements — particularly in the Bantem (West Java) area — to threaten and coerce otherwise indifferent segments of the population into giving it support.[69] Moscow protested against the direction in which the Indonesian Communist Party was moving in 1925, but to no avail. In June 1925 Alimin openly suggested revolt; from then on control seemed to be in the hands of Communists of the far left.

In the latter half of 1925 a series of strikes led the government to limit the right of assembly[70] and finally to arrest Darsono and other leaders.[71] Alimin escaped to Singapore.[72] The action of the government disrupted the Communist Party, now believed to contain about 3,000 members, and made the retention of rural support ever more dependent upon terroristic methods. The Communist leaders attempted to win the approval of Moscow for the proposed revolution but this seems not to have been forthcoming. The party became divided and ever more confused. Finally in November 1926 revolts broke out around Batavia and in Bantem (West Java), to be followed some two months later (January 1927) by revolts on the west coast of Sumatra. Both uprisings were put down by the government, the Batavia-Bantem revolt rather easily, the Sumatra incident with slightly more effort. Neither, however, seems to have been more than a local threat. Numerous arrests were made and about a thousand persons were sent off to New Guinea. The nature of the uprisings and their participants will be analyzed below (see pp. 231–236). For the present, suffice it to say that the Communist Party was so broken by these arrests following upon the revolts that it ceased to play a role in East Indian affairs until after the Second World War.

The Budi Utomo also suffered from internal dissensions during the early 1920's. Some of its members had pulled it into the political arena in the years of the First World War, but this position was by no means unanimously accepted (see above, p. 169 ff.). The government's thrift measures and reluctance to grant greater autonomy had given the politically minded members of the group the opportunity to participate in various alliances with left wing associations.[73] As a cultural organization with wide support from the intellectuals, the Budi Utomo was particularly hostile to the cuts in the educational budget which accompanied the thrift program.[74] All this resulted in early 1923 in the Budi Utomo's seriously considering non-cooperation in the style of Gandhi. But the bulk of the membership was not prepared to countenance the label of 'left wing' which now came to be applied to the Budi Utomo. In the April/March 1923 meeting the organization rejected non-cooperation and followed the lead of a center group which was able to placate both the radicals and moderates within the organization.[75]

Despite this wavering course and indecisiveness of policy the Budi Utomo continued to be the organization which drew the intellectuals. In large part this was probably due to Budi Utomo's cultural role which seemed to solidify Javanese culture for those who felt torn loose from it through their training. But in even larger measure it was probably due to the fact that there was no other organization for the Western-trained intellectual to join.[76] Sarekat Islam with its religious appeal could win no great popularity among intellectuals who stemmed from a religiously-indifferent prijaji class which oriented itself about the Javanese-Hindu traditions. Nor could the revolutionary appeal of the Communists expect much support from persons who envisioned their future within the existing social order. Budi Utomo was by no means the perfect home for the expanding intellectual group, however, for its administrator and civil servant membership tended to cling to the old ways and traditions longer than the intellectuals thought wise. The intellectuals came to have a sense of mission about guiding the Indonesian people on the path to a new life; they were very conscious of their need to assume positions of leadership. In December 1923, Dr. Satiman Wirjosandjojo, founder of Young Java, suggested forming an organization of intellectual elite which would take the lead in guiding the destiny of the Indonesian people. His choice of words was unfortunate, for he succeeded in making his plan sound snobbish and esoteric; among socialistically inclined, politically minded Indonesians this could not be tolerated. He was attacked in the Indonesian press and had to retract.[77] In less than one year, however, Dr. Satiman's idea had become a reality, but under another guise and with more fortunate phrasing. It came to form the rallying point for Indonesian national sentiments (see below, p. 223 ff.).

The Budi Utomo, meanwhile, wavered in its attitude toward the issue of cooperation or non-cooperation, and was uncertain on the extent of its political activity. Its attitudes and policies seemed to be shaped by immediate events, and it moved in the direction that seemed most expedient. In this regard it was probably quite representative of the attitudes of that great bulk of the Indonesian elite who joined none of the Indonesian organizations. When in May 1923 the government resolutely suppressed the Railway strike, the Budi Utomo remained aloof and neutral. When in the course of the following year (1924), however, there was a growth in Pan-Islamic and Communistic activity and it appeared as if the Indonesian organizations were gaining in strength, the Budi Utomo intensified its Indo-centric educational and welfare activity and reflected the heightened radical feeling. In April 1925 the Budi Utomo moved its headquarters to Semarang. The younger, intellectual members in control moved the organization into increasingly more radical lines. This radical inclination continued until December 1925, when the

Communist inspired labor unrest was at its height. The Budi Utomo leadership went so far as to renounce their representative in the Volksraad (Dwidjosewojo) at this time.[78]

Suddenly everything changed again. The government moved; strikes were quashed, radical Communist leaders arrested, and the right of assembly limited. Suddenly, Sutopo, the radical leader of the young intellectuals in the Budi Utomo returned to government service (December 1925). In April 1926 the organization decided to withdraw from all political activity and devote attention to its social task. If there was some doubt about this withdrawal being non-cooperative, the matter was clarified in June 1926 when non-cooperation was definitely rejected and those who opposed the government left the organization. By this time other parties had been formed which the radical intellectuals could join. The Budi Utomo regained a certain stability; under its new leader R. M. A. A. Koesoemo Oetoyo the organization seemed once again to be on a steady path. The instability and indecision of the early 1920's had passed; not only for the Budi Utomo, but also for the other Indonesian organizations. The Budi Utomo, probably more than any other organization, fitted its plan of action rather closely into the newly developed government policy which came to be clarified in the late 1920's (see below, p. 246 ff.).

In surveying the activities of the three Indonesian organizations which had sprung into life prior to 1920 certain general features concerning their fate during the 1920's appear. In a time of a changing government policy the activity of the parties was also confused. The trend of government policy away from recognition and encouragement of the Indonesian organizational movement elicited the expected response of non-cooperation. Actually this made ever less difference to the government, for it was formulating a policy in which the Indonesian organizations would play a diminishing role. The organizations through their policies, on the one hand, and through the government policy on the other, were divorced ever farther from any mass support they might have had. As a result they could reformulate their actions to suit the more limited membership they now served. This reformulation cost the Communist Party its life largely because of the manner in which radical and revolutionary concepts tended to snowball among certain elements in Indonesian society. The Communist Party could no longer contain its own left wing. In the 1926/27 uprisings the party signed its own death warrant. The Sarekat Islam and Budi Utomo were more fortunate in their reorientation procedure. The Sarekat Islam Party along with its youth organization, the *Jong-Islamieten Bond* (Union of Young Moslems) which had split away from Young Java in January 1925,[79] became the political exponent of modernism and reformism in Islam. It would be a few years before full cooperation with the government was undertaken but it would soon be seeking its future within the existing political relationships. As a counter measure to the Sarekat Islam Party the orthodox religious elements formed the *Nahdatul Ulama* (Council of Moslem Teachers) in January 1926.

The Budi Utomo finally regrouped itself around the concept of a reintegrated Javanese culture with certain of its members emerging to take a hand in strengthening the economic fiber of that society. 'Javanese society' came to have an ever less exclusive connotation for the Budi Utomo, and it came for all intents and purposes to mean the same thing as Indonesian society. This cultural-economic orientation of the organization was not entirely new, but it was a change from its political dabblings of a few years earlier. It was something to which its civil servant oriented membership could agree and also something which fitted into the new concepts of colonial policy. Those persons who fell away from the Indonesian organizations in the process of reorientation were in large part content to remain within that large mass of expanding elite who were and always had been unaffiliated with political movements, and were in lesser part taken up in some of the newly formed groups of younger, politically-conscious Indonesians.[80]

The regrouping of these Indonesian political groups and the development of their new doctrines and policies was an uneven process which at anytime directly affected only a small number of the growing elite group. Yet they are important, for many of the present-day top echelon leaders moved into prominence through these groups. It is possible to recognize a common ground of understanding among these groups during the early 1920's. They almost all envisioned an autonomous state freed from the economic burdens imposed by the colonial relationship. They also envisioned a more active political role for Indonesians. These common goals were logical albeit more radical expressions of the ideals and aims which had been generated during the preceding decade.

There is little doubt that the nationalistic concepts of Douwes Dekker influenced the thinking of these newer groups, for he stood in close association with many of the aspiring elite. But such influences at the Protestant and Catholic missions, the Masons, the Theosophical Society and the various Dutch political parties and factions also affected the thinking of the various segments of the elite. Yet all these groups were losing influence among the Indonesian elite during the 1920's. What they had in common was that they sought a more meaningful life for Indonesians through the process of association. The new Indonesian groups which came into existence during the 1920's tended to reject the outward manifestations of association and preferred to strive toward Indonesian-centered goals.

The older Indonesian organizations had long been aware of the necessity of winning the support of the Indonesian youth. Through scout organizations and youth groups they set out to reach this objective. In practically all instances the youth organizations were circumspectly kept outside the realm of politics.[81] Most of them forbade their members to engage in political activity during their student days. The youth organizations were formed and flourished among students at the Westernized schools, particularly the more advanced schools. Efforts to gain the adherence of the non-student youth was less successful.

Around 1920 certain factors began to affect students and graduates of Westernized schools who had formulated their plans for the future in terms of employment within the Westernized sphere of East Indian Life.[82] Government jobs, which were highly coveted, began to grow scarce. Or, to state the matter in other terms, the value of the diplomas began to decrease.[83] Where once a primary school certificate would have sufficed for entry into the lower ranks of the civil service, it would now no longer serve that purpose. Something would have to be done to channel off the growing surplus of educated Indonesians.[84] The Regency Councils and extension of self-administration at the local level, which the Van Limburg Stirum government had advocated, was designed to do this, but these measures had not been advanced by the Fock government. Instead the government had economized and had reduced the rate of expansion of organs of government which had absorbed at least a part of the Western educated Indonesians.

Meanwhile the desire among Indonesians to partake of Westernized education continued to grow;[85] in fact, it began to exceed the expansion rate of the school system.[86] It became apparent to a growing number of Indonesians that by adopting Western manners and attributes, life would become generally easier. The wish to go the way of the West began to move ever deeper into Indonesian society. Following 1920, however, the Fock government began to curtail the practicalities (economic possibilities) which made this Westernization possible and desirable, and at the same time failed to take positive measures to rechannel the Westernization process which was allowed to continue pushing toward the same goals as previously. This was probably the most serious failing of the Fock government and one which was bound to lead to an explosive situation.[87] The necessary rechanneling was being devised, but the Fock government either could not or would not undertake its adoption. As a consequence the deeper aspects of Dutch colonial policy during the early 1920's remained confused.

Resulting from the failure of the government to meet or rechannel the growing demand for Westernized education, a large number of what were termed 'wild schools' sprang into existence. These schools did not meet the requirements of staff or curricula as established by the government and could consequently not grant diplomas which would be recognized by any official agency. They are further characterized by being in large part directed against the nature and principles of the colonial government. They were almost always established by Indonesians — usually intellectual idealists who did not wish to work for the colonial government — and were attended by Indonesians who either could not be accommodated by recognized schools or could not meet the requirements of such schools. Not all schools operated by Indonesians were 'wild schools', however. The Muhammadijah schools, for instance, were recognized and subsidized by the government. Some of the primary schools established by the Sarekat Islam were also not regarded as 'wild schools'; at least not until the Communists infiltrated them and used them for indoctrination purposes.

In the midst of the 'wild school' mêlée, an institution which in its methods, depth of purpose, and vitality distinguished itself from the others appeared. This was the *Taman Siswâ* (Garden of Learning) School of Soewardi Soerianingrat. While exiled in the Netherlands from 1913 to 1918, Soewardi had applied himself to further schooling and had acquired a teacher's certificate before returning to his homeland. The hope of an autonomous Indonesia which had inspired him while in the Indische Partij had not faded, but his views on how this could best be achieved had altered radically. The failure of the association principles of the refurbished Indische Partij after the war and the degeneration of the Indonesian organizations into forums for the political bickerings of self-centered personalities, probably strengthened his conviction that another approach was badly needed.[88] The growing self-awareness of the Indonesians was spinning in a void — it was necessary to provide some content to the new feelings. Influenced greatly by the educational theories of Maria Montessori and Rabindranath Tagore, Soewardi came to feel that education of the youth of Java along Javanese national lines was the most sensible manner to prepare the way for autonomy and self-expression. [89]

"In this cultural confusion," said Soewardi in setting forth the principles of his school, "let our cultural history be a starting point from which to advance. On the basis of our own culture only can the work of construction be advanced in peace. In a nonimitative national form let our people appear on the stage of international relations."[90] On this basis the Taman Siswå School spread its roots in the Javanese cultural tradition. In physical nature the school steered toward an informality that was unknown in Western schools, encouraging a close relationship between student and teacher. Much emphasis was placed on the traditional skills and values of Javanese life; music, dance, and character formation were as highly regarded as the usual Western subjects of learning. Once the basis of the pupil's education had been laid in Javanese life there should be an adoption of the usable elements of Western culture in order to prepare him to meet the requirements of modern life.[91] It was felt that only in this manner could a new culture be formed, a culture which might be made the property of all the people. This cultural nationalism was the ideal to which the Taman Siswå was dedicated, but this nationalism could only be valid if it involved a struggle of the individual toward a harmonious integration in life. The aim of the Taman Siswå can best be expressed in one word, the same word that typifies so much of Javanese life: harmony.[92]

In actual operation the Taman Siswå School was beset with difficulties. At the time of its creation (July 3, 1922) the government was uncertain and hesitant, almost hostile, toward this type of schooling. In a few years, with the changing government attitude and with the improvement in the caliber of the school, this attitude was to soften until before the outbreak of the Second World War the Taman Siswå was receiving government subsidy. As funds were lacking in the early years the teachers whom Soewardi assembled worked more from conviction than from prospect of material gain. Assembling a student body was also not easy, for the school was unrecognized, but persons of some power, including members of some of the princely families, had faith in

Soewardi's experiment and sent their children to his school.[93]

The beginnings were slow. It became necessary to compromise on ideals since the great demand was for Westernized education. The Taman Siswå Schools (soon there were more than one) subsequently established an educational program on a par with Western primary schools so that Taman Siswå graduates could compete for entry into the government's secondary schools.[94] Ideally this was not the chief aim of the Taman Siswå School, but it became one of its principal functions and was probably the root of the financial support which permitted it to survive. Even so the Taman Siswå remained distinctive from the usual Western style schools and can only be regarded as Javanese. The Taman Siswå remained outside the realm of politics. It can, however, be in a certain sense regarded as one facet of the aims and goals of the Budi Utomo. The Taman Siswå Schools were certainly an influence in the formation of a positive national consciousness among Indonesians. Taman Siswå pupils were soon counted in the thousands. It must not be lost from sight, however, that the government schools counted their enrollment in the hundreds of thousands.[95]

One new development in the government's primary education system after 1920 was the establishment of the Connecting School (*Schakelschool*) in 1921, which permitted students from the Second Class Native Schools or Standard Schools, formerly a dead end, to make the shift into the regular, Westernized, secondary school system.[96] For the rest it was a matter of retaining the existing forms and making new additions in the same pattern as already existed.[97] University education was extended after 1920 when the groundwork had been laid with the establishment of the Engineering College in Bandung (see above, p. 179). In 1924 the Law School was replaced by a faculty of Law, and in 1927 the Doctors' School gave way to a faculty of Medicine. Both these faculties were later integrated into a university.

Through a growing desire to participate in the highest education available, and by means of scholarships and study funds bestowed by a number of philanthropic organizations, an increasing number of Indonesians went to the Netherlands to complete their academic training at one of the Dutch universities.[98] During the First World War the flow of students to the Netherlands had been disrupted, but once the war had ended and normal communications were restored the flow recommenced. Indonesian students in the Netherlands had early formed an *Indische Vereeniging* (Indies Club) as a meeting ground for students away from their homeland. The students who arrived after 1919 became increasingly dissatisfied with the mild nature of this organization. These students had undergone experiences in the East Indies which made them desire something stronger than a friendly society.[99] Most of them had been members of one of the youth organizations in Indonesia and as such had followed events closely and had come to feel that they were the future elite of the Indonesian people.[100] For these dedicated, elite-conscious young Indonesians there would have to be an organization of political action.[101] In 1922 the younger groups were strong enough to force the issue and the new orientation was indicated by changing the name of the non-political *Indische Vereeniging* to *Perhimpunan Indonesia:* this means Indonesian Organization and carries nationalist overtones.[102]

The Indonesian students in the Netherlands were motivated in their politically conscious course of action by any number of factors. Their very presence in the Netherlands was one factor. How many of them were amazed at the greater degree of personal freedom they found in the Netherlands? How many did not fail to notice the difference between Hollanders at home and Hollanders in the East Indies?[103] This post war generation of Indonesian students was, for the most part from a lower social milieu than their prewar predecessors in the Netherlands, and as such they felt more keenly the difficulties involved in battling their way upward in a society dominated by a colonial relationship. While still in Indonesia they had encountered the growing radicalism of the Sarekat Islam movement and had witnessed the creation and progress of the Volksraad. The Reform Commission had raised their hopes, but the hesitant attitude of the government after 1920 toward granting Indonesians a share in the affairs of state had disillusioned them. They keenly sensed the limitations which the colonial relationship placed upon social mobility (and more particularly political mobility). They were convinced that European capitalism was incompatible with the best interests of Indonesians. They were interested in the teachings of Marx and Lenin, and were unhappy over the failure of President Wilson's Fourteen Points to apply to all peoples of the world. And they were stimulated by the support they received for a united Indonesia concept from academic circles in the Netherlands. These and many other realities inherent in their student position in particular and in the colonial relationship in general, made many of them feel their goals could not be achieved by working with the colonial government. From occurrences in the British Empire — Gandhi's non-cooperation and civil disobedience (announced July 1920), but even more the Sinn Fein movement of the Irish — they learned of the possibility of resistance to the will of a government.

So it was that in 1922 the Perhimpunan Indonesia was formed and launched on its radical program. The names of the *formateurs* and leaders during the early years of the organization have become well known in Indonesian annals. They not only became active in political movements upon their return to Indonesia, but they also became dominant in the independent Indonesia which came after the Second World War. Two Mangoenkoesoemos, sons of a Javanese school teacher; R. Iwa Koesoema Soemantri, R. Sastromoeljono, and R. M. Sartono from the prijaji class; Mohammed Hatta and Soekiman Wirjosandjojo from merchant families; and A. I. Z. Momonutu: all played a leading part in the early organization. One person, who nowhere appears on the records, but who played the role of mentor and prime stimulator to the younger men, was Dr. R. Soetomo. It is doubtful if any one man was of greater importance in shaping Indonesian life during the 1920's.

Soetomo, after participating in the formation of the Budi Utomo during his student days at the medical school (STOVIA), finished his studies in 1911 and became a doctor in service of the government. Until 1919 he served in this capacity in various towns of the archipelago. Then he went to Europe to continue his studies. He remained in Europe until mid-1923 when he returned to the East Indies and became a teacher at the medical school (NIAS) in Surabaya. While in Europe he had taken an active part in the Indonesian Organization and was a leader and guide for the younger Indonesian students.[104] His ideas were in large part reflected in the declaration of principles which accompanied the change in the organization's name to *Perhimpunan Indonesia* in late 1922. This declaration read:

> The future of the people of Indonesia is exclusively and solely vested in a form of government that is responsible to that people in the true sense of the word, because only such a form of government is acceptable to the people. Every Indonesian should strive for this goal in conformity with his ability and capacities, through his own power and own endeavor, independent of the help of outsiders. Every dilution of Indonesian powers, in whatever form, is most firmly disapproved, for only the closest unification of Indonesia's sons can lead to a realization of the common goal.[105]

Here was a clear expression of the general goals to which the young politically-minded intellectuals of the growing elite of Indonesia aspired. The call for representative Indonesian government was not new. What was new, however, was the delegation of responsibility for action to the individual Indonesian. No longer was the stimulant to come from an Ethical colonial government. This new program was directed to Indonesians as worthy, self-integrated persons who were to arouse themselves and to work for their own future without relying upon outsiders. This somewhat resembles the concept of auto-activity, to be discussed below (see p. 246 ff.), which was being advanced at just this time in Dutch academic circles.

Whether this new united effort among Indonesians was to be directed chiefly toward political ends was never clearly indicated. Most likely it was not, but various interpretations were possible and came to be applied. For Soetomo and many others the struggle toward a responsible state was cultural, economic, and social much more than political. For others, however, following the thought of Douwes Dekker, the political struggle was paramount; once political independence was achieved, all other things would follow.[106]

It has been debated whether or not the principles of the Perhimpunan Indonesia were a declaration of non-cooperation. The rejection of outside help is certainly non-cooperative in tone, but may well be a barb directed against the Ethical Policy and the meddling in Indonesian life which accompanied it. Whatever the case, the Perhimpunan Indonesia clarified its stand in a separate statement which declared that a policy of non-cooperation with the colonial government would be followed as long as President Wilson's principles of self-determination of peoples were disregarded.[107]

In 1924, after the departure of Soetomo, the Perhimpunan Indonesia leaders came into contact with the exiled Semaoen and Tan Malaka. The influence of these men is shown by the issuance of a new platform calling for "the creation of a conscious, nationalist mass action supported by internal strength."[108] The revolutionary flirtations of the Perhimpunan Indonesia need not be recorded in detail here. Suffice it to say, the organization grew ever more hostile to the government and favored immediate independence and freedom (1925). All effort was to be directed toward crushing the colonial power. More intimate relations with the Communists were undertaken in December 1926 when a covenant was arranged between the Perhimpunan Indonesia and the Indonesian Communist Party whereby the former was to take over the guidance of the entire Communist organization in the East Indies.[109] The Perhimpunan Indonesia may have wanted to control the entire revolutionary independence movement, but as might be expected, the Comintern could not agree to this type of commitment and the contract was soon annulled. In 1927 the Perhimpunan Indonesia became affiliated with the Moscow-inspired League Against Colonial Oppression, but it withdrew from this organization when the Dutch left-wing Socialists left it. A few members of the Perhimpunan Indonesia retained close contacts with the Communist Party, but for the majority the affiliation with the Communists was dictated more by practical considerations regarding common aims than by a conviction of the wisdom of Communist doctrine. Most of the Perhimpunan Indonesia members were Socialists and favored direct action against the government in order to achieve independence, but they had no desire to receive their orders from Moscow. In later years, beyond the scope of this essay, the Perhimpunan Indonesia seems to have become a tool of the Comintern.[110]

Meanwhile Dr. Soetomo had returned to the East Indies and began reorienting himself to the activities of the politically conscious Indonesians. In January 1924 he attended the Surabaya meeting of the All Indies Congress which Tjokroaminoto hoped would bring unity for all people of the archipelago under the aegis of Islam. Soetomo listened to the high-flown phrases and the usual plans and proposals, and then rose to voice his challenge: when was there to be some really constructive work toward freedom by doing first that which was both necessary and attainable — preparing the people socially and economically for participation in a responsible government? This was a note foreign to the political leaders of the earlier Indonesian organizations. It was really the call of what was best within the new intellectual elite. It was so strange that it completely shattered the concept of an All Indies Congress.[111]

Soetomo not only sought to destroy the old ineffectual Indonesian political concepts, but also sought means to implement the new, as typified by the Perhimpunan Indonesia platform of 1922. He became convinced that leadership would have to emanate from the intellectuals, but it must be a leadership that embraced the Indonesian people, not one that left them behind. His inclination and experience toward organizing intellectuals was fortified by the fact that the Indonesian intellectuals seemed the only group capable, through faith and training, of moving the Indonesian organizational movement into new and fruitful lines.[112] Indonesians must help themselves and must prepare themselves. In July 1924 Dr. Soetomo relinquished his post on the Surabaya city council and founded the Indonesian Study Club (*Indonesische Studieclub*).[113]

The Study Club, as conceived by Soetomo, had as its purpose the stimulation of a sense of social responsibility and political awareness among the better educated Indonesians. Discussions were directed to questions of national and local concern, and in an attempt to stimulate constructive work the Study Club stood prepared to give advice to other organizations. The Study Club did not limit its activities to discussion and advice. It actively participated in seeking solutions to pressing problems, and in so doing founded schools, banks, health clinics, foundling homes, and took measures to limit child marriage and prostitution.[114] It was politically indifferent to the Netherlands Indian government, rather than assuming a positive position of non-coopera-tion. As regards other Indonesian organizations, the Study Club stood closest to the Budi Utomo, drawing its members from the young intellectuals who would normally have leaned toward the Budi Utomo, and having many joint members with the Budi Utomo, including Dr. Soetomo himself.

The concept of the Study Club spread from Surabaya to other cities and soon there were similar organizations in Surakarta, Jogjakarta, Batavia (Djakarta), Semarang, and Buitenzorg (Bo-gor). The best known of the remaining study clubs, however, came to be the *Algemeene Studieclub* (General Study Club), founded in Bandung in 1926 by a young graduate of the Engineering College by the name of Soekarno.

Soekarno (born Koesno Sosro Soekarno) was the son of a West-ern educated schoolteacher of lesser prijaji lineage.[115] Starting his education in the desa schools, Soekarno was, through the help of private teachers, able to make the transition into the European educational system.[116] He attended secondary school in Sura-baya, living in the home of Tjokroaminoto where he met many of the leading Sarekat Islam figures and eventually married Tjok-roaminoto's daughter. As Soekarno was an apt student, he was able to enter the newly created Engineering College in Bandung in 1920 where he received his degree in civil engineering in 1925.[117] He had dabbled in political affairs and written some articles before his graduation, but he had not actively joined any one of the political groups seeking his membership. A handsome man with a popular and winning personality, he soon discovered that he had potential talent for swaying and inspiring men with his words. He established a private engineering office in Bandung and began feeling his way into political life for which he felt himself destined. The General Study Club which he founded in 1926 was his first positive step into politics. Administered in close liaison with Perhimpunan Indonesia members who had returned to Java, the Study Club reflected the positive principles of this student organization.

The General Study Club of Soekarno was a political organization. It was only in outward form modeled after Dr. Soetomo's club in Surabaya. It made no pretense of concerning itself with social and economic problems and had even less interest in seeking positive solutions to these. Its program and plan of action were definite: non-cooperation with the government and complete and immediate independence for Indonesia. The Bandung group became a focal point for the returning political-activists of the Perhimpunan Indonesia. Non-cooperation was the key to the entire organization and self-help (or autoactivity) was the dynamic force which was to give it strength. In February 1927 all non-Indonesians were excluded and the movement became exclusively Indonesian, though Western in its tone and texture.

Here (and in the other study clubs too) were young men who had partaken of the best of Western education. They were not men who had to fear for their personal economic or social security under the colonial government, for they could have held government posts if they had wished. Nor were they men who had failed in their careers as many earlier leaders. In general they came from the lesser prijaji group — sons of men employed by the Netherlands Indian government. Many of their families had sacrificed much for their education and were shocked by their attitude of non-cooperation. It had been the parents' hope that their sons, through education, would gain positions of prestige; it was inconceivable to them that their sons would reject all this for an ideal. They little understood the individualistic course which their sons had chosen. It was a course which split them away from their family; it was a course dictated through Western formulated ideals and principles; it was a course that would have been unthinkable in Indonesian life only a few generations earlier.

These young men had chosen consciously to defy the colonial government and to seek a free future for Indonesia in which they might give full play to the ideals and capacities instilled in them by the West. Their program was closely tied to all shades of Marxist thinking, as had been the programs of most other Indonesian organizations. In part this was perhaps due to the feeling that they had little stake in the present economic arrangement in which foreign capital profited from Indonesian labor and produce. This is an obvious factor, but of less influence than a desire on the part of most politically minded Indonesians to seek friends and allies among those persons and doctrines most actively opposed to the existing colonial relationship. These young men were not satisfied merely to engage in revolution for the sake of World Communism or the advancement of Socialistic principles; their aim lay elsewhere.[118] They were particularly grieved by the racial duality of East Indian life, feeling that it was an insult to them in particular and to their people in general.[119] Furthermore they felt capable of doing everything themselves that was now being done for them by Europeans. They no longer wanted guidance, they wanted to lead. They hated the duality of Indonesian life. As long as they were unable to destroy this duality and the colonial relationship on which it rested, they would at least retain their dignity and refuse to have any relations with the existing government.

The General Study Club in Bandung was but newly formed when the poorly coordinated Communist inspired uprisings of 1926/27 occurred (see above, p. 213). Many of the General Study Club's members felt themselves closely allied to much in the Communist program, and the uprisings had an influence on the Study Club. In order to be able to tie in all factors, the discussion of the nature of the Communist revolts on Java (November 1926) and on Sumatra (January 1927) has been postponed to this point.

The Communist uprising in November 1926 on Java was a disorganized fiasco. Even those Communists with a smattering of reality realized it to be a senseless endeavor.[120] As one reads over the official government report on the event (and there is no reason for this report to minimize events) one is struck by the uprising's feeble, sporadic, disorganized, and, one might almost say, insignificant nature.[121] In Batavia the most exciting occurrence was the seizure of the telephone office by an armed group; for the rest the Batavia part of the uprising consisted of little more than marauding bands milling confusedly in the streets. Almost all the demonstrators were in the custody of the police by the next day. The greatest loss of life was in Bantam (West Java) where several civil servants were murdered by terrorist bands which continued their plundering and robbing tactics on into the month of December. Never, however, was there even a serious threat of control being surrendered to the rebel bands. Behind the Bantam disorders lay a certain amount of unrest created by taxation pressure, but for the most part it was the socially outcast bandit elements which the Communists had mobilized that caused most of the trouble.[122]

There is some question as to whether the West Coast of Sumatra trouble two months later (January 1927), which it was thought was meant to be coordinated with the Java uprising, had anything at all to do with Communism. This is not to deny the presence of a Communist Party, but is a questioning of whether Communist doctrine was in any sense at issue. The Minangkabau area of Sumatra had for some time been experiencing a mounting internal tension which was caused by conflicts stemming from the administration, from Islamic factions, from social changes, and from traditional customs. The Sarekat Islam in trying to enter the area had split and proved ineffectual. The situation was made more tense by an unwise government policy of work recruitment and taxation. Those groups beset by the greatest tensions in this situation found there was but one party which seemed prepared to take action toward relieving their grievances. They joined the Communist Party in the hope of gaining wider support for their stand in a strictly local affair. The troubles which broke out in January 1927 were more bloody than in Java and necessitated a greater exertion of force by the government before order could be restored, but even here it was not a major effort. Communist symbols seem to have been employed (almost as *djimat*), but there was no attempt to tie the show of force into a pattern of planned Communist thinking. It seemed to be a case of the Minangkabau insurgents using the Communist Party as much as the party was using them.[123]

The Communist disturbances evoked a firm and resolute reaction from the Netherlands Indian government. Some 13,000 persons were arrested — of these about one half were immediately released, another 4,500 received prison sentences, and about 1,300 were interned in New Guinea at Tanahmerah on the Upper Digul River.[124] These sentences were approved by the new Governor General A. C. D. de Graeff (not to be confused with Minister S. de Graaff who was out of office at this time) who had arrived only a few months before the disturbances. Known as a liberal and sympathetic man who had been close to Van Limburg Stirum, he began his term of office with a clear indication that he would suffer no forceful violation of the established order. He made it evident in his inaugural speech, however, that the government would be sympathetic toward those political wishes and ideals showing a sincere desire to achieve good.[125] Thus he did not in first instance close the door to all cooperation.

The discontent which the Communists sought to exploit was not great enough to cause great masses of people to rise against established authority. Nor were the terroristic methods employed by the Communists successful in winning the support of the more stable elements of the population or inducing them to make great sacrifices. Communist indoctrination remained limited to a handful of persons who were not even completely agreed among themselves on the methods and aims of Communism. Interning about 1300 persons, more than half of whom were released within five years after the event, was sufficient to remove Communism as an active force in East Indian politics for the remaining years of Dutch rule. Naturally police measures hampered the free flow of incendiary ideas and the free circulation of suspected persons during Dutch rule, but such measures were neither severe nor concerted enough to hold back a really heartfelt movement.

Of the persons to be interned, nearly 1000, mostly from Java, were interrogated on various subjects including their education, occupation, etc. The results of this questioning appeared in statistical form which, although incomplete (some refused to answer questions) and probably partly inaccurate (some might for personal reasons have given false answers), gives a fair idea of the type of person who was attracted to Communism.[126] It must be kept in mind that the internees were not necessarily all the persons who actively participated in riotous activity: they were rather the persons who through word and deed stimulated and guided the activities of November 1926. It must also be remembered that the top Communist Party leaders had either fled or been exiled from the East Indies prior to the revolts and are therefore not included among the internees. It would seem that the bulk of these internees were the second echelon party members (the party probably numbered about 3,000 by November 1926,[127] but probably only about 1,000 were old stalwarts who had been in the party for some years),[128] propagandists, and active members of some of the Sarekat Rakjats.[129]

As Western education was highlighted as one of the factors leading to Communism, much data is available on the educational background of the 1000 internees. Of the group, 761 were literate — that is to say, had had some schooling — an amazingly high percentage when compared to a general literacy rate usually placed in the neighborhood of five percent. Of those who had attended school the breakdown is approximately as follows:[130]

	Total Attending	Graduated
College	0	0
Secondary School	24	1
Vocational Educ. (Secondary)	97	37
Primary Education		
Primary Only	640	396
Moh. Rel.	—	45
Desa Sch.	40(?)	—
Sec. Cl. Native School	400+	250+
Dutch Native School (HIS)	128	67
European Primary	32	10

Viewing this education in relation to the age of the persons involved, some 613 of the 761 literate persons fall between the ages of twenty and thirty-five years. This would mean that the bulk of the educated persons finished their schooling from five to twenty years prior to the uprising, the variance depending upon age and type of schooling.

As regards the occupations of the internees, there were some 1,907 occupations given, or an average of about two per person. These occupations, in general categories, are:[131]

I. Government Service 518
II. Western Industry and Commerce 374
III. Native Industry and Commerce 858
IV. Native Society (Teacher, Journalist, etc.) 157

In addition there were 108 accounts of long term unemployment.[132] In the entire group there were 57 persons from the prijaji class and 59 persons who had made the pilgrimage (hadj) to Mecca.[133]

Not all of these statistics lend themselves to ready analysis. It is the educational factor which seems remarkable, however, for the high degree of education represented in the above statistics must have some significance. Recognizing that the above statistics are based upon an unusual segment of Indonesian society in that the literacy figures are exceedingly high, one must in turn recognize that the guiding and stimulating force behind a revolutionary movement in the East Indies lay in the hands of persons with some education. None of the internees could be classed as be-

longing to the highest Indonesian intellectual level although the
one secondary school graduate would approach this. The degree
of failure to complete secondary school training is unusually high
even when compared with the general average of failures. Outstanding in these figures is the high percentage of persons with
Second Class Native School primary education. In light of what
has previously been said about the Second Class Native Schools,
however, this should not be too startling (see above, pp. 68–70
and 178–9), particularly when it is realized that the Connecting
Schools (*Schakelschool* — see p. 222) were founded too late to
affect the persons involved in the Communist uprisings. The
number of persons attending the more decidedly Western style
schools: Dutch Native (H.I.S.) and European Primary, is also quite
high. Their participation in part must be a cultural disorientation
problem, but must also in part be economic.[134] The Dutch Native
Schools founded in 1914, did not begin turning out students in
appreciable numbers until after the First World War. These
students were in large measure interested in employment in the
government service, but there was at this time a decided shortage
of positions (see above, p. 219). That the unemployment possibility proved to be quite real is shown by the fact that more than
100 of the internees claimed to have suffered from lengthy unemployment in the period before the uprising. Since unemployment in the positive sense was practically unheard of in Indonesian society, and since any lengthy unemployment would drive
those who could make the transition back into rural Indonesian
society, it seems quite plausible to assume that these unemployment complaints originated largely with the Western educated,
Western employed elements who could not easily make the
transition back into traditional life patterns. There is little more
that can be said about the employment of the internees: the
number of positions held is indicative of a fairly high degree of
instability, but there is nothing that permits an analysis of trends
from one employment category to another. Further investigation
into the positions held with the government shows what would
be expected: that the greatest numbers were or had been in serv-

ice of the railways, pawnshops and public works departments —
all, of course, divisions of service which had been most active in
labor union and strike activity in previous years.[135]

Before leaving this analysis of the persons involved in the Communist uprisings, the general educational achievements in the
East Indies should be surveyed lest there be a tendency to view
the above figures out of context. Starting in 1914 and counting
up through 1925, there were some 23,000 Indonesians who had
received diplomas from Dutch Native Schools (H.I.S.) or European Primary Schools;[136] of this number, 77 were among the
Communist internees. Looking at education from another angle,
at the end of 1926 when the revolt occurred there were 406,000
Indonesian pupils enrolled in Moslem religious schools, 917,000
Indonesian pupils enrolled in desa schools, 313,000 Indonesian
pupils enrolled in Second Class Native Schools, and 79,000 Indonesian pupils enrolled in Dutch language primary schools.[137]
In relation to this total school enrollment at a given instant,
stands the rather insignificant figure of 716 literate Communist
internees whose educational experience ranged over a thirty year
period. It seems justified to conclude that the number of persons
with education who engaged in the Communist movement was
exceedingly small compared with the impact of that education.
Yet the removal of the internees from Indonesian society succeeded in putting an end to an active Communist movement of any
importance during the Dutch colonial period. The Communist
uprising merely bore out a fact already well understood in Indonesian life: namely, that a handful of dedicated and clever
men can win a following and create trouble. This is not to deny
that there were grievances and injustices and police surveillance,
but the relative strength and appeal of revolutionary sentiments
must not be overestimated. The Communist movement was a
spectacular event, but it was only of limited significance.

Returning to the General Study Club in Bandung which served
as the point of departure for the digression into the Communist
uprisings, one finds it actively concerned with the fate of the
Communist Party. Closely linked to the Perhimpunan Indonesia,

which toward the end of 1926 was seeking closer affiliation with the Communists,[138] the General Study Club began forming a political party which could pick up the pieces left from the shattering of the Communist Party. In April 1927 a preparatory committee was organized, and on July 4, 1927 the *Perserikatan Nasional Indonesia* (Indonesian National Union — P.N.I.) was formed.[139]

The P.N.I. was an extension of the Bandung Study Club and the Perhimpunan Indonesia, and promoted the same ideas. The program and platform of the P.N.I. shows this connection to be very real. The goal was the freedom of Indonesia which was to be achieved through a conscious, national, popular movement founded upon indigenous strength and ability and in cooperation with other organizations of like purpose.[140] Of primary importance was the struggle for political freedom which entailed non-cooperation with the government and which had to be achieved through the efforts of the Indonesian people.

The actual operations and functions of the P.N.I. fall outside the scope of this study but one factor should be emphasized: namely, the trend toward uniting the various political groups participating in the movement of a growing Indonesian self-consciousness. Douwes Dekker and his Indische Partij had tried on an associational basis to unify those groups of liberals and progressives who sought the welfare of the Indies, the Dutch Socialists had tried on a political basis by taking the lead in two Radical Concentrations (1918 and 1922) and the Autonomy Action of 1921, the progressive leaders of the Sarekat Islam and Communist Party had tried on a proletarian basis through the united labor movement (1920-22), the Sarekat Islam had furthermore tried on a religious basis during 1923/24: all these efforts ended in failure and left the Indonesian movement as much divided as ever. The revolutionary nationalists now tried to create unity on a nationalistic basis. In September 1926 several groups assembled to form the *Persatuan Indonesia* (Indonesian Unity) but this seemed to create no permanent, close ties.

A great sense of the need for unity seems also to have gripped the youth organizations.[141] They were composed of students from all parts of the archipelago. In facing common problems arising from the confrontation with European culture, the Indonesian youth who were engaged in the Westernized educational process were drawn more closely together than would normally have occurred. The need for active participation in Indonesian life was also becoming clearer to the students, particularly after the formation of the various study clubs.[142] The unity of the youth, however, could come only after the unity of the political parties.

Feelers in the direction of unity were coming from Surabaya and Bandung, but it was particularly after the creation of the P.N.I. (July 1927), that a sense of urgency seemed to attach itself to the unification of various Indonesian groups and parties. Finally at a meeting in Bandung in December 1927 under the guidance of Soekarno there came into being the *Permufakatan Perhimpunan-perhimpunan Politiek Kebangsaan Indonesia* (Consolidated Political Organizations of the Indonesian People), better known as P.P.P.K.I.[143] The story of the P.P.P.K.I. also falls beyond the limits of this study. For our purposes, the P.P.P.K.I. is symbolic of the culmination, in a sense also 'fruition', of the political aims of Indonesian organizations in the early twentieth century. The fact that the P.P.P.K.I. soon broke apart and that Indonesian political groups would spend the next fifteen years seeking unity in no way detracts from its significance. The symbol of united action under nationalist principles retained its appeal to politically conscious Indonesians after 1927, and served as a vague goal for an increasing number of the newly developed elite from that time forward.

The P.N.I. which gave the P.P.P.K.I. its chief symbolic content of national unity, was, it must be realized, a small group of at the most a few hundred members. When the Communist Party was annihilated by the Netherlands Indian government, the P.N.I. determined to gain a wider following. It was able to pick up members from the Sarekat Rakjats and to win a following of sorts among the Indonesian masses. However, this membership was not of the most desirable sort, and lost the P.N.I. much of the more stable mass following which it might have hoped to win. The asocial aspects of much of its following failed to deter the P.N.I. leadership, however, for it could use such elements in its zeal to further non-cooperation, and meanwhile seemed completely convinced that it had stirred the masses of Indonesia. The nature of the P.N.I. following rather than its program, led to perpetual difficulties with the authorities. Tjipto Mangoenkoesoemo, who was one of the early party founders, was exiled for attempting to foment revolt among Indonesian troops of the Netherlands Indian army. Iwa Koesoema Soemantri, one of the founders of the Perhimpunan Indonesia and later associated with the P.N.I., was arrested for stirring up Communists on the East Coast of Sumatra. In various areas of Java the party's activities occasioned open resistance against the party by the people because of the collusion of the P.N.I. with terrorist elements. Yet all this is secondary, since the significance of the party lay not in its revolutionary activities and certainly not in the number of its adherents, for it always remained a small group.

The real significance of the P.N.I. lay in its ideal and in the small nucleus of dedicated leaders. This had nothing to do with either its actual or relative strength in the late 1920's, but lay rather in its symbolic influence.[144] The fact that a handful of well-educated, competent persons of Indonesian blood would openly defy the colonial government, would seek their strength in the Indonesian people, and would openly proclaim a desire for independence from the Netherlands made an impression among Indonesians of various levels of society, but particularly among those on higher levels. The majority so influenced never joined the P.N.I. or actively supported it, but they were moved by the example of Indonesians acting with force and dignity — among these persons were a number of administrators and other government personnel. The flame of independence which the P.N.I. had kindled more intensely than any earlier party continued to brighten the hearts of many Indonesians long after that organization had become defunct. They no longer thought of the deeds of the P.N.I., they no longer thought of its motives; they thought of it only as the symbol of a free Indonesia, a better Indonesia, an Indonesia for the Indonesians. This symbol was personified in the leader of the P.N.I., Soekarno — in so far as his significance was founded on this vague emotional appeal, the P.N.I. can be said to have certain *ratu adil* aspects.[145]

Of greater significance in reshaping and strengthening Indonesian society during the 1920's was a group of less radical Indonesians who were just as convinced of the desirability of Indonesian independence as the P.N.I. people, but who went about their work in an entirely different manner. To them non-cooperation was not a primary principle of honor. Although many of them may have had non-cooperative periods, they felt in general that the destructive aspects of non-cooperation failed to justify its moral value. These people were the constructive elements of the new Indonesian society. Although they never had the symbolic impact of the P.N.I., they were far more instrumental in laying the groundwork for the functioning of the new elite and in providing a firm social structure on which this elite might function. Their efforts were directed toward the economic and social strengthening of Indonesian society, with political activity relegated to a secondary position. Their names are many, their type of activity varied, and their influence usually localized. Foremost among them stood Dr. Soetomo, but also operative in this manner were Hadji Agus Salim, Soewardi Soerianingrat (Ki Hadjar Dewantoro), and Hoesein Thamrin — to name but a few. This group came to form an essential facet in the newly evolving colonial relationship, and the Netherlands Indian government directed special attention to them in its new policy.

Before discussing this new policy, a few concluding remarks about the development of the Indonesian elite up to about 1927 seem appropriate. The discusssion of Indonesian elite development which has been presented here has proceeded principally through Indonesian organizations. These organizations, either directly or indirectly, became involved in political activities. That the newly developing Indonesian elite should be viewed in such organizational-political forms is necessary, but unfortunate (see above, p. 165 ff.). The great majority of the new Indonesian elite joined no organization and had no active political views. At most the Indonesian organizations reflected or stimulated ideas and ideals among the broader group of the expanding elite, but there is no certainty of the extent or direction of this influence. This organizational presentation of elite development has probably also tended to give a political tinge to the social changes occurring in Indonesia during these years. Actually most of the social change took place within the framework of the Dutch colonial system and was mostly apolitical.

The broad group of the newly developing elite might for immediate purpose be described as the functional elite. This would serve to separate them from the political leaders whose symbolic and idealistic influence may have been widespread, but whose practical significance, especially after 1920, was slight. The functional elite, by the very nature of Indonesian social realities, would consist of administrators and civil servants (many of whom would be classified as intellectuals) in all branches of government service, but it would also include Indonesians outside direct government service who had developed a leadership role in Indonesian society. This latter group would include professional men, certain entrepreneurs, religious teachers, and persons of social prominence. These were the people who held Indonesian society together while it was undergoing the changes of the early twentieth century, and these are also the people who have kept an independent Indonesia functioning after 1945.

The great majority of the Western trained Indonesians were, during the first quarter of the twentieth century, forming themselves into such a functional elite. Indonesian society had always had an elite but this new elite was expanded, was extended into new fields of operation, and was imbued with new concepts of service and efficiency. The prestige of the traditional elite had been lessened, though not completely eliminated, by government policy and by social change. Hereditary claims to status and position, though not to be discounted, played a less important role than formerly. The rights of the functional elite came to be tied closely to Western style education and the possession of diplomas. Actually the same elite families participated in this group as in former days, for the prijaji families had been best able to obtain and afford the necessary education for their children. But now there was more room for additional family members and for those who pushed their way upward from the lesser prijaji group.[146]

The functional elite certainly followed Indonesian and Dutch political events, but was not prepared to participate in these events.[147] At most they were prepared to participate in the administrative-political process which was provided them through the continuing decentralization process. The removal of tutelage from the Regencies provided some political experience for members of the functional elite, and the creation of Regency Councils after 1924 added additional opportunities.[148] But this was all rather distant from the aggressive political plans and actions of many of the Indonesian organizations during the 1920's. This does not mean that the functional elite did not sympathize with the ideals of the Indonesian political leaders, for they felt many of the same grievances and were inspired by the symbol of national unity. But they viewed Indonesia's future in more conservative terms; that is to say, in terms of preserving the functioning, administrative state and society in which they were coming to play an ever more important role. They too probably thought of future independence, but they wanted to be prepared for it through further extensions of autonomy, for they viewed themselves as the necessary component of any modern state. These men were not inclined to take idealistic excursions; they were practical administrators. As long as Dutch authority was unshaken, they stayed with it and sought their future within the colonial system, limiting their demands to attainable objectives within the existing system.[149] Until they gave their support, the Indonesian political leaders would remain only symbols.

A New Colonial Policy

The new policy of the Dutch government toward Indonesia began to emerge clearly about 1925 although its origins go back
earlier than this. The new policy was based on the realities of
East Indian colonial life after the First World War and on a
reconsideration of the Ethical Colonial Policy. The years of
Governor General Fock's administration (1921–1926) were years
of readjustment which would in any event have been confused
enough, but the inconsistencies and shortcomings of this administration as described above (see p. 207) added to the difficulty
in comprehending the new policy. A growing confusion in the use
of descriptive language added even further to the problem.[150] The
fact that the new policy was launched just when the East Indian
economy began to suffer a serious decline meant that this new
policy had to be revised before it had an opportunity to stand the
test of time. All this leads to a somewhat more vague policy than
had characterized Dutch colonial attitudes in earlier periods, but
nevertheless a change in both mood and direction became quite
real.

One basic reality of East Indian life after the First World War
was the shift in emphasis to the outer islands. In these islands
Dutch and other Western nations' capital was used to develop
raw material production for world markets and industries. Naturally there had been capitalistic enterprises in the outer islands at
earlier dates, but after the First World War the investments in
these areas were greatly expanded.[151] The opening of the Djambi
(Southeast Sumatra) oil concessions in 1920 forms a convenient
point of division from the earlier Java-centered interests of Western capital. The government naturally encouraged this shift and
tended to limit the extension of foreign plantation or agrarian
enterprises in Java, for it was becoming very clear that the
population pressure on this island was making land a scarce
commodity. This study makes no attempt to analyze the effects
of this population increase at the various levels of Indonesian
society — enough has been said of the elite to indicate that their

numbers increased and had to be provided for. Nor is it possible here to expand this study of the developing elite to include the outer islands of the archipelago. Suffice it for our purposes to note that after the First World War Dutch interests and policies began to shift their primary emphasis from Java to the outer islands; many Indonesians also began to reorient their vision in a similar manner.

The second basic reality of East Indian colonial life in the post war decade was the widespread feeling that the Ethical Colonial Policy, as conceived and as applied during the past two decades, had shown numerous defects and weaknesses. The disturbances in various parts of the archipelago in the years following the First World War were a painful shock to many persons. The tendency of the native movement to take on a more radical nature and to direct its energies against the established government was also a factor which led to a diminishing popularity of the Ethical Policy among Europeans. The radical democratic notion of allowing Indonesian political organizations to seek their own form became discredited. It became apparent that the dislocated masses were a fertile ground for varying degrees of irresponsible political activity, and the conservative view that the more one ceded, the more was demanded, seemed to be borne out in fact. More painful than all of this, however, was the failure of the Ethical Policy to raise living standards. By about 1920 many persons had come to realize that the energies of men and money which had been expended to raise the general welfare of Indonesian life had not succeeded to any appreciable extent. The goal seemed just as far removed as ever. It was almost as if one were working against a Malthusian natural law which tended to swallow up any advance in welfare by an increase in population. Yet the concept of raising welfare remained an inherent part of Western thought, and it was primarily with this essentially good goal in view that revisions were made which led to a new policy.

The new policy emerged in large part from the reflective, academic atmosphere of the University of Leiden. The Faculty of Indology at Leiden had served as the training center for the

European civil administrators in the East Indies. Through these administrators the new policy began to make itself felt.[152] It found little favor with many politicians in The Hague, who were laying down the repressive and thrift measures being followed by Governor General Fock.[153] But the new policy had wide support among administrative circles in the East Indies. It can be summarized as a desire to promote the welfare of the Indonesian people, while at the same time seeking to restore or strengthen (depending on the locality) the Indonesian culture pattern.

The new policy was applied in various branches of the Netherlands Indian government service starting about 1920, and came to affect overall policy about 1925. An example of the application of the new trend which came to typify the policy is shown by developments in the People's Credit System (Volkscredietwezen).

The Volkscredietwezen (see above, pp. 73–75) had originally sought to fortify and strengthen indigenous cooperative institutions in order to bolster native finances and prosperity. The system unfortunately became tied to the gentle pressure methods used by the administrators and civil servants to bring about change. The village grain sheds were the most successful part of the Credit System. Both the village banks and the district banks missed their goals.[154] The village banks sought to use the cooperative aspects of village life, but instead of viewing cooperation in indigenous terms, applied Westernized concepts of cooperation. The culmination of this Western oriented desire to further cooperation in the money-poor, land-centered economy of Indonesia came in 1915 with a law providing for a legal framework within which cooperatives might be established.[155] This law was also one facet of the great drive toward legal unification, which will be discussed shortly (see below, pp. 247–8). It was a complete failure, for it missed the realities of Indonesian social and economic life and failed to realize that indigenous cooperation was rooted in the customary (adat) moral feelings rather than in an expression of free will of the members of an individualistic society. The district banks missed their mark because they were not designed or prepared to extend credit to the earliest manifestations of an Indonesian middle class which began to appear after the First World War. This latter shortcoming was not remedied for more than a decade.[156]

The failure of the effort to inspire cooperative endeavor among Indonesians underwent complete revision in 1920 with the establishment, under the chairmanship of Dr. J. H. Boeke, of the Cooperative Commission. Dr. Boeke was a member of the Leiden group. Very shortly success began to replace failure as Indonesian cooperatives were established on a simple basis with Indonesian rather than European legal status.[157] The new methods did not receive immediate and unanimous approval since they did not fit too well with the concepts of unification and association which still found adherents. However, the recognition of two separate levels of legal and practical operation, the Indonesian and the Western, was so succesful that it was widely acknowledged as a solution to the many problems posed by the colonial dilemma. The cooperative legislation of 1927 abolished the unification concepts of the old law.[158]

Boeke's ideas on Indonesian economics were not limited to the stimulation of native cooperatives. He attributed the failure of the government's entire credit and welfare program to the prevailing atmosphere of impersonality, which sought to apply rules of development and improvement to the entire Indonesian population uniformly. What happened in practice was that a few individuals showed themselves willing to utilize the facilities for economic advancement provided by the government, while the great majority remained indifferent. Boeke felt that the government should direct its attention to these energetic individuals, concentrating upon helping them rather than continuing the prodigious and thankless task of attempting to raise the level of the entire population. The creation of a solid core of economically viable individuals would then act as a base for further economic development. This process, according to Boeke in 1922, should be dependent upon the efforts, energies and capacities of individual Indonesians to seek self-improvement — he employed the term 'auto-activity' — and government pressures (*perentah halus*) which attempted to force improvements should be abandoned.[159] Here was the idea which several months later was embodied in the program of the Perhimpunan Indonesia and which came to form such an important facet of the new, intellectually-guided, nationalist-oriented Indonesian political organizations.

This new view of colonial activity found favor in other branches of the government. An example of the more individualized approach is seen in the program of agrarian information. In 1922 the Department of Agriculture changed its entire program of rural extension work. Previously the department had conducted a uniform developmental program on largely theoretical or generalized foundations. The new program was directed to localized situations with greater emphasis upon practical procedures.[160]

The de-emphasis on forcing improvement is illustrated by the work in the program of health education. When Dr. J. L. Hydrick, supported by funds from the Rockefeller Foundation, started a program of local health information bureaus in 1924, he was permitted to run a test on the relative effectiveness of coercion and explanation. He was rapidly convinced that the latter procedure would render the most permanent results.[161] And so the concept of auto-activity came to be applied in modified forms to most of the government services.

By 1925 this new trend had progressed so far that the new Law on the Organization of the State (Wet op de Staatsinrichting) which came into being that year, abolished the lowest rank of the European civil administration (Contrôleur), thus removing the source of pressures. This last move went a little too far, however, and in 1931 the Contrôleur, with curtailed powers, was fitted back into the system.[162]

These changes toward individualization, designed to appeal largely to the more Western-oriented Indonesians, parallel another deep current of change — also emanating from Leiden — which sought to re-stabilize the indigenous community through developing the adat (customary) law. These developments which form the second aspect of the new policy are intimately bound to the name of the famous Dutch jurist, C. van Vollenhoven. Since 1901 a professor at the University of Leiden, Van Vollenhoven had directed his attention to the study of the adat of the Indonesian people. Adat law was not a new concept, but due to its complexity and confusing aspects it was not highly regarded by the jurists of the first two decades of the 20th century.[163] The Fundamental Law of 1854 had allowed great leeway in the application of Western law to the archipelago, but with the advent of the Ethical Policy, the letter rather than the spirit of this earlier regulation was followed. The result was a tremendous surge toward unification and equalization of the law for all peoples of the archipelago.[164] Van Vollenhoven opposed this process in various ways and with varying success. A turning point came about 1918 to 1920. In 1918 the first volume of his great work on the adat law, begun in 1906, was completed. It would be more than a decade before the second volume appeared, but it was the first volume that caused the profound effect. Van Vollenhoven had succeeded in systematizing the adat law of the East Indies so that it could be used as a practical system of jurisprudence to be applied to Indonesians.

Once again the change was not immediate. The work of legal unification carried on under the Fock government brought forth a unified civil law code in 1923 to complete the work which had started with the unified criminal law in 1916. But the civil law code had great and obvious shortcomings. These were heightened by the advances that Van Vollenhoven's concepts were making among persons in important positions in the East Indies.[165] Between 1923 and 1927 some of the unified legislation was withdrawn while other parts were disregarded in practice.[166] By 1927 one can speak of the application of adat law to the Indonesian community being the accepted policy.[167]

Van Vollenhoven was in no sense a reactionary who wished to force back the clock, nor must he be confused with the advocates of repressive measures to keep the Indonesian in his secondary position. On the contrary, he favored far-reaching autonomy for the Indonesian people (he was one of the supporters of the May

1922 proposals, see above, pp. 206–7), but he conceived of this as a development from out of their own culture through the growth of a living and changing *adat*.[168] The Dutch and the Indonesian people were different, not superior or inferior, but different — culturally different; they had different needs and institutions. Indonesian autonomy must not be based upon equality or assimilation with European concepts.[169] The application of adat law was envisioned as occurring principally at the village level — studies by Van Vollenhoven's students indicated the strong practicability of this[170] — where those traditions and patterns that still lived would be supported and would be allowed to develop naturally toward the top levels of Indonesian society which were in large measure Westernized.

The Dutch colonial policy, as applied by the civil administration which was almost entirely Leiden trained, began to stress the reintegration of Indonesian life at the village level.[171] Reintegration was not an even or immediate process.[172] It was most thoroughly applied in parts of the outer islands where Western influence had penetrated less deeply.[173] But it also led to a village autonomy investigation on Java and Madura (instituted in 1926) which prepared the way for a reorientation of Javanese village life into the new policy pattern.[174] Its influence was clearly shown in 1928 when the application of adat law and reestablishment of traditional Indonesian institutions was proposed by B. Schrieke as a solution to the problems of the West Coast of Sumatra which had led to the uprising of early 1927.[175]

Underlying the application of adat law to native Indonesian communities and the application of self-motivation and removal of pressure from the Western educated Indonesian groups was an implicit understanding that Indonesian society should be reintegrated, and that the colonial relationship should be founded upon an openly recognized duality.[176] The term association had lost all political and social meaning: Indonesians showed little interest in taking on European legal status (at the most they placed themselves under European law for certain occasions),[177] the new nationalist feeling of the political-minded Indonesians was decidedly exclusive, the political parties based on association were losing popularity,[178] and as though this were not already enough the Fock government assumed a hostile and insulting attitude toward the advocates of association. Association became a concept that was limited to the Cultural field; various institutions of arts and learning continued to advance the best traditions of association.[179] Here it continued to be supported by scholarly Europeans and some of the highly educated Indonesians, but it was no longer a concept which wielded great social or political power.[180]

In recognizing a duality within the colonial relationship, the new policy did not force a rigid division along ethnic lines. An ethnic separateness was already contained in the tripartite division of the population dating from 1919 (see above, p. 205), but this type of legislation did not seek to seal off Western influence and penetration into Indonesian life. Nor did the new recognized duality attempt to do this. Those Indonesians, particularly of the rising middle class, who felt the desire to enter the Westernized sphere of life might quite easily do so.[181]

The functional elite for the most part, however, remained within the Indonesian orbit of life, though continuing to receive the best of Western educations. The idea was to have the masses move upward toward the elite, and to have the elite in turn move downward to the masses, thus joining and forming a new cultural synthesis which would include all the Indonesian people rather than all the people of the East Indies.[182] This process was started with the creation of the Regency Councils at one end, and the extension of village autonomy at the other.[183] The group left standing outside the door throughout this entire process was the non-cooperating, politically-inclined Indonesians. The new policy pushed them and their movement into the background and during the 1930's they were diminishing in significance.[184] It was the Japanese invasion in 1942 which gave them a new lease on life.

Once it is understood that the new colonial policy operated on a recognized duality, much of the legislation which came in the late 1920's becomes much clearer. In June 1925 the new Organization of the State became law [185] (see above p. 204ff.). The left wing groups opposed the law because they felt it failed to provide the East Indies with a sufficient measure of autonomy. The law did not make many deep-seated changes;[186] these were coming about in another manner, as just described. The new Organization of the State did provide for semi-legislative powers for the Volksraad, in which room for greater representation of Indonesians was eventually made.[187] There is great question, however, if under the new policy of recognized duality the Volksraad had any real or vital power or influence in Indonesian life.[188]

The government, under the new policy, tacitly approved of the type of activity in which Dr. Soetomo was engaged as the means of advancing the Western-oriented Indonesians. Soetomo saw the need of directing Indonesian energies toward economic and social improvement, and, although not directly cooperating with the government, his efforts were leading in the same direction as that of the new policy. Other Indonesians, too, saw the aim of the government and were inclined to work toward the creation of the new syncretic culture which would stand on a groundwork of adat communities and autonomous districts, and which would eventually be able completely to dispense with the government's civil administration.[189]

That the aims and intentions of this new policy were never fully realized is attributable to numerous factors which lie outside the scope of this study. It can never be fully determined how far the new policy of a recognized duality would have succeeded in solving the colonial problem, for just as the new policy was gaining control the world depression intervened.[190] The depression disrupted plans and policies at all levels. The economic aspects of the duality became so distorted that the other aspects of duality tended to appear bigoted and foolish throughout the next decade. At the time of its formulation, however, the new policy was a sincere effort to find an answer to one of Western civilization's thorniest problems: how to deal with colonial areas.[191]

Notes

1 W. F. Wertheim, *Effects of Western Civilization on Indonesian Society* (New York, 1950), p. 5.

2 See: W. R. van Hoëvell, *Parlementaire redevoeringen over koloniale belangen 1849–1859*, 4 volumes (Zalt Bommel, 1862–5), and any one of numerous editions of the *Max Havelaar* by Multatuli (Eduard Douwes Dekker) which first appeared in 1860.

3 *Staatsblad van Nederlandsch Indië* (Henceforth *Ind. Stbl.*) 1915, No. 491.

4 J. S. Furnivall, *Netherlands India: a study of plural economy* (Cambridge, 1944), p. 212. "...by reason of the strong financial, mercantile and planting interests in Parliament, with its close control over Indian policy and over even the details of Indian administration, the non-officials had more real power than the officials." In the light of actual practices this statement seems exaggerated and must be viewed as part of Furnivall's overall thesis. That there was influence from outside upon the East Indian civil administration is beyond question.

5 Ordonnance... (9 Avril 1894) "Le Main-d'Oeuvre aux colonies", *Bibliothèque Coloniale Internationale* 1re Série, Tome I (1895), 506–512. Also see: *Ind. Stbl.* 1899, No. 263.

6 G. J. Nolst Trenité, "Verhuring van grond door Inlanders aan niet-Inlanders op Java en Madoera", *Indisch Genootschap*, 27 Maart 1906, pp. 131–8. See also: *Ind. Stbl.* 1866, No. 80.

7 P. Kasteel, *Abraham Kuyper* (Kampen, 1938), p. 300.

8 Furnivall, *loc.cit.* In 1852 there were perhaps about 600 non-civil servants in a European population of about 22,000. By 1900 there were approximately 76,000 European civilians the majority of whom were non-official.

9 J. Chailley-Bert, *Java et ses habitants* (Paris, 1900), p. 67 ff.

10 Brooshooft, Memorie over den toestand in Indië, ter begeleiding van den open brief op 7 Maart 1888 door 1255 ingezetenen van Nederlandsch-Indië gezonden aan 12 Nederlandsche Heeren.

11 "Een Eereschuld" (1899) in H. T. Colenbrander en J. E. Stokvis, *Leven en Arbeid van Mr. C. Th. van Deventer*, vol. II (Amsterdam, 1917?), pp. 1–43.

12 A draft program for party policy advanced by Van Kol in 1901 embodied many of the aims of the Ethical Policy. The physical, mental and moral development of the native was the highest aim. Freedom of speech, press and

assembly, equitable justice, development of native crafts, improvement of roads, rivers and irrigation systems, better regulation of taxes, increased health measures, free education, and separation of colonial and home finances were advanced as the principle points in the program. "Ontwerp-program voor de Nederlandsche Koloniale Politiek", *Verslag van het Congres S.D.A.P.*, 1901, pp. 197-220.

13 E. Moresco, "Onze politiek ten aanzien van de Inlandsche zelfbesturen", *Indisch Genootschap*, 7 April 1908, p. 205. See also: R. Emerson, *Malaysia* (New York, 1937), p. 379.

14 D. Fock, "De Algemeene Sekretarie in Nederlandsch-Indië", *De Indische Gids* XXII (1900), 832-8.

15 Chailley-Bert, *op. cit.*, pp. 171-4.

16 C. Snouck Hurgronje, *Verspreide Geschriften* IV, (Bonn u. Leipzig, 1924), pp. 423-4.

17 Emerson, *op. cit.*, p. 421.

18 H. Carpentier Alting, "Bestuursonthouding of Bestuursbemoeienis?", *Tijdschrift voor het Binnenlandsch Bestuur* XXVI (1904), 48-53.

19 Snouck Hurgronje, *op. cit.*, pp. 60-68.

20 In 1883 regular civil service examinations were instituted for judicial and administrative posts in the East Indies, and in 1893 the requirements were raised. Koninklijk Besluit van 29 Augustus 1883 (*Ned. Stbl.*, No. 133) and Koninklijk Besluit van 20 Juli 1893 (*Ned. Stbl.*, No. 117). See also: R. A. van Sandick, "De Regeeringsvoorstellen betreffende de ambetnaarsopleiding", *De Indische Gids* XXIV (1902), 4-5.

21 Snouck Hurgronje, *op. cit.*, p. 151.

22 A. van Marle, "De groep der Europeanen in Ned. Indië, iets over ontstaan en groei", *Indonesië* V (1951-52), 487-8.

23 D. M. G. Koch, "De Indische Bond", *Indische Koloniale Vraagstukken* (Weltevreden, 1919), pp. 113-121.

24 C. O. van der Plas, "De maatschappelijke, cultureele en politieke ontwikkeling van Insulinde in heden en toekomst", *Koloniaal Tijdschrift* VIII (1919), 556-8.

25 *Indisch Verslag* 1940 vol. II, p. 42.

26 Liem Twan Djie, *De distribueerende tusschenhandel der Chineezen op Java* ('s-Gravenhage, 1947), *passim*.

27 *Indisch Verslag* 1940, vol. II, p. 39.

28 R. A. Kern, *De Islam in Indonesië* ('s-Gravenhage, 1947), pp. 110-111.

29 Today Indonesians sometimes divide their compatriots into a secular and into a staunchly religious group. This division does not seem to have been much employed around 1900 even though religion did then play a part in Indonesian life and often did conflict with secular interests. Perhaps the growth and development of Reformist doctrines within the Indonesian Islamic community during the 20th century are reflected in this newer social division.

30 R. Kennedy, "Contours of Culture in Indonesia", *The Far Eastern Quarterly* II (1942), 11.

31 J. H. Boeke, *Dorp en desa* (Leiden, 1934), p. 54.

32 P. A. van de Lith, "Introduction historique", Le Régime foncier aux Colonies — *Bibliothèque Coloniale Internationale*, 3me Serie, Tome IV. *Indes Orientales Néerlandaises* (1899), pp. 7–26.

33 B. Schrieke, "Uit de geschiedenis van het Adatgrondenrecht", *Tijdschrift voor Indische Taal-, Land- en Volkenkunde* LIX (1919–21), 122 ff.

34 J. R. Lette, *Proeve eener vergelijkende studie van grondbezit in Rusland, zoals dit zich heeft ontwikkeld tot de Russische Revolutie, en op Java* (Leiden, 1928), pp. 100–102.

35 C. van Vollenhoven, *De Indonesier en zijn grond* (Leiden, 1919), pp. 5–6.

36 G. J. Vink, *De grondslagen van het Indonesische landbouwbedrijf* (Wageningen, 1939?), pp. 44–45.

37 C. van Vollenhoven, *Het Adatrecht van Nederlandsch Indië* I (Leiden, 1918), p. 524 ff.

38 Vink, *loc. cit.*

39 D. H. Burger, *De Ontsluiting van Java's binnenland voor het Wereldverkeer* (Wageningen, 1939), p. 6.

40 B. Schrieke, "Native Society in the Transformation Period", *The Effect of Western Influence...* (Batavia, 1929), p. 238. For an interesting sidelight on the subtle fashion in which Western influences might affect village patterns see: W. F. Engelbert van Bevervoorde, "De vlechtindistrie in de residentie Jogjakarta", *Tijdschrift voor het Binnenlandsch Bestuur* XXIX (1905), 2–3.

41 Burger, *op. cit.*, pp. 80–81, 163 and 178–180.

42 P. A. A. Djajadiningrat, *Herinneringen van Pangeran Aria Achmad Djajadiningrat* (Amsterdam-Batavia, 1936?), p. 182, and R. Toemenggoeng Koesoemo Dikdo, "Nog iets over dessahoofdverkiezingen", *Tijdschrift voor het Binnenlandsch Bestuur* XXIV (1903), p. 10.

43 R. M. Toemenggoeng Ario Koesoemo di Poetro, "Bestuursonthouding of (en) bestuursbemoeienis", *Tijdschrift voor het Binnenlandsch Bestuur* XXVI (1904), 351–2.

44 G. W. J. Drewes, *Drie Javaansche Goeroe's, hun leven, onderricht en messias-prediking* (Leiden, 1925), pp. 191–2.

45 A. W. Nieuwenhuis, "De godsdienst op Java in zijne oeconomische en politieke beteekenis", *Indisch Genootschap*, 27 Maart 1906, pp. 131–138.

46 *Ibid.*, p. 141.

47 W. F. Wertheim, "Oude en nieuwe Islamieten in Indonesië", *De Nieuwe Stem* VI (1951), 328–331. See also: Djajadiningrat, *op. cit.*, p. 20.

48 Kern, *op. cit.*, pp. 88–89.

49 C. O. van der Plas, "Mededeelingen over de stroomingen in de Moslimsche gemeenschap in Nederlandsch-Indië en de Nederlandsche Islampolitiek", *Indisch Genootschap*, 16 Februari 1934, p. 254, speaks of an annual average

of 40,000 pilgrims in the early 20th century. An article in *De Indische Gids* XXVI (1904), p. 105, entitled "Mekkagangers op Nederlandsche stoomsche-pen", mentions that the pilgrims had numerous complaints against the Nether-lands' shipping lines on grounds they were being overcharged. The round trip from Java to Jeddah with food was 250 francs.

50 Van der Plas, "Mededeelingen...", *op. cit.*, p. 257.

51 Kern, *op. cit.*, pp. 107–8.

52 Van der Plas, "Mededeelingen...", *op. cit.*, p. 258.

53 Hamka, *Sedjarah Islam di Sumatera* (Medan, 1950), p. 38 ff.

54 Wertheim, "Oude en nieuwe...", *op. cit.*, p. 331 and 396.

55 Towns and cities had existed in Java before Europeans arrived. These had centered either around the courts of sultans and princes or about a favorable harbor along the coast. These towns and cities did not, however, display the functional diversity and cultural intermingling which character-ized the urban centers created by the West. See: J. H. Boeke, *The structure of the Netherlands Indian Economy* (New York, 1942), p. 8.

56 J. P. Duyvendak, *Inleiding tot de Ethnologie van de Indonesische Archipel* (Djakarta/Groningen, 1946), p. 177.

57 J. van Gelderen, "Welvaart en welvaartsmeting in Nederlandsch-Indië", *Indisch Genootschap*, 21 Januari 1927, pp. 4–8, points out that proletarian Indonesians employed by the government and Western enterprises were most amenable to agitation and radical organizational influence directed against the capitalistic West. This might in part be due to the nature of Western employment which brought people together in an impersonal fashion and failed to supply the *camaraderie* so prevalent in Indonesian employment.

58 Dr. Radjiman (R. T. Wedijodiningrat), *Een bijdrage tot het reconstructie-idee van de Javaansche maatschappij*. XIIIe Congres van Boedi Oetomo te Soera-karta, 24–26 December 1921 (Djokja, 1921), pp. 14–15.

59 R. A. A. A. Djajadiningrat, "De positie van de regenten op Java en Ma-doera in het huidige bestuursstelsel", *Indisch Genootschap*, 15 November 1929, pp. 84–86.

60 D. W. van Welderen Rengers, *The Failure of a Liberal Colonial Policy: Netherlands East Indies*, 1816–1830 (The Hague, 1947), *passim*.

61 A. Jonkers, *Welvaartszorg in Indonesië* ('s-Gravenhage, 1948), p. 170.

62 N. A. C. Slotemaker de Bruïne, "De cultureele beteekenis van het onder-wijs in Ned.Indië", *Indisch Genootschap*, 27 November 1931, p. 121.

63 J. C. van Eerde, *Ethnologie Coloniale* (L'Européen et l'Indigène) (Paris, 1927), pp. 157–8.

64 Snouck Hurgronje, *op. cit.*, p. 158. Also see: C. Day. *The policy and administration of the Dutch in Java* (New York, 1904), p. 426.

65 Gouvernements Besluit van 30 Maart 1878, No. 21.

66 In many instances the Regent was no longer the real head of the people but merely a high ranking civil servant. Boeka, "De Hoofden op Java: een

studie", *De Indische Gids* XXVI (1904), 333-339. See also: Djajadiningrat, "De positie van de regenten...', *op. cit.*, p. 102.

67 R. Tjokroamprodjo, "Het voornemen van de Regeering van Neder-landsch Indië om Inlanders tot het aanleeren en de studie der Hollandsche taal aan te moedigen", *Tijdschrift voor het Binnenlandsch Bestuur* XXIII (1902), 145-52. R. M. T. Tjokro Adi Koesoemo, "Pengatoeran boeat menambahi kemadjoean bagei orang Djawa", *Tijdschrift voor het Binnenlandsch Bestuur* XXXIII (1907), 454-456.

68 *Ontwikkeling van het Geneeskundig Onderwijs te Weltevreden 1851-1926* (Wel-tevreden, 1926), p. 3.

69 *Ibid.*, pp. 3-4.

70 Conversation with Dr. Radjiman Wedijodiningrat, Djakarta, March 26, 1952.

71 *Gedenkboek M.O.S.V.I.A. 1879-1929* (Bandoeng, ca. 1929), pp. 21-22. After 1886 Dutch became the language of instruction in the upper grades of these advanced schools.

72. J. Habbema, "Hollandsch voor aanstaande inlandsche ambtenaren en onderwijzers", *De Indische Gids* XXIII (1901), 839.

73 W. K. Terhupeiory, "Iets over de Inlandsche geneeskundigen", *Indisch Genootschap*, 28 Januari 1908, pp. 110-111.

74 In 1891 Dr. Snouck Hurgronje was made Adviser for Eastern Languages and Moslem Law to the government of Netherlands India. In 1899 this title was changed to Adviser for Native and Arab Affairs.

75 *Ind. Stbl.* 1893, No. 125.

CHAPTER II

1 H. H. van Kol, "Geen 'Indische Bijdragen' meer!" and "Bestaat er schei-ding of eenheid van Nederlandsche en Indische financiën?", *De Indische Gids* XXII (1900), pp. 697-708 and 1142-9.

2 J. S. Furnivall, *Progress and welfare in Southeast Asia* (New York, 1941), p. 38.

3 J. J. Schrieke, *De Indische Politiek* (Amsterdam, 1929), p. 10.

4 Quoted in H. A. Idema, *Parlementaire Geschiedenis van Nederlandsch Indië 1891-1918* ('s-Gravenhage, 1924), p. 159 ff.

5 C. T. van Deventer, "De eereschuld in het Parlement" (Feb. 1900) and "Indië en de democratie" (April 1902) in H. T. Colenbrander en J. E. Stok-vis, *Leven en Arbeid... op. cit.*, vol. II, pp(48-65 and 88-113.

6 H. J. de Graaf, *Geschiedenis van Indonesië* ('s-Gravenhage/Bandung, 1949), p. 460.

7 This is clearly shown in the reply Van Deventer made to Maurice Chotard at the meeting of the Institut Colonial International in May 1901. See: H. T.

Colenbrander and J. E. Stokvis, *Leven en Arbeid... op. cit.*, vol. I (Amsterdam, 1916), pp. 225-6.

8 P. Brooshooft, *De ethische koers in de koloniale politiek* (Amsterdam, 1901), pp. 9-25.

9 Koloniaal-Economische Bijdragen (I) *Overzicht van den Economischen toestand der Inlandsche Bevolking van Java en Madoera...* door Mr. C. Th. van Deventer met aanhangsel: *De voornaamste industrieën der Inlandsche Bevolking van Java en Madoera* door G. P. Rouffaer, (II) *De Financiën van Nederlandsch-Indië* door Dr. E. B. Kielstra, and (III) *Beschouwingen en voorstellen ter verbetering van den Economischen toestand der Inlandsche Bevolking van Java en Madoera* door Mr. D. Fock ('s-Gravenhage, 1904).

9A Idema, *op. cit.*, p. 167.

10 W. J. A. Kernkamp, "Regeering en Islam", *Daar Werd Wat Groots Verricht* (Amsterdam, 1941), p. 206.

11 W. P. D. de Wolff van Westerrode, "Eene credietinstelling voor Inlanders", *Tijdschrift voor Nijverheid en Landbouw* LVI (1899), 35 ff.

12 Conversation with Abdoel Moeis, Bandung, June 5, 1952.

13 Raden Adjeng Kartini, *Door duisternis tot licht* ('s-Gravenhage, 1912). English translation under title *Letters of a Javanese Princess* (London, 1921).

14 Unfortunately Abendanon has written no major work setting forth his ideas, but samplings of his thought can be found in the following places: Introduction to Kartini's letters, a chapter on education in *Neerlands Indië* vol. 2 under editorship of H. Colijn, in the meetings of the *Indisch Genootschap* of March 27, 1906 (pp. 146-8), February 14, 1911 (pp. 172-4), and November 16, 1914 (pp. 20-2).

15 "Een dankbare herinnering aan wijlen Mr. J. H. Abendanon", *Oedaya* (Feb., 1926).

16 G. A. M. Meijer, "Een bestuursambtenaar, die veel voor den Inlander deed", *De Indische Gids* XLII (1920), pp. 507-36, and F. Fokkens, "Onze naaste plicht ten aanzien van de Inlandsche bevolking op Java en daarbuiten, naar aanleiding van de Indische begrooting voor 1903", *Indisch Genootschap*, 11 November 1902, pp. 79-106, also his *Bescheiden wenken voor de verbetering van den economischen toestand der Inlandsche bevolking op Java en daar buiten* ('s-Gravenhage, 1904).

17 P. H. Fromberg, *Verspreide Geschriften* (Leiden, 1926).

18 Brooshooft, *op. cit.*, p. 7.

18a *Encyclopaedie van Nederlandsch-Indië* (2d printing), vol. I, p. 67.

19 H. Colijn, who firmly opposed the progressive notions, spoke of "the influence of the association idea spoiling the belief in our calling...", *Staatkundige Hervormingen in Nederlandsch Indië* (Kampen, 1918), p. 11.

20 W. Walraven, *Op de Grens* (Amsterdam, 1952), *passim*.

21 D. A. Rinkes, "Oude en nieuwe stroomingen onder de bevolking", *Indisch Genootschap*, 18 November 1916, pp. 63-4.

22 See: [G. L. Gonggrijp Sr.], *Honderd brieven van opheffer aan het Bataviaasch Handelsblad* (Batavia, 1913), *passim*.

23 See especially S. J. Rutgers, *Indonesië*, 2 volumes (Amsterdam, 1947).

24 G. Gonggrijp, *Schets eener economische geschiedenis van Nederlandsch-Indië* (Haarlem, 1928), p. 196.

25 G. H. van der Kolff, "European Influence on Native Agriculture", *The Effect of Western Influence on the Malay Archipelago* (Batavia, 1929), pp. 123–5. See also: G. Gonggrijp, *Over de invloed van het westerse grootbedrijf op de inheemse samenleving in Nederlands-Indië* (Haarlem, 1930), pp. 15–18.

26 J. H. Benjamin, *Opmerkingen over de suikercultuur en omtrent hetgeen gedaan kan worden, om de inlandsche bevolking in de gouvernementslanden van Java, speciaal voor zoover zij den landbouw beoefent, vooruit te brengen*. [Overgedrukt uit de April/Mei-aflevering van het *Tijdschrift voor Nijverheid en Landbouw in Ned. Indië*, deel LXXVI] (Batavia, 1908), pp. 107–9.

27 Ki Hadjar Dewantara, *Een en ander over "Nationaal Onderwijs" en het Instituut "Taman Siswà" te Jogjakarta* (Jogjakarta, 1935), pp. 4–5, complains bitterly of the attachment and dependence of the Indonesian to Western ways of action and thought.

28 "Conventions avec des Princes Indigènes de l'Archipel des Indes Orientales", *Bibliothèque Coloniale Internationale* 4me Serie, Tome I, Le Régime des protectorats (1899), pp. 67–143.

29 E. Moresco, "De Inlandsche zelfbesturen en de rechterlijke organisatie", *De Indische Gids* XXV (1903), p. 535.

30 C. Lulofs, "Gezagsuitbreiding", *De Indische Gids* XXVIII (1906), pp. 1342–54.

31 Moresco, *op. cit.*, *Ind. Genootschap* (1908), pp. 210–1, also see N. Adriani, "De Hoofden der Toradja's van Midden-Celebes", *Indisch Genootschap*, 16 Februari 1916, p. 108.

32 J. de Louter, *Handleiding Staats- en Administratief Recht van Nederlandsch Indië* 4e druk ('s-Gravenhage, 1895), footnote p. 158. See also J. M. Somer, *De korte verklaring* (Breda, 1934), pp. 295–8.

33 Emerson, *op. cit.*, pp. 394–8.

34 The first positive example of the new policy of securing a hold over the outer islands was the Lombok Expedition of 1894.

35 F. H. Visman, "Staatkundige ontwikkeling van Indonesië", *Vijftig Jaren: Officieel Gedenkboek* (Amsterdam, 1948), p. 458.

36 D. Fock, "Decentralisatie in Nederlands-Indië", *De Indische Gids* XXII (1900), pp. 153–73.

37 Idema, *op. cit.*, pp. 164–5.

38 *Verslag van de Commissie tot herziening van de Staatsinrichting van Nederlandsch-Indië ingesteld bij Gouvernementsbesluit van den 17en December 1918 No. 1.* (Weltevreden, 1920), pp. 30–1. (Henceforth *Verslag Herziening Commissie*).

39 J. J. Schrieke, *Ontstaan en groei der stads- en landgemeenten in Nederlandsch-Indië* (Amsterdam, 1918), pp. 73–4.

40 A. B. Cohen Stuart, "Hedendaagsch decentralisatiewerk in Neder-landsch-Indië", *Leiding* I (1931), pp. 208–10.

41 *25 Jaren Decentralisatie in Nederlandsch-Indië, 1905–1930* (Semarang, 1930?), p. 14 ff.

42. J. T. Petrus Blumberger, "De Sarekat Islam, en hare beteekenis voor den Bestuursambtenaar", *Koloniaal Tijdschrift* VIII (1919), p. 280.

43 Circular No. 2014, August 22, 1913.

44 P. H. Fromberg, *Verspreide Geschriften* (Leiden, 1926), p. 542.

45 E. A. A. van Heekeren, "Nederlandsch Oost-Indië in 1914", *De Indische Gids* XXXVII (1915), pp. 145–6.

46 Colenbrander and Stokvis, *Leven en Arbeid van Mr. C. Th. van Deventer, op. cit.* II, p. 421.

47 *Gedenkboek M.O.S.V.I.A., op. cit.*, p. 23.

48 M. S. Koster, "De opleiding der Inlandsche administratieve en rechter-lijke ambtenaren op Java en Madoera", *Indisch Genootschap*, 19 Januari 1904, p. 16.

49 Djajadiningrat, *op. cit.*, p. 62 ff.

50 Furnivall, *op. cit.*, p. 76, gives the figure of 19 non-Europeans in European secondary schools in the East Indies.

51 Before being sent to Holland to study, Hoessein, through his brother Achmad, had asked the government if he could be placed in a judical post if he studied law in Europe. The government issued a decree making this possible. However, Hoessein studied Liberal Arts instead because he found the naturalization clause of the decree too limiting. *De Indische Gids* XXVIII (1906), pp. 432–3.

52 Djajadiningrat, *Herinneringen, op. cit.*, pp. 62 and 263.

53 Conversation with R. A. A. Wiranatakusumah, Bandung, March 6, 1952.

54 Furnivall, *op. cit.*, p. 79, states that in 1900 there were five Indonesians studying in Holland.

55 Conversation with P. A. A. Koesoemo Joedo, The Hague, January 10, 1952.

56 Parada Harahap, *Riwajat Dr. A. Rivai* (Medan, 1939), pp. 9–10.

57 Conversation with Abdoel Moeis, Bandung, June 5, 1952.

58 Furnivall, *loc. cit.*, sets the number at twenty-three.

59 Conversation with Prof. R. M. Wreksodiningrat, Jogjakarta, May 29, 1952.

60 J. van Gelderen, "Maatschappelijke veranderingen in Indië in de na-oorlogsjaren", *De Vakbeweging* (Mei, 1927), p. 201.

61 *Ontwikkeling van het Geneeskundig Onderwijs... op. cit.*, p, 26.

62 *Ibid.*, p. 19.

63 *Ibid.*, p. 42.

64 *Ibid.*, pp. 43–4.

65 *Ibid.*, p. 54.

66 Conversation with Hadji Agus Salim, Djakarta, March 13, 1952.

67 Conversation with Abdoel Moeis, Bandung, June 5, 1952.

68 W. K. Terhupeiory, "Iets over de Inlandsche geneeskundigen", *Indisch Genootschap*, 28 Januari 1908, pp. 105–6 and 115.

69 Conversation with Dr. Radjiman Widijodiningrat, Djakarta, March 26, 1952.

70 Duyvendak, *op. cit.*, pp. 174–5.

71 Terhupeiory, *op. cit.*, p. 120.

72 Mr. Balfas, *Dr. Tjipto Mangoenkoesoemo: demokrat sedjati* (Djakarta/Amsterdam, 1952), p. 29.

73 Terhupeiory, *op. cit.*, pp. 112–4.

74 Tjokro Adi Koesoemo, *op. cit.*, pp. 456–64, gives an account of one of the organizations of prijaji which preceded the Budi Utomo.

75 "Boedi Oetama", *De Indische Gids* XXX (1908), pp. 1417–8.

76 Duyvendak, *op. cit.*, p. 173.

77 B. J. Haga, *Indonesische en Indische democratie* (Den Haag, 1924), pp. 123–6 and 207.

78 *Ibid.*

79 A. C. Kruijt, *Het Animisme in den Indischen Archipel* ('s-Gravenhage, 1906).

80 Rinkes, "Oude en nieuwe...", *op. cit.*, p. 59.

81 A. van Velsen, "Eenige opmerkingen over de cultureele verhouding Indonesië-Nederland", *De Gids* CX, No. 4 (1947), pp. 165–6. The Javanese is not conscious of his culture; he is his culture, he lives it...

82 "Boedi Oetama", *De Indische Gids* XXX (1908), p. 1417.

83 Some of the Javanese prijaji were, in the years just preceding the formation of the Boedi Oetomo, forming clubs and organizations directed at self-improvement and reorientation with the Western concepts penetrating their lives. Tjokro Adi Koesoemo, *op. cit.*, passim.

84 L. M. Sitorus, *Sedjarah Pergerakan Kebangsaan Indonesia* (Djakarta, 1947), p. 9.

85 *Ibid.*

86 The circular announcing the First Javanese Congress is reproduced in *Soembangsih: Gedenkboek Boedi-Oetomo 1908 — 20 Mei — 1918* (Amsterdam, 1918), p. 15.

87 "De Javanenbond", *De Indische Gids* XXX (1908), p.1563.

88 Balfas, *op. cit.*, p. 43 ff.

89 *Ibid.*, p. 44.

90 Terhupeiory, *op. cit.*, pp. 116–7.

91 Balfas, *op. cit.*, pp. 28 and 45–7.

92 Goenawan Mangoenkoesoemo, "Boedi Oetomo in de Periode 1908–1918", *Soembangsih*, pp. 17–25.

93 A. Cabaton, *Java, Sumatra, and the other islands of the Dutch East Indies* (London, 1911), p. 151.

94 *Soembangsih*, p. 34.

95 For sketches out of his life as well as a view of his personality see: E. F. E. Douwes Dekker, *70 Jaar Konsekwent* (Bandung, 1950), *passim*.

96 Sitorus, *op. cit.*, p. 12.

97 E. F. E. Douwes Dekker, "Aansluiting tusschen Blank en Bruin", Reden uitgesproken te Batavia op 12(?) December 1911 (Batavia, 1912), *passim*. and *Een Sociogenetische Grondwet: een der hoeksteenen voor het gebouw onzer revolutionaire maatschappij* (Semarang, n.d.), *passim*.

98 E. F. E. Douwes Dekker, *De Indische Partij, haar wezen en haar doel* [Herdrukt uit *De Expres*] gevolgd door de op 25 December 1912, gearresteerde Statuten der Partijen en het verslag der Constitutievergadering op dien datum (Bandoeng, 1913), pp. 1–33.

99 Sitorus, *op. cit.*, p. 13.

100 Van der Plas, "De maatschappelijke...", *op. cit.*, p. 567.

101 In 1913 the Indische Partij claimed 7300 Indo-European and 1500 Indonesian members. Balfas, *op. cit.*, p. 51.

102 Sitorus, *loc. cit.*

103 *Ons Standpunt* ('s-Gravenhage, 1913). Reprint out of *De Expres* of an audience which G. G. Idenburg granted the three leaders of the Indische Partij, March 13, 1913.

104 E. F. E. Douwes Dekker, *Het Jaar 1913 in zijn beteekenis voor de Indische Beweging* (Schiedam, 1914).

105 *Onze Verbanning:* Publicatie der Officiëele Bescheiden, toegelicht met Verslagen en Commentaren, betrekking hebbende op de Gouvernements-Besluiten van den 18en Augustus 1913, nos. 1a en 2a, regelen- de de toepassing van artikel 47 R.R. (interneering) op E. F. E. Douwes Dekker, Tjipto Mangoenkoesoemo en R. M. Soewardi Soerjaningrat (Schiedam, 1913). See also: E. F. E. Douwes Dekker, Tjipto Mangoenkoesoemo en R. M. Suardy Suryaningrat, *Mijmeringen van Indiërs over Hollands Feestvierdag in de Kolonie* (Vlugschriften van het Comité Boemi Poetra No. 2) (Schiedam, 1913), pp. 1–33.

106 J. Habbema, "Een pleidooi voor het Inlandsch Onderwijs", *De Indische Gids* XXII (1900), p. 844.

107 K. Neijs, *Westerse acculturisatie en Oosters volksonderwijs* (Leiden, 1945), pp. 219–20.

108 *Ibid.*, p. 221.

109 J. E. Jasper, "Het Inlandsch Volksonderwijs op Java", *Indisch Genootschap*, 1 November 1910, pp. 2–3.

110 Idema, *op. cit.*, p. 196.

111 *Ibid.*

112 Snouck Hurgronje, *op. cit.*, p. 289.

113 J. H. Abendanon, "Het onderwijs in Nederlandsch India", *Neerlands Indië*, vol. II (Amsterdam, 1912), p. 269.

114 *Ind. Stbl.* 1906, No. 241.

115 K. F. Creutzberg, "Enkele grepen uit de Indische onderwijspolitiek", *Indisch Genootschap*, 19 Januari 1923, p. 7 ff.

116 Fromberg, *op. cit.*, p. 538 is one of the more optimistic persons on the value of the village schools, for he regards them as a symbol of the fact that education is not reserved for a privileged few.

117 Jasper, *op. cit.*, p. 3. "The Second Class Native School gives the students the power to think logically... It gives him the power of associative thought... It forms in the brightest students the beginnings of a desire for higher intellectual development."

118 *Ibid.*, p. 4.

119 G. Gonggrijp, "The economic position of the indigenous population", *The Asiatic Review* XXIII (1927), p. 23.

120 A brilliant discussion of the difficulties involved for the Indonesians in the breakdown of their traditional cultural pattern is contained in: C. A. O. van Nieuwenhuijze, *Mens en vrijheid in Indonesië* ('s-Gravenhage/Bandung, 1949), pp. 102-112.

121 M. Vastenhouw, "Inleiding tot de vooroorlogse paedagogische problemen van Indonesië", *Indonesische Paedagogische Monografieën* No. 1 (Groningen/Djakarta, 1949), pp. 23-6. This pamphlet contains the statistics and concepts with regard to education which are used throughout the remainder of this essay. It will not be cited again except to substatiate direct quotations.

122 Slotemaker de Bruïne, *op. cit.*, pp. 126-7. "It is generally recognized that the difference between 'Western' and 'Native' education is only a matter of language of instruction and the quantity of material presented... ...all education which emanates from the government is Western in spirit."

123 W. H. Vliegen in the Netherlands' Parliament in 1911 quoted in Idema, *op. cit.*, p. 255.

124 Idema, *op. cit.*, p. 240.

125 *Ibid.*, p. 241.

126 *Verslag omtrent de verdere voorbereiding eener hervorming van het bestuurswezen in Nederlandsch-Indië* (Weltevreden, 1914), *passim.* This report is based on the findings of S. de Graaff who from 1910-14 was Government Commissioner for investigating the administrative system. Of the proposals he makes, Regency Councils and *ontvoogding* (detutelization) were put into plan or operation by 1920.

127 D. H. Burger, "Structuurveranderingen in de Javaanse samenleving", *Indonesië* II (1948/49), p. 398.

128 *Ind. Stbl.* 1903, Nos. 337, 402 and 403.

129 *Bijblad op het Staatsblad van Nederlandsch Indië* 1906, No. 6462 (Henceforth *Bijblad*).

130 Gonggrijp, *op. cit.*, p. 200.

131 W. F. Lutter, "De loemboeng-desa in de Afdeeling Grobogan", *Tijdschrift voor het Binnenlandsch Bestuur* XXVIII (1905), p. 342.

132 In fifteen years of operation there were almost 10,000 *lumbung* (grain sheds) in Java and Madura with more than six million guilders in rice. *Encyclopaedie van Nederlandsch-Indië* IV, p. 606.

133 In fifteen years of operation there were about 2,000 desa banks in Java and Madura with a capital of almost two million guilders. *Ibid.*

134 "Een inlandsch controleur B. B.", *De Indische Gids* XXIX (1907), p. 1874.

135 Conversation with P. A. A. Koesoemo Joedo, The Hague, January 10, 1952.

136 A. D. A. de Kat Angelino, *Staatkundig beleid en bestuurszorg in Nederlandsch-Indië*, vol. II ('s-Gravenhage, 1930), p. 384.

137 *Encyclopaedie van Nederlandsch-Indië* II, p. 524.

138 G. J. Vink, "De Inheemsche Landbouw", *Daar Werd Wat Groots Verricht* (Amsterdam, 1941), p. 364.

139. *Encyclopaedie van Nederlandsch-Indië* III, pp. 160-1.

140 Colenbrander and Stokvis, *Leven en Arbeid van Mr. C. Th. van Deventer, op. cit.* II, p. 406.

141 Moresco, *Indisch Genootschap* (1908), *loc. cit.*

142 *Publicaties Hollandsch-Inlandsch Onderwijs-Commissie, No. 6A*, p. 18 ff. Chart on p. 23 shows following native employment in European enterprises as of approximately 1928.

	Office Personnel	Remaining Personnel
Positions which require Dutch language	2,677	923
Positions which require literacy	8,438	22,650
Positions which can be filled by illiterates	973	88,096

143 J. E. Jasper, "Ambachtsscholen voor Inlanders", *De Indische Gids* XXIX (1907), pp. 674-5, points to the need for consciously and purposely drawing Indonesians with vocational training out of the orbit of their villages.

144 Schrieke, "Native Society...", *op. cit.*, pp. 239-40.

145 *Ind. Stbl.* 1893, No. 186, ran a test case in Pasuruan. Thereafter numerous 'feudal services' were eliminated or reduced although they were not entirely abolished and replaced by a head tax until 1916. *Encyclopaedie van Nederlandsch-Indië* II, pp. 79-80.

146 Heerendiensten (feudal or vertical services) were regulated by the Fundamental Law of 1854 (Regeerings Reglement) Article 57 as amended, but, as P. Kleintjes, *Staatsinstellingen van Nederlandsch-Indië* II, 63 (Amsterdam, 1933), pp. 386-7, points out, nothing was said regarding village services. Evidently the distinction between *heerendiensten* and *desadiensten* was not clear to some people about 1903. See also F. Fokkens, "Voortvarendheid der Indische Regering", *De Indische Gids* XXVI (1904), p. 30.

147 C. J. Hasselman, *Eindverslag over het onderzoek naar den druk der Dessa-diensten* (1905), p. 86.

148 Burger, *op. cit.*, p. 233.

149 *Ind. Stbl.* 1906, No. 83, Article 8, Part 1.

150 *Ibid.*, Article 4.

151 *Ibid.*, Article 3; 5; 8, Part 3; 9, Part 2; 11; 12, Part 2; 15, and 18.

152 *Ibid.*, Articles 5, 7, and 10.

153 *Ibid.*, Articles 16 and 17.

154 *Bijblad* 24 November 1906, No. 6576.

155 Quoted in Furnivall, *op. cit.*, p. 294.

156 R. A. Kern, "De Inlandsche Gemeente-Ordonnantie", *De Indische Gids* XXVIII (1906), 1473–88.

157 Petrus Blumberger, "De Sarekat Islam, en hare beteekenis...", *op. cit.*, p. 280.

158 Furnivall, *op. cit.*, p. 383.

159 G. L. Gonggrijp, Sr., *op. cit.*, see especially letters 32, 39 and 42.

160 J. W. Meijer Ranneft, "Scheiding van bestuur en politierechtspraak op Java", *Koloniaal Tijdschrift* VI (1917), pp. 897–916.

161 J. W. Meijer Ranneft, "Reglementeering van zachten dwang", *Tijd-schrift voor het Binnenlandsch Bestuur* IXL (1910), pp. 57–70.

162 J. H. Nieuwenhuijs, "Kan het aantal Controleurs bij het Binnenlandsch Bestuur op Java en Madoera worden ingekrompen?", *De Indische Gids* XXX (1908), pp. 581–93.

163 H. Carpentier Alting, *loc. cit.*

164 Van der Plas, "De maatschappelijke...", *op. cit.*, pp. 558–9.

165 *Verslag betreffende het onderzoek in zake de Saminbeweging, ingesteld ingevolge het G. B. van 1 Juni 1917, No. 20,* See also: *Encyclopaedie van Nederlandsch-Indië* III, 2e druk, p. 684, "De Saminbeweging", *De Indische Gids* XLI (1919), pp. 1309–10, Tjipto Mangoenkoesoemo, *Het Saminisme* (Semarang, 1918), and J. Bijleveld, "De Saminbeweging", *Koloniaal Tijdschrift* XII (1923), pp. 10–24.

166 Visman, *loc. cit.*

167 Raden Achmad: "The people have joined the Sarekat Islam because they seek justice. They have sought it vainly from their traditional chiefs."; and R. Soedjono: "This [the Sarekat Islam] is more than an economic or moral movement; it means the natives are seeking justice which they find nowhere." (1914) quoted in Fromberg, *op. cit.*, p. 543.

168 Letter from Dr. N. Adriani quoted in Idema, *op. cit.*, p. 284. See also Fromberg, *op. cit.*, p. 543.

169 G. J. Lammers, *A. W. F. Idenburg: in zijn leven en werken geschetst* (Amsterdam, 1935), pp. 19 and 26.

170 Idema, *op, cit.*, p. 242.

171 *Ibid.*, pp. 252–3.

172 "Licht en Donker: De Indisch Ontwerp", *De Locomotief*, July 9, 1912.

173 Lammers, *op. cit.*, p. 27.

174 Van der Plas, "De maatschappelijke...", *op. cit.*, p. 562.

175 Van der Plas, "Mededeelingen...", *op. cit.*, p. 260.

176 Kwee Tek Hoy writing in Ho Po, quoted in *De Indische Gids* XXVIII (1906), pp. 88–9.

177 Conversation with Dr. Yap Hong Tjoen, The Hague, November 19, 1951.

178 *Ibid.*

179 Conversation with Hadji Agus Salim, Djakarta, April 8, 1952.

180 "Arabische scholen", *De Indische Gids* XXX (1908), 1251–2.

181 J. T. Petrus Blumberger, *De Nationalistische Beweging in Nederlandsch Indië* (Haarlem, 1931), p. 92.

182 The influence of Jam Yat Khair on the Budi Utomo and Sarekat Islam is difficult to determine. Hadji Salim felt that many B.U. and S.I. members had formerly been members of the Jam Yat Khair, but no other evidence in this regard has been uncovered. Conversation, Djakarta, April 8, 1952.

183 Amelz, *H. O. S. Tjokroaminoto, Hidup dan Perdjuanannja* I (Djakarta, 1952), pp. 88–9.

184 Statutory Regulation of November 9, 1911 given in *Encyclopaedie van Nederlandsch-Indië* III, p. 695.

185 Petrus Blumberger, *op. cit.*, pp. 56–7.

186 Conversation with Abdoel Moeis, Bandung, June 18, 1952.

187 Conversation with Hadji Agus Salim, Ithaca, New York, April 1953.

188 Petrus Blumberger, *op. cit.*, pp. 58–9.

189 Fromberg, *op. cit.*, p. 547.

190 Tjokroaminoto: "The Sarekat Islam uses religion like a rope, as a means to bind, and what is wanted, all-out progress, is not hindered by that religion." quoted in Fromberg, *op. cit.*, p. 545.

191 J. E. Stokvis, "Van Limburg Stirum", *Indonesië* I (1948), p. 19. Also: Conversation with Prof. Dr. R. A. Hoessein Djajadiningrat, Djakarta, August 12, 1952.

192 Letter from G. G. Idenburg to Min. of Colonies De Waal Malefijt on January 9, 1911 quoted in F. L. Rutgers, *Idenburg en de Sarekat Islam in 1913* (Amsterdam, 1939), p. 36.

193 Letter from G. G. Idenburg to Min. of Colonies De Waal Malefijt on November 12, 1911 quoted in Rutgers, *loc. cit.*

194 Petrus Blumberger, *op. cit.*, p. 61.

195 Conversation with P. J. A. Idenburg, The Hague, November 19, 1951.

196 Organizations with legal status which deviated from their statutes might be subject to legal prosecution. Fromberg, *op. cit.*, p. 541.

In 1913 there had been disturbances caused by local Sarekat Islam groups in Tangerang, Meester-Cornelis (Djatinegara), Indramaju, Cheribon, Tuban and Sapudi which would have placed a central body in a difficult legal position. *Verslag Herziening Commissie*, p. 295.

197 Accusations of 'divide and rule' politics designed to crush the formation of a united people under the guidance of the Sarekat Islam have been brought forward by some Indonesians: see Sitorus, *op. cit.*, p. 16. These arguments make better propaganda than history.

198 Letter of July 4, 1913 quoted in Rutgers, *op. cit.*, p. 54.

199 Fromberg, *op. cit.*, p. 543.

200 Idema, *op. cit.*, p. 279.

201 *Ind. Stbl.* 1909, No. 238 and 1913, No. 524.

202 Idema, *op. cit.*, p. 282.

203 In large measure the return of prosperity was due to budgetary regulations which permitted the East Indies to arrange her own loans for unusual expenditures. See: "Licht en Donker: De Indisch Ontwerp", *De Locomotief*, July 20, 1913.

204 *Onderzoek naar de Mindere Welvaart der Inlandsche Bevolking op Java en Madoera.* 10 volumes. Batavia, 1905–1914.

CHAPTER III

1 J. H. Carpentier Alting and W. de Cock Buning, *The Effect of the War upon the Colonies* [The Netherlands and the World War, vol. III] (New Haven, 1928), pp. 64–5 and 109–111.

2 Cecile Rothe, "De Nijverheid", *Daar Werd Wat Groots Verricht* (Amsterdam, 1941), p. 380.

3 "De Javasche Bank in 1918", *De Indische Gids* XLI (1919), 1287.

4 B. H. M. Vlekke, *Nusantara: a history of the East Indian archipelago* (Cambridge, Mass., 1943), p. 328. See also: G. Gonggrijp, *Over de invloed van het westerse grootbedrijf... op. cit.*, p. 5.

5 In 1919 the following indigenous enterprises were in operation:

Type of Indigenous Enterprise	Number of Enterprises	Number of Employees
Brick and tile bakeries	904	3,458
Lime kilns	247	1,210
Rice mills	214	232
Smiths	659	1,476
Gold Smiths	298	188
Carpentry shops	325	209
Textile and batik enterprises	362	6,139
Shoemakers	67	287
Tailors	138	88

This must be compared to 5,703 non-indigenous enterprises employing 323,707 indigenous personnel. *Mededeelingen omtrent enkele onderwerpen...* (1920), *op. cit.*, p. 96.

6 C. Snouck Hurgronje, "Een belangrijk document betreffende den heiligen oorlog van de Islam (1914) en eene officiëele correctie", *Bijdragen tot de Taal-, Land- en Volkenkunde van Nederlandsch-Indië* LXXIII (1917), 255–84.

7 Numerous short contributions in the polemical journal *De Indische Gids* during the war years point up the Japanese threat (See Note 52, below).

8 One aspect of this Western cultural problem is displayed in the short-lived magazine, *Orient* (1923–25), in which such Western thinkers as Romain Rolland, Bertrand Russell, AE (G. W. Russell), Don Miguel de Unamuno and others express their fear of Western collapse unless some form of cultural synthesis with Asia is achieved.

9 Conversation with Hadji Agus Salim, Ithaca, New York, May 1953.

10 Much of the biographical information given in the following pages on persons associated with the early Sarekat Islam has been obtained from a secret government report prepared by the Adjunct adviser for Native Affairs, D. Rinkes. *Bescheiden betreffende de Vereeniging Sarekat Islam.* Zeer Geheime Missive van den Adviseur voor Inlandsche Zaken aan den Gouverneur-General, 13 Mei 1913, No. 46.

11 Conversation with Abdoel Moeis, Bandung, June 18, 1952.

12 Balfas, *op. cit.*, pp. 1–8.

13 W. de Cock Buning, "De Indische Beweging van den economischen kant", *De Opbouw* (July, 1924), 4.

14 Conversation with R. A. A. Wiranatakusumah, Bandung, March 6, 1952.

15 Archive Van Limburg Stirum, Folio 35, Letter from Regent of Tjandjur, Wiranatakusumah, to Mr. Filet, November 1, 1919.

16 *Ibid.*

17 *Verslag Herziening Commissie, op. cit.*, p. 297 (See also above, p. 163).

18 Archive Van Limburg Stirum, Folio 19, Letter from F. A. Liefrinck to Van Limburg Stirum, December 26, 1917. Written while investigating conditions in Besoeki (Java), this letter points to the justice of many of the S. I. grievances and the recalcitrant attitude of the civil administrators.

19 Personality sketch based upon talks with A. C. D. de Graeff, F. M. van Asbeck, Th. B. Fruin and J. E. Stokvis — May–July, 1949.

20 *Javasche Courant*, 28 Maart 1916, no. 25.

21 Conversation with Hadji Agus Salim, Ithaca, New York, May 1953.

22 Conversation with Hadji Agus Salim, Ithaca, New York, April 1953.

23 Conversation with Hadji Agus Salim, Ithaca, New York, May 1953.

24 Petrus Blumberger, *op. cit.*, p. 76.

25 Conversation with Abdoel Moeis, Bandung, June 18, 1952.

26 *Verslag Herziening Commissie, op. cit.*, p. 295. See also: Van Heekeren, *op. cit.*, p. 147.

27 Looking only at the leaders of revolutionary socialism, Sneevliet had come to work with the government railways, Brandsteder was in charge of

the government naval buildings in Surabaya, Baars was a teacher and was later employed as an engineer by the Department of Public Works (B.O.W.) in Semarang, and Van Burink was a teacher at a European primary school.

28 *Javasche Courant*, 19 Februari 1909, no. 14 and 22 November 1912, no. 94. See also: "Vereeniging van Spoor- en Tramweg-personeel in N.-I.", *De Indische Gids* XXXI (1909), 1240–1.

29 *Javasche Courant*, 28 April 1911, no. 34.

30 *Ibid.*, 31 December 1912, no. 105.

31 *Ibid.*, 17 November 1916, no. 92.

32 *Ibid.*, 21 Januari 1916, no. 6.

33 *Ibid.*, 23 Februari 1917, no. 16.

34 *Ibid.*, 16 November 1917, no. 92.

35 Petrus Blumberger, *op. cit.*, p. 106.

36 Sarekat Islam Congres (1e Nationaal Congres) 17–24 Juni 1916 te Bandoeng. [Behoort bij de Geheime Missive van den Wd. Adviseur voor Inlandsche Zaken dd. 29 September 1916, No. 226.]

37 *Ibid.*, p. 1.

38 Djajadiningrat, *Herinneringen... op. cit.*, p. 286.

39 Archive Van Limburg Stirum, Folio 20, Supplement to the investigation of the Garut Affair, July 26, 1919.

40 Sarekat Islam Congres (1e...), *loc. cit.*

41 Sarekat Islam Congres (1e...), *op. cit.*, p. 62.

42 Sarekat Islam Congres (1e...), *op. cit.*, p. 3.

43 *Ibid.*, p. 7. Vlekke, *op. cit.*, p. 339, translates this as "Cooperation with the government for the welfare of the Indies", which makes for more readable English but is not exactly the way Tjokroaminoto said it.

44 Sarekat Islam Congres (1e...), *op. cit.*, pp. 8–10.

45 *Ibid.*, pp. 13–14.

46 See speech of G. de Raad, *De Indische Gids* XLI (1919), 1160–1163.

47 *Ind. Stbl.* 1917, no. 114.

48 Sarekat Islam Congres (1e...), *op. cit.*, p. 32.

49 *Ibid.*, p. 36.

50 *Ibid.*, p. 20.

51 Archive Van Limburg Stirum, Folio 6, Letter from Pleyte to Van Limburg Stirum, August 29, 1916.

52 Any number of newspaper articles around 1916 pointed up the Japanese threat. As a sampling: "Japan begeerig naar Java en Sumatra", "Tegen het Japansche gevaar", "De verdediging van Indië", and "Indie's verdediging", *De Indische Gids* XXXVIII (1916), 608–18.

53 Van der Plas, "De maatschappelijke...", *op. cit.*, p. 569.

54 "De Oetoesan Hindia over de militieplannen", *De Indische Gids* XXXVII (1915), 75–6.

55 Archive Van Limburg Stirum, Folio 48, Letter from H. 's Jacob to Van

Limburg Stirum, August 4, 1916. See also: O. Collet, *L'Évolution de L'Esprit Indigène aux Indes Orientales Néerlandaises* (Bruxelles, 1921), pp. 76–77.

56 Archive Van Limburg Stirum, Folio 7, Letter from Idenburg to Van Limburg Stirum, May 15, 1917.

57 Conversation with Abdoel Moeis, Bandung, June 5, 1952.

58 Djajadiningrat, *op. cit.*, p. 289.

59 Sarekat Islam Congres (2e Nationaal Congres) 20–27 October 1917. [Behoort bij de Geheime Missive van den Regeeringscommissaris voor In-landsche en Arabische Zaken van 22 Augustus 1918, No. 416.]

60 Djajadiningrat, *Herinneringen...*, *op. cit.*, p. 288.

61 Sarekat Islam Congres (2e...), *op. cit.*, pp. 2–4.

62 *Ibid.*, p. 13. Salim's views on Socialism and Islam are to be found in *Bataviaasch Nieuwsblad*, 18 Augustus 1918, no. 7.

63 Conversation with Hadji Agus Salim, Djakarta, July 18, 1952.

64 Sarekat Islam Congres (2e...), *op cit.*, Bijlage IV, *Neratja*, 25 October 1917, No. 80.

65 "De Sarikat Islam", *Koloniale Studiën* I (1917) (Extra Politiek Nummer), 35–6.

66 Sarekat Islam Congres (2e...), *op. cit.*, p. 5.

67 Neijs, *op. cit.*, pp. 219 and 225.

68 Sarekat Islam Congres (2e...), *op. cit.*, p. 27.

69 Stokvis, *Van Wingewest naar Zelfbestuur in Nederlandsch-Indië* (Amsterdam, 1922), p. 124, feels that the concessions made by the government were in response to the power politics of the native movement. There is little evidence for this view, and one is led to suspect that the radical Stokvis was, at this time (1922), trying too hard to prove that the Ethical Policy ended in 1913, on the assumption that after that time the initiative came from Indonesian groups.

70 Stokvis, "Van Limburg Stirum", *op. cit.*, p. 23.

71 Van der Plas, "De maatschappelijke...", *op. cit.*, p. 566.

72 Conversation with Abdoel Moeis, Bandung, June 5, 1952.

73 Sarekat Islam Congres (2e...), *op. cit.*, pp. 19 and 25.

74 Quite another opinion of Soerjopranoto's actions and character is given by the editor of the Bataviaasch Handelsblad. See *De Indische Gids* XLII (1920), 551.

75 A. Baars en H. Sneevliet, *Het proces Sneevliet. De Sociaal-democratie in Ne-derlandsch-Indië* (Semarang, 1917).

76 Conversation with Darsono, Djakarta, March 12, 1952.

77 Secret letter of Dr. Hazeu quoted in Secret Report, *Overzicht van de gestie der Centraal Sarikat Islam in het jaar 1921* (Weltevreden, 1922), p. 2.

78 *Ibid.*

79 Sarekat Islam Congres (3e Nationaal Congres) 29 September–6 October 1918 te Soerabaya. [Behoort bij de Geheime Missive van den Regeeringscom-

missaris voor Inlandsche en Arabische Zaken van 9 December 1918, No. 599.]

80 *Handelingen Volksraad.* Tweede Gewone Zitting 1919, Bijlagen, onderwerp 4.

81 Sarekat Islam Congres (3d...), *op. cit.*, pp. 2–6.

82 *Ibid.*, p. 12.

83 *Ibid.*, pp. 20–1.

84 *Ibid.*, pp. 22–5.

85 *Ibid.*, p. 30.

86 *Ind. Stbl.* 1918, no. 772.

87 Archive Van Limburg Stirum, Folio 19, Letters from F. A. Liefrinck to Van Limburg Stirum, January 2, March 7, and March 19, 1917.

88 Archive Van Limburg Stirum, Folio 37, Letter from Hazeu to Hulshof Pol, March 2, 1918.

89 Stokvis, "Van Limburg Stirum", *op. cit.*, p. 25.

90 Soekanto, *Het gewas in Indonesië Religieus-Adatrechtelijk Beschouwd* (Leiden, 1933), pp. 13–4, and A. W. Nieuwenhuis, "De godsdienst op Java in zijne oeconomische en politieke beteekenis", *Indisch Genootschap,* 27 Maart 1906, p. 131.

91 For details see: "De Regeering over het verzet te Garoet", *De Indische Gids* XLI (1919), 1269–72.

92 An Indonesian writing in *De Locomotief,* "De Inlandsche beweging", quoted in *De Indische Gids* XLI (1919), 1570–2, tells of reactions in native society.

93 M. W. "De opstand in Leles", *Soer. Hbl.* quoted in *De Indische Gids* XLI (1919), 1303–5. This Social Democratic organ had continuously opposed the government action in the Garut area, Dr. Hazeu in letters to the Governor-General (Archive Van Limburg Stirum, Folio 27) also criticizes the action of the administration.

94 Archive Van Limburg Stirum, Folio 20, Supplement to the investigation of the Garut Affair, July 26, 1919.

95 On *djimat* see Noto Soeroto in *Het Vaderland* and S. Soeriokoesoemo in *Wederopbouw* quoted in *De Indische Gids* XLII (1920), 161–2.

96 Archive Van Limburg Stirum, Folio 27, Letter from Hazeu to Van Limburg Stirum, August 29, 1919. "Hadji Hasan is vain and greedy. He was not a member of the S.I. A change came in him through his son-in-law, Hadji Gadjali. The latter engaged in all sorts of mystic practices (ilmu koe-koesoemahan, i.e., the art of incorporating a spirit in his body, invulnerability, etc.). He was a member of the S.I."

97 "Wat de 'Zaak Hadji Ismail' leerde", *Soer. Hbl.* quoted in *De Indische Gids* XLII (1920), 652–8.

98 Archive Van Limburg Stirum, Folio 32, Letter from Resident Schippers to Van Limburg Stirum, September 17, 1919.

99 Van de Kamer, "De Centraal Sarekat Islam", *Bataviaasch Nieuwsblad* quoted in *De Indische Gids* XLI (1919), 1299–1301.

100 E. J., "Het Garoet-Drama en de Afdeeling B", *De Locomotief* quoted in *De Indische Gids* XLII (1920), 449–58.

101 Archive Van Limburg Stirum, Folio 25, Letter from W. Muurling to Van Limburg Stirum, January 5, 1920. See also: *Overzicht van de Gestie der C.S.I., op. cit.*, pp. 39–40.

102 *Overzicht van de Gestie der C.S.I., op. cit.*, p. 1.

103 *Ind. Stbl.*, 1920, no. 67 and 1921, no. 78.

104 Archive Van Limburg Stirum, Folio 27, Letter from Hazeu to Van Limburg Stirum, November 21, 1918.

105 Archive Van Limburg Stirum, Folio 8, *passim*.

106 About 1920 the *Nationale Bond tegen Revolutie* (National Union against Revolution) was formed in the Netherlands and gained support among Europeans in the East Indies. This organization, among others, issued numerous brochures which overplayed the Communist menace.

107 *Encyclopaedie van Nederlandsch-Indië* V, p. 370.

108 Platoek, "De stand der Inlandsche beweging", in *Bat. Nbl.* quoted in *De Indische Gids* XLI (1919), 1023–7.

109 *Encyclopaedie van Nederlandsch-Indië* VII, p. 430.

110 *Ibid.*

111 *Overzicht van de Gestie der C.S.I., op. cit.*, p. 5.

112 Alimin Prawirodirdjo, *Louteren Wij Ons! — Open Brief aan elk lid van de Sarekat Islam* (Bandoeng, 1919), *passim*.

113 *Encyclopaedie van Nederlandsch-Indië* V, p. 372.

114 *Overzicht van de Gestie der C.S.I., op. cit.*, p. 3.

115 *Encyclopaedie van Nederlandsch-Indië* V, p. 374.

116 Archive Van Limburg Stirum, Folio 33, Letters from Resident Schippers to Van Limburg Stirum, March 30, April 11 and April 16, 1920.

117 Petrus Blumberger, *op. cit.*, p. 137. See also: *Verslag van de arbeidscommissie betreffende de wettelijke vaststelling van Minimumloonen voor werknemers op Java en Madoera* (Weltevreden, 1920).

118 *Overzicht van de Gestie der C.S.I., op. cit.*, p. 4.

119 *Ibid.*   120 *Ibid.*

121 Communists who were held on charges of press excesses or disturbing the peace.

122 In November, Sosrokardono was sentenced to four years in jail for his part in the Section B Affair. The Sarekat Islam had begun a campaign to raise money for his trial, but this was stopped when his brother Rachmat ran off with a large share of the money.

123 Sanoesi was editor of a West Java newspaper, *Sora Merdika* (Voice of Freedom) owned by one Hadji Azhoeri. Both men were linked with the Section B of the Sarekat Islam. A few years later, Sanoesi was instrumental in dissuading Soekarno from joining the Sarekat Islam which the latter seems seriously to have considered doing.

124 Bratanata was a South Sumatran, Tirtodanoedjo, a Javanese who was active in the Djawadipa language movement, and Hadisoebroto, a Javanese who had more cultural than political ambitions. These three men, of the more moderate direction, had been swept along by leftist propaganda and a growing resentment against the government policies, until they were briefly taken into custody in connection with propaganda speeches.

125 *Overzicht van de Gestie der C.S.I.*, *op. cit.*, p. 7.

126 *Encyclopaedie van Nederlandsch-Indië* V, p. 373.

127 *Overzicht van de Gestie der C.S.I.*, *op. cit.*, pp. 8–10.

128 When the Garut Affair was investigated, Sarekat Islam propaganda materials were uncovered which, according to Dr. Hazeu, spoke of the Sarekat Islam as "a paradise, sweet incense, and a delightful garden". This was followed by terms of sexual endearment which were applied to the Sarekat Islam. According to Hazeu this type of propaganda was not unusual. Archive Van Limburg Stirum, Folio 20.

129 J. J. Puister, "Een Javaansch oordeel over den toestand in Indië", in *Algemeen Handelsblad* quoted in *De Indische Gids* XLI (1919), 1573–6.

130 A. K. Pringgodigdo, *Sedjarah pergerakan rakjat Indonesia* (Djakarta, 1950), p. 23. Dr. Tjipto had been permitted to return in 1914 for reasons of health. Douwes Dekker returned in August 1917 and Soewardi in July 1918.

131 Archive Van Limburg Stirum, Folio 25, Letter from W. Muurling to Van Limburg Stirum, June 17, 1919.

132 For concepts of D.D.'s program in 1919 see summary of his speech to Eighth Indiërs Congress. *De Indische Gids* XLI (1919), 1168–9, and his answer to Bergsma, p. 1170.

133 *Ibid.* D.D. speaks of hindering economic development so that progress might occur through the conflict of opposing economic forces. He does not favor forceful revolution, for his association concepts would bring about change before force was necessary.

134 "De z.g. 'Volksbeweging' in Solo", *De Indische Gids* XLI (1919), 1145.

135 "D.D. in het Solosche", in *De Locomotief* quoted in *De Indische Gids* XLI (1919), 1305–6.

136 "Het Achtste Indiërs congres", (Tweede dag, 8 Juni 1919), *De Indische Gids* XLI (1919), 1165.

137 "Kentering?", in *De Telegraaf* quoted in *De Indische Gids* XLI (1919), 1307–8.

138 *Deli Courant* quoted in *De Indische Gids* XLI (1919), 1195.

139 J. T. Koks, *De Indo* (Amsterdam, 1931), p. 261.

140 J. T. Petrus Blumberger, *De Indo-Europeesche Beweging in Nederlandsch-Indië* (Haarlem, 1939), pp. 61–2.

141 Conversation with D. M. G. Koch, Bandung, February 22, 1952. Koch claimed that the only Indos who continued to support Douwes Dekker were

those who had fallen to the level of native life but who still wanted to be regarded as Europeans.

142 Balfas, *op. cit.*, p. 108 ff.

143 Conversation with Mas Darnakoesoema, Bandung, June 27, 1952.

144 Narpowandowo (Sunanate), Prinsenbond Mataram (Sultanate), Darah Mangkoenegaran, and Habdi Dalem Wargo Pakoealam.

145 Rede van Mr. J. P. graaf van Limburg Stirum, 6 november 1925, uitgesproken in het groot-auditorium der Leidsche Hoogeschool. "...among the leading natives in the Volksraad there are persons who can certainly be regarded as representatives of the people; they stand for the rights of the native people. The orientation of the younger civil servants is in general patterned after them..."

145a Rinkes, *Bescheiden...op. cit.* (1913) speaks of Dachlan's school in Jogjakarta already receiving a nominal subsidy which was much appreciated since it showed the government was not limiting its aid to Christian schools. By 1915 it was generally known that the Muhammadijah School was being subsidized.

146 "De Javasche Bank in 1918", *De Indische Gids* XLI (1919), 1284–5. Also see "De Rede van den Gouverneur-Generaal" (May 18, 1920), *De Indische Gids* XLII (1920), 749. "Good harvests and high price of products brought prosperity to quite a large part of the agricultural and commercial population..."

147 Conversation with Sutan Sjahrir, Djakarta, March 28, 1952.

148 Conversation with M. Tabrani, Djatinegara, March 27, 1952.

149 Conversation with Hadji Agus Salim, Djakarta, July 18, 1952. See also: "De theosophie en Boedi-Oetama", *De Indische Gids* XXXI (1909), 534–5.

150 Archive Van Limburg Stirum, Folio 27, Letter from Hazeu to Van Limburg Stirum, November 21, 1918.

151 Conversation with E. Gobée, Leiden, November 17, 1951.

152 Political program of June 1917 quoted in Petrus Blumberger, *op. cit.*, p. 25.

153 Soembangsih, *op. cit., passim.*

154 *Ibid.*, p. 20.

155 *Ibid.*, p. 10.

156 *Ibid.*, pp. 27–48.

157 *Ibid.*, p. 43.

158 The psychological aspects of the shift in educational and thought patterns is nowhere exhaustively treated. However, it is touched upon by Neijs, *op. cit.*, p. 226 ff., who has taken much from Stutterheim, *Mededeeling van het Bureau van de Onderwijs raad* VI (1931), p. 5 ff. This problem is also touched upon by Djajadiningrat, *Herinneringen... op. cit.*, p. 352 and was reinforced by interviews with various Western educated Indonesians, particularly with R. Sastromuljono, (Djakarta) April 9, 1952.

159 C. C. Berg, "Critische beschouwing van Neerlands cultureelen invloed en Neerlands cultureele taak in Oost-Indië", *Indisch Genootschap*, 6 April 1934, p. 283.

160 D. J. A. Westerveld, "De vernederlandsching van het Inlandsch Onderwijs in Nederlandsch-Indië", *De Indische Gids* XXXVII (1915), 305–25.

161 Tan Malaka, *Dari pendjara ke pendjara* I (Djakarta, n.d.), p. 68.

162 J. E. Stokvis, "Uitkomsten en vooruitzichten van den ethischen koers in onze Koloniale Staatkunde", *Indisch Genootschap*, 25 Maart 1919, p. 133.

163 H. J. van Mook, *Indonesië, Nederland en de Wereld* (Amsterdam, 1949), p. 37.

164 Stokvis, *op. cit.*, p. 141. See also his *Van Wingewest naar Zelfbestuur in Nederlandsch-Indië*, p. 117.

165 The government regarded its policy as rather clear cut; namely, "the slow but certain movement toward changing the old bureaucratic authority of this land into a form of government in which representation and responsibility in the administration will be given to the people." Archive Van Limburg Stirum, Folio 15, Bouwstoffen (1920). This in no sense alters the paradoxes which arose, and fails to answer the questions which most persons had concerning the government's policies.

166 "Indische Problemen", *Koloniale Studiën* III (1919), 265–304.

167 Bijblad 1913, no. 8579. See also Kleintjes, *op. cit.*, II, p. 36.

168 H. G. Heijting, "Staat de adel op Java nog steeds aan de spits van het volk?", *De Indische Gids* XLVII (1925), 786.

169 Neijs, *op. cit.*, p. 238 quotes C. O. van der Plas at Tweede Koloniale Onderwijs Congres 1919. Stenografisch Verslag pp. 212–3.

170 *Mededeelingen omtrent enkele onderwerpen van algemeen belang* (Afgesloten, 1 Januari 1920), p. 12.

171 Neijs, *op. cit.*, p. 241.

172 *Overzicht van de Gestie der C.S.I.*, *op. cit.*, p. 50.

173 *Mededeelingen omtrent enkele onderwerpen...* (1920), *op. cit.*, Hoofdstuk XIII "Personeel- en Bezoldigingsvraagstuk", p. 75 ff.

174 *Javasche Courant* 22 Augustus 1913, no. 67.

175 Colenbrander and Stokvis, *Leven en Arbeid van Mr. C. Th. van Deventer*, *op. cit.*, II, pp. 408–9.

176 J. M. Pieters, *De zoogenaamde ontvoogding van het Inlandsch Bestuur* (Wageningen, 1932), pp. 130–1.

177 Djajadiningrat, "De positie van de regenten...", *op. cit.*, p. 88.

178 "Memorie van antwoord nopens het wetsontwerp op de instelling der regentschapsraden", *Handelingen Volksraad*, Tweede gewone zitting 1919, Onderwerp 11, stuk 2.

179 R. A. A. Achmad Djajadiningrat, "Vorst en volk", *Djawa* III (1924), 62–3.

180 Archive Van Limburg Stirum, Folio 8, Telegram from Van Limburg Stirum to Pleyte, April 16, 1918 clearly shows his intention of pushing the Volksraad in the direction of a responsible governing organ.

181 The July 1918 elections resulted in the following arrangement in the Second Chamber of the States General which met in September 1918.

Revolutionary Group	4	Protestant group	20
Social Democrats	22	Christian group	2
Radical Concentration	15	Neutral Group	7
Catholics	30		

182 *Dagverhaal van Mr. Dr. H. H. A. van Gijbland Oosterhoff over de periode 8–15 November 1918* ('s-Gravenhage, 1918).

183 Archive Van Limburg Stirum, Folio 8, Letter from Idenburg to Van Limburg Stirum, December 11, 1918.

184 Archive Ministry of Colonies, Kab. 41. Telegrams November 15, 1918, no. 411 and November 18, 1918, no. 36 from Minister of Colonies to the Governor General.

185 Archive Ministry of Colonies, 923 K32. Telegram November 19, 1918, no. 462 (Secret) from Governor General to the Minister of Colonies.

186 Archive Van Limburg Stirum, Folio 14. Speech of Van Limburg Stirum at installation of the Reform Commission, December 17, 1918.

187 "Rede van den Regeeringsgevolmachtigde, den Heer W. Muurling, in den vergadering van den Volksraad van 2 Juli 1919", *De Indische Gids* XLI (1919), 1258–9.

188 P. J. Oud, *Honderd Jaren (1840–1940)* (Assen, 1946), p. 247.

189 *Ibid.*

190 Archive Van Limburg Stirum, letter December 11, 1918, *op. cit.*

191 Archive Van Limburg Stirum, Folio 9, Letter from Idenburg to Van Limburg Stirum, March 7, 1919.

192 Archive Van Limburg Stirum, letter December 11, 1918, *op. cit.*

193 Archive Van Limburg Stirum, Folio 9. Letter from Idenburg to Van Limburg Stirum, January 17, 1919.

194 Archive Van Limburg Stirum, Folio 10, Letter from Idenburg to Van Limburg Stirum, February 19, 1920.

195 *De Locomotief* quoted in *De Indische Gids* XLII (1920), 152.

196 Archive Van Limburg Stirum, Folio 10, Letter from De Graaff to Van Limburg Stirum, August 25, 1920.

197 The man who stood behind many of the changes formulated during the 1920's was H. Colijn, personally distasteful to Van Limburg Stirum, but a man with wider vision and greater ability than De Graaff.

198 Archive Van Limburg Stirum, Folio 10. Letters from March 12 through October 1, 1920 which De Graaff wrote to, Van Limburg Stirum clearly show the lack of understanding between the two men.

199 Stokvis, "Van Limburg Stirum", *op. cit.*, p. 21.

200 F. van Lith, S. J., *De politiek van Nederland ten opzichte van Nederlandsch-Indië* ('s-Hertogenbosch-Antwerpen, n.d.), p. 28. "The great majority of the Netherlanders in the Indies have grown accustomed to their favored position... they will oppose all efforts at equality with the natives."

201 Archive Van Limburg Stirum, Folios 6–11, *passim*. Numerous letters show the impossibility of finding proper men for the leading positions of government. Many of the highest appointments were desperation choices in order to have the office filled.

202 Archive Van Limburg Stirum, Folio 21, Letter from K. F. Creutzberg to Van Limburg Stirum, March 21, 1920.

203 Archive Van Limburg Stirum, Folio 27, Letters from Hazeu to Van Limburg Stirum, September 1, 1919 and January 10, 1920.

204 Muurling in the Volksraad, July 1919, quoted in *De Indische Gids* XLI (1919), 1256 and 1266.

205 "Redevoering van Zijne Excellentie den Gouverneur-Generaal bij gelegenheid van het openbaar gehoor op 1 September 1919", *De Indische Gids* XLI (1919), 1438–9.

206 The hostility between De Graaff and Van Limburg Stirum reached its culmination and was openly expressed in the final letter which the Governor General sent to the Minister. Archive Van Limburg Stirum, Folio II, January 28, 1921.

207 K. L. Mitchell, *Industrialization of the Western Pacific* (New York, 1942), p. 197.

208 J. van Gelderen, "Maatschappelijke veranderingen in Indië in de na-oorlogsjaren", *De Vakbeweging* (Mei, 1927), 194.

209 G. Angoulvant, *Les Indes Néerlandaises leur role dans l'économie internationale* II (Paris, 1926), pp. 653–9.

210 Archive Van Limburg Stirum, Folio 9, Letter from Idenburg to Van Limburg Stirum, July 23, 1919.

211 "De Rede van den Gouverneur–Generaal", *De Indische Gids* XLII (1920), 750.

212 *Ibid.*, pp. 750–1.

213 *Ibid.*, p. 754. See press comments on speech, *De Indische Gids* XLII (1920), 717–22. The same note prevailed a few months later, See: "Het Openbaar Gehoor op 31 Augustus", *Ibid.*, p. 1058.

214 Furnivall, *op. cit.*, p. 277.

215 Nota III signed by Kan, Kindermann and Welter. *Verslag Herziening Commissie, op. cit.*, pp. 407–28. This particular dissenting view was regarded as the best part of the Report by Minister of Colonies De Graaff. Archive Van Limburg Stirum, Folio 10. Letter of October 1, 1920.

216 Verslag Herziening Commissie, *op. cit.*, p. 1.

217 *Ibid.*, pp. 7–8 and 19.

218 *Ibid.*, p. 8.

219 *Ibid.*, pp. 9–12, 18 and 59.

220 *Ibid.*, pp. 15–6.

221 *Ibid.*, p. 13. See also C. van Vollenhoven, "De ontvoogding van Indië, samenhang der maatregelen en plannen", *Indisch Genootschap*, 24 October 1919, p. 177.

222 Verslag Herziening Commissie, *op. cit.*, pp. 39–43.

223 Vlekke, *op. cit.*, p. 48. The term 'association' was coming ever more in practice to mean really 'Assimilation'. Van Eerde, *op. cit.*, p. 170, makes the point that the constant flow of new and fresh persons from the Netherlands worked against the creation of a viable, composite culture which would really be 'association' in its best sense.

224 Verslag Herziening Commissie, *op. cit.*, p. 33 ff.

225 Koninklijk Besluit van 20 December 1918.

226 Oud, *loc. cit.*

CHAPTER IV

1 Conversation with Hadji Agus Salim, Ithaca, New York, May 1952.

2 *Overzicht van de Gestie der C.S.I.*, *op. cit.*, p. 11. According to this report Salim had formulated the new Islamic-socialistic basis for the Sarekat Islam in correspondence with Hasan Djajadiningrat, who had died in December 1920.

3 *Overzicht van de Gestie der C.S.I.*, *op. cit.*, p. 13.

4 *Ibid.*, p. 16.

5 Petrus Blumberger, *op. cit.*, pp. 30 and 74.

6 Tan Malaka, *op. cit.*, pp. 19–46.

7 *Handelingen Volksraad*, Eerste Buitengewone Zitting 1921, pp. 28–72 and 79–124.

8 Petrus Blumberger, *op. cit.*, pp. 30 and 74.

9 "De 'prentah haloes' " and "De autonomie voor Oost-Indië: de reactie ontmaskerd: de leden van het comité", *De Indische Gids* XLIV (1922), 353–5.

10 *Overzicht van de Gestie der C.S.I.*, *op. cit.*, p. 21.

11 D. M. G. Koch, *Om de Vrijheid* (Djakarta, 1950), p. 67.

12 Conversation with Abdoel Moeis, Bandung, June 11, 1952.

13 Gouvernements Besluit van 2 Maart 1922.

14 *Ind. Stbl.* 1922, no. 71.

15 Koch, *Om de Vrijheid*, *loc. cit.*

16 J. T. Petrus Blumberger, *De Communistische Beweging in Nederlandsch-Indië* (Haarlem, 1935), p. 35.

17 About this time (1922) the *Sarekat Islam hidjau* (Green Sarekat Islam) began to be formed in some parts of Java as a reaction against Communist activities. Conversation with R. A. A. Wiranatakusumah, Bandung, March 6, 1952.

18 E. Moresco, "The New Constitution of the Netherlands Indies", *The Asiatic Review* XXIII (1927), 216–24. Moresco was Secretary General of the Ministry of Colonies during the 1920's. Here he clearly expresses the fear that the Indonesian masses would become dependent upon the educated and wealthy classes working through disguised Western institutions. Sentiments similar to this form one part of the trend, explained below, to reintegrate and revitalize the traditional strengths of Indonesian life.

19 J. L. Vleming Jr., "De financieele positie van Nederlandsch-Indië en de belastingpolitiek van de laatste jaren", *De Socialistische Gids* XI (1926), 963–75.

20 Conversation with P. J. Gerke, Djakarta, July 31, 1952.

21 Oud, *op. cit.*, p. 248.

22 Conversation with P. J. Gerke, Djakarta, July 31, 1952.

23 W. Huender, *Overzicht van den economischen toestand der Inheemse Bevolking op Java en Madoera* ('s-Gravenhage, 1921), p. 244.

24 Koch, *Om de Vrijheid, op. cit.*, p. 77.

25 E. P. Wellenstein, "Het onderzoek naar den belastingdruk op de inheemsche bevolking van Nederlandsch-Indië", *Koloniale Studiën* IX$_2$ (1925), 23ff.

26 J. W. Meijer Ranneft en W. Huender, *Onderzoek naar den belastingdruk op de Inlandsche bevolking* (Weltevreden, 1926), *passim*.

27 H. Fievez de Malines van Ginkel en J. W. Meijer Ranneft, *Verslag van den economischen toestand der Inlandsche bevolking 1924*, 2 volumes (Weltevreden, 1926), *passim*.

28 *Ibid.*, vol. I, pp. 8–9.

29 G. Gonggrijp, "The Economic position...", *op. cit.*, pp. 29–32. See also: "Prijzen, Indexcijfers en Wisselkoersen op Java 1913–1929", *Mededelingen van het Centraal Kantoor voor de Statistiek* No. 88. Tabel VIII, pp. 76–7.

30 *Ind. Stbl.* 1922, no. 216. For Minister De Graaff's side of the story on the administrative reform see: S. de Graaff, *Parlementaire Geschiedenis van de Wet tot hervorming der grondslagen van het gewestelijk en plaatselijk bestuur in Nederlandsch-Indië, 1922* ('s-Gravenhage, 1939), *passim*.

31 Colenbrander and Stokvis, *Leven en Arbeid van Mr. C. Th. van Deventer, op. cit.* II, pp. 408–9.

32 Kleintjes, *op. cit.*, II, p. 19.

33 *Ind. Stbl.* 1919, no. 816.

34 Kleintjes, *op. cit.*, p. 25.

35 *Ned. Stbl.* 1922, no. 736; *Ind. Stbl.* 1923, no. 259.

36 *Ibid.*, Artikel 60.

37 Kleintjes, *op. cit.*, I, pp. 23–4.

38 *Ind. Stbl.* 1923, no. 259, Artikel 61.

39 The home government was playing an ever diminishing role in East Indian affairs, but it is nonetheless interesting to note the growing conservative nature of the Netherlands parliament, even when compared to the situation in 1918, see footnote no. 181, Chap. III. By the elections of 1922 the political

distribution in the Second Chamber of the States General was as follows:

Revolutionary Group	2	Protestant group	27
Social Democrats	20	Christian splinter	1
Radicals	5	Center	11
Catholics	32		

40 *Ind. Stbl.* 1919, no. 816.

41 J. Visser, *Hoofdzaken van het Staatsrecht van Nederland en Nederlandsch-Indië*, vol. 2 (Batavia, 1931), p. 10.

42 Archive Van Limburg Stirum, Folio 9, Letter from Idenburg to Van Limburg Stirum, February 6, 1919.

43 W. de Cock Buning, "De Indische beweging van den economischen kant", *De Opbouw* (1924), p. 6.

44 *Encyclopaedie van Nederlandsch-Indië* V, p. 36.

45 Kleintjes, *op. cit.*, p. 26.

46 J. Oppenheim, J. H. Carpentier Alting, Ph. Kleintjes, C. Snouck Hurgronje, C. van Vollenhoven, en Raden Oerip Kartodirdjo, *Proeve van eene staatsregeling voor Nederlandsch-Indië* (Leiden, 1922).

47 In 1922 the government slowed up the ontvoogding process. W. P. Hillen, "De verhouding tusschen het Inlandsche en het Europeesch Bestuur op Java en Madoera", *Indisch Genootschap*, 11 Mei 1934, p. 302.

48 Archive Van Limburg Stirum, Folio 60, Letter from Creutzberg to Van Limburg Stirum, January 1924. "I have the feeling that it is far more the tone of the new government than what one does or does not do with regard to legislative and administrative matters which is driving — I fear irrevocably — the youth of the Indies into the harness against the Netherlands. The disillusionment in the more or less intellectual native circles, and especially among those studying in the Netherlands, is increasing in alarming measure."

49 Petrus Blumberger, *Nationalistische Beweging... op. cit.*, pp. 32 and 78.

50 *Ibid.*, p. 82.

51 *Ibid.*, p. 95.

52 E. Gobée, "Hedendaagsche strijd over het chalifaat", *Koloniale Studien* VIII (1924), 503–545.

53 At the Seventh National Congress, 17–20 February 1923, Petrus Blumberger, *op. cit.*, p. 78.

54 This in no sense implies that there was unanimity in the world of Reformist Islam. In 1928 there was a fierce controversy between the Ahmadiah and Muhammadijah movements which called forth some nasty denunciations of Muhammadijah from Sarekat Islam members. See: Van der Plas, "Mededeelingen...", *op. cit.*, p. 263.

55 Petrus Blumberger, *op. cit.*, pp. 79–80.

56 A. von Arx, *L'Évolution politique en Indonésie de 1900 à 1942* (Fribourg, 1949), p. 194.

57 G. McT. Kahin, *Nationalism and Revolution in Indonesia* (Ithaca, N.Y., 1952), p. 77.

58 Petrus Blumberger, *op. cit.*, pp. 142–3.

59 *Ibid.*, pp. 32 and 78.

60 *Ibid.*, pp. 113–5.

61 *Ind. Stbl.* 1923, nos. 222 and 452.

62 *Ind. Stbl.* 1923, no. 136.

63 Petrus Blumberger, *op. cit.*, pp. 116–7.

64 *Ibid.*, pp. 120–2.

65 *Ibid.*, p. 117.

66 *Annuaire de Documentation Coloniale Comparée année 1927*, vol. II, p. 200.

67 Kahin, *op. cit.*, p. 78.

68 Petrus Blumberger, *op. cit.*, p. 116.

69 H. Kraemer, "Beschouwingen met betrekking tot de Inlandsche Beweging", *Koloniale Studiën* XI$_1$ (1927), pp. 7–8.

70 *Ind. Stbl.* 1925, no. 582 (17 November 1925).

71 Gouvernements Besluit van 17 December 1925.

72 Petrus Blumberger, *op. cit.*, p. 147.

73 *Ibid.*, pp. 30–1.

74 *Ibid.*, p. 32.

75 *Ibid.*

76 Conversation with Koentjoro Purbopranoto, Djakarta, April 9, 1952.

77 Petrus Blumberger, *op. cit.*, pp. 34–5 and 197–8.

78 *Ibid.*, p. 37.

79 *Ibid.*, p. 171 ff.

80 Conversations with R. Sastromuljono, Djakarta, April 9, 1942, M. Tabrani, Djatinegara, March 27, 1952, and Abdoel Moeis, June 18, 1952.

81 Pringgodigdo, *op. cit.*, pp. 32–4.

82 *Overzicht van de Gestie der C.S.I.*, *op. cit.*, pp. 47–50.

83 *Publicaties Hollandsch-Inlandsch Onderwijs-Commissie, No. 6A*, p. 35 ff.

84 *Publicaties Hollandsch-Inlandsch Onderwijs-Commissie, No. 12.*

Average Annual School Population for Indonesians

	1900/04	1905/09	1910/14	1915/19	1920/24
Native Lower Education (Desa + 2d Class Native Schools)	125,444	203,382	458,959	708,742	987,413
Western Lower Education (Dutch Native + European Primary Schools)	2,987	5,175	23,910	33,516	51,308
Intermediate Education (MULO and HBS)	25	45	135	675	2,602

85 In the later 1920's the desire for education continued, but it was now, at least at the higher levels, directed more toward intellectual development

than to winning a specific government post. See Djajadiningrat, "De positie van de regenten...", *op. cit.*, p. 101.

86 Ki Hadjar Dewantara (Soewardi Suryaningrat), "Beginselverklaring, Opvoedingssysteem en Leerplan voor Nationale Scholen", *Brochuren-Serie-Wasita*, No. N V — 1937 (Jogjakarta, 1937), p. 1.

87 Creutzberg, *op. cit.*, (1923), p. 17.

88 Ki Hadjar Dewantara, "Een en ander over 'Nationaal Onderwijs' en het Instituut 'Taman Siswå' te Jogjakarta", *Brochuren-Serie-Wasita*, No. N II — 1935 (Jogjakarta, 1935), p. 4.

89 Conversation with Ki Hadjar Dewantara, Djakarta, June 6, 1952.

90 S. Mangoensarkoro, "Het Nationalisme in de Taman Siswå-beweging", *Koloniale Studiën* XXI (1937), 288.

91 "We have gone up the wrong path; we must go back a couple of decades to find our starting point and reorient ourselves; back to the national, to the own." Ki Hadjar Dewantara quoted in Vastenhouw, *op. cit.*, p. 15.

92 Ki Hadjar Dewantara, *op. cit.*, (Beginselprogram "Taman Siswå"), pp. 3–4.

93 Conversation with Ki Hadjar Dewantara, Djakarta, June 6, 1952.

94 Mangoensarkoro, *op. cit.*, p. 290.

95 Vastenhouw, *loc. cit.* In 1933 Taman Siswå had 17,000 students. At the same time there were 1,813,286 students in the government's native primary schools, 144,019 in the Western primary schools, and 17,331 in the Western intermediate and secondary schools.

96 *Publicaties Hollandsch-Inlandsch Onderwijs-Commissie, No. 9* (2e stuk) (Batavia, 1931), pp. 81–3.

97 *Ibid.*, p. 82.

98 The Free Masons and the Theosophical Society, operating through an organization known as the "Dienaren van Indië", helped Indonesians to bear the costs of studying in Europe.

99 Djajadiningrat, *Herinneringen...*, *op. cit.*, p. 352.

100 G. S. S. J. Ratu Langie, "Het nieuw Aziatisme", *Koloniaal Tijdschrift* VIII (1919), p. 49.

101 An interesting article in *Oedaya* by Noto Soeroto, member of the House of Paku Alam and firm believer in association, telling of his expulsion from the *Perhimpunan Indonesia* because he was too Dutch is quoted in *De Indische Gids* XLVII (1925), 246–7.

102 *Gedenkboek 1908–1923 Indonesische Vereeniging* (n.p., n.d.), pp. 17–18.

103 Conversation with R. Sastromuljono, Djakarta, April 9, 1952.

104 Imam Supardi, *Dr. Soetomo: riwajat hidup dan perduangannja* (Djakarta/Amsterdam, 1951), pp. 2–3 and 33.

105 *Hindia Poetra*, March 1923, quoted in Petrus Blumberger, *op. cit.*, pp. 185–6.

106 Conversation with A. K. Pringgodigdo, Djakarta, March 28, 1952.

107 Petrus Blumberger, *op. cit.*, p. 186.

108 *Ibid.*, pp. 190–1.

109 *Ibid.*

110 Kahin, *op. cit.*, p. 89.

111 Petrus Blumberger, *op. cit.*, p. 82.

112 It was natural for Dr. R. Soetomo to regard Western education as the key to becoming a leader of people and nation. More than ten years later he still thought in terms of Western education for the elite. R. Soetomo, "Onderwijsvraagstukken in Indonesië", *Indisch Genootschap*, 16 October 1936, p. 101.

113 Supardi, *op. cit.*, pp. 3–4.

114 Petrus Blumberger, *op. cit.*, pp. 198–200.

115 M. Y. Nasution, *Penghidupan dan perdjuangan Ir. Sukarno* (Djakarta, 1951), p. 11.

116 *Ibid.*, p. 13.

117 *Ibid.*, p. 15.

118 J. A. Verdoorn, *De zending en het Indonesisch Nationalisme* (Amsterdam, 1945), p. 23 ff.

119 Conversation with Mohammed Hatta, Djakarta, October 8, 1952.

120 B. Schrieke, *Het Communisme ter Sumatra's Westkust* (Overdruk uit het Rapport van de Commissie van Onderzoek, ingesteld bij het Gouvernementsbesluit van 13 Februari 1927 No 1a) (Weltevreden, 1928), p. xii.

121 *Officiëel Rapport der Nederlandsch-Indische Regeering over de Communistische Woelingen in November 1926* (Weltevreden, 1927). This report was presented without essential change to the Volksraad. From the Volksraad report, Petrus Blumberger has made it easily accessible in his *Communistische Beweging...* *op. cit.*, pp. 70–9.

122 Djajadiningrat, *Herinneringen...*, *op. cit.*, pp. 338–40.

123 Kraemer, *op. cit.*, p. 7. makes the point that nationalism in general sought to use Communism and Communism in turn sought to use nationalism. This symbiotic relationship was certainly not limited to the Minangkabau area.

124 Koch, *Om de Vrijheid*, *op. cit.*, p. 93.

125 Speech of September 7, 1926.

126 W. M. F. Mansvelt, "Onderwijs en Communisme", *Koloniale Studiën* XII (1928), 203–25.

127 Annuaire de Documentation... *loc. cit.*

128 See Darsono's estimate of party strength in June 1924 given above, p. 212.

129 Only 601 of the 1000 would give any information on their position in the Communist movement. These 601 listed 747 functions (some had two or more functions) as follows:

Central administration P.K.I.	4
Terrorist leaders	4
Administrative members of the P.K.I.	71
Administrative members of Sarekat Rakjat	53
Administrative members of labor unions	44

Members P.K.I.	249
Members Sarekat Rakjat	216
Members labor unions	45
Propagandists	61

Mansvelt, *op. cit.*, pp. 221–2.

130 *Ibid., passim.*

131 *Ibid.*, pp. 214–6.

132 *Ibid.*, p. 220.

133 *Ibid.*, p. 219.

134 *Publicaties Hollandsch-Inlandsch Onderwijs-Commissie, No. 6A*, p. 36, concludes that only a few persons with Dutch Native education or better seek employment in the laboring class. Among these, however, the percentage of persons with 'extremist' tendencies is rather high.

135 Mansvelt, *op. cit.*, p. 216.

136 This total is derived from a chart loaned the writer by Mr. A. K. Pringgodigdo who worked at the Bureau of Statistics before 1942.

137 *Centraal Kantoor voor de Statistiek in Nederlandsch-Indië*, Statistisch Jaaroverzicht 1926, p. 100 ff.

138 The Semaoen-Hatta Convention followed upon proposals for creating a joint revolutionary-nationalist people's party [S.R.N.I.] with headquarters in Bandung, Petrus Blumberger, *Nationalistische Beweging... op. cit.*, p. 205.

139 *Ibid.*, p. 206. In May 1928 the name was changed to *Partai Nasional Indonesia* (P.N.I.) under which name the organization is more widely known. *Ibid.*, p. 213.

140 *Ibid.*, p. 206.

141 *Ibid.*, p. 397.

142 Conversations with Koentjoro Purbopranoto, Djakarta, April 9 and July 16, 1952.

143 Petrus Blumberger, *op. cit.*, p. 251.

144 Verdoorn, *op. cit.*, pp. 17–19.

145 C. C. Berg, "Indonesia", *Whither Islam* (H. Gibb, ed.) (London, 1932), p. 277.

146 Heijting, *op. cit.*, p. 788.

147 Conversation with Djumhana Wiriaatmadja, The Hague, January 10, 1952.

148 Djajadiningrat, "De positie van de regenten...", *op. cit.*, pp. 89–95.

149 Carpentier Alting and De Cock Buning, *op. cit.*, p. 109.

150 J. H. Boeke, "De begrippen dualisme, unificatie en associate in de koloniale politiek", *Koloniale Studiën* VII (1923), 153 ff.

151 H. H. van Kol, *Het Nederlandsch-Indisch Land-Syndicaat* (Amsterdam, 1921), pp. 1–31.

152 H. Colijn, the man who stood behind many of the actions of the "De Graaff-Fock" administration clearly recognized the powerful influence of the

University of Leiden and saw this influence was working against his interests. Through his connections in the petroleum industry he made money available for the establishment of a Faculty of Indology at the University of Utrecht. This faculty, established in 1925, sought to counteract the influence of the Leiden School, but the Leiden School remained dominant throughout the 1920's. See: "Utrecht contra Leiden", *Koloniale Studiën* IX (1925), 78–80.

153 Archive Van Limburg Stirum, Folio 60, Letter from Creutzberg to Van Limburg Stirum, January 1924. "The lack of understanding between The Hague and Leiden is phenomenal."

154 G.H. van der Kolff, "European Influence on Native Agriculture", *The Effects of Western Influence... op. cit.*, p. 118.

155 *Ind. Stbl.* 1915, no. 431.

156 A. H. Ballendux, *Bijdrage tot de kennis van de Credietverlening aan de "Indonesische Middenstand"* ('s-Gravenhage, 1951), pp. 5–9. See also Tan Goan Po, "De vorming van een Indonesische Middenstand", *Semangat Baroe — De Nieuwe Geest* I, no. 12 (April, 1946), 8.

157 Teko Sumodiwirjo, *Koperasi dan artinja bagi masjarakat Indonesia* (Djakarta, 1951), p. 33.

158 Van der Kolff, *loc. cit.*

159 J. H. Boeke, "Auto-activiteit naast autonomie", *Indisch Genootschap*, 13 October 1922, pp. 46–65.

160 Vink, "De Inheemse landbouw", *op. cit.*, pp. 364–5. See also J. G. Hoekman, "Het tweede tienjarig tijdvak van het bestaan van het Landbouw Departement", *Koloniale Studiën* IX (1925), 132 & 134–5.

161 J. L. Hydrick, "Intensive Rural Hygiene Work in the Netherlands East Indies", Paper, Eighth Conference of the Institute of Pacific Relations, December 1942, pp. 18 and 37.

162 Kleintjes, *Staatsinstellingen..., op. cit.* II, p. 70.

163 J. C. Kielstra, "Betere Rechtspraak over de Inlandsche Bevolking", *De Indische Gids* XXIX (1907), 1021, points to the difficulty in recruiting legal personnel for government service and how the jurists created and applied legal codes and practices which were confusing to the native community.

164 J. H. A. Logemann, "Direct gebied met inheemsche rechtspraak", *Feestbundel uitgegeven door het Koninklijk Bataviaasch Genootschap van Kunsten en Wetenschappen bij gelegenheid van zijn 150 jarig bestaan 1778–1928* (Weltevreden, 1929), p. 122.

165 C. van Vollenhoven, "Juridisch confectiewerk (eenheidsprivaatrecht voor Indië)", *Koloniale Studiën* LX₁ (1925), 293–318.

166 B. ter Haar Bzn., "Een keerpunt in de adatrecht-politiek: Toekomstbeschouwingen", *Koloniale Studiën* XII₁ (1928), 245–53.

167 Van Eerde, *op. cit.*, (1927), pp. 137–41.

168 Van Vollenhoven, "De ontvoogding van Indië...", *op. cit.*, p. 173.

169 *Ibid.*, See also Boeke, *The structure..., op. cit.*, p. 23.

170 L. Adam, *De autonomie van het Indonesisch dorp* (Amersfoort, 1924) and B. J. Haga, *Indonesische en Indische Democratie* (Den Haag, 1924).

171 D. J. Hulshoff Pol, *De strijd tegen het Communisme in Nederlandsch-Indië en het gewijzigde Regeeringsreglement* (Haarlem, 1925), pp. 1–24. Also see: J. H. Boeke, "Dorpsherstel", *Indisch Genootschap*, 20 Februari 1931, pp. 31–35.

172 The reestablishment of adat often came into conflict with Moslem religious law — this conflict became one of the more important aspects of Dutch Islamic Policy during the 1930's. Inconclusive evidence points to the trend running against Islamic law with a resulting alienation of the staunch Moslems by the Netherlands Indian government. H. Westra, "Custom and Muslim Law in the Netherlands Indies", *The Netherlands Indies:* Bulletin of the Colonial Institute Amsterdam III (June-August, 1940), 174–88.

173 Logemann, *op. cit.*, p. 123.

174 F. A. E. Laceulle, *Eindverslag over het desa-autonomie-onderzoek op Java en Madoera:* samengesteld ingevolge het gouvernementsbesluit van 8 Mei 1926 No. 3x (Weltevreden, 1929).

175 B. Schrieke, *Het Communisme ter Sumatra's Westkust* (Overdruk uit het Rapport van de Commissie van Onderzoek, ingesteld bij het Gouvernementsbesluit van 13 Februari 1927 No. 1a) (Weltevreden, 1928), pp. 93–133.

176 Boeke, *Ind. Genootschap*, 13 October 1922, *op. cit.*, p. 55.

177 Van Vollenhoven, "Juridisch Confectiewerk", *op. cit.*, p. 304.

178 When the electoral laws for the Volksraad were changed, the political parties based on association lost their influence. *Ind. Stbl.* 1925, no. 673.

179 Speech of Hoessein Djajadiningrat to the Congress of the Java-Instituut, June 18, 1921, *Djawa* I (1921), 254–6.

180 P. A. Soerjodiningrat, "De ontwakende cultuur van Java", *Indisch Genootschap*, 18 Juni 1926, pp 48–9, points to the Cultural work being conducted by Europeans in conjunction with the Javanese, but he is primarily concerned with the revival of interest by the Javanese in their own Culture.

181 It was not Boeke's idea that the Indonesian would care to move into the Westernized economic order, for he laid great emphasis upon the social aspects of economic needs. However, he was severely criticized on this point, and in practice the line of economic duality never exactly coincided with the ethnic groups, but it was close. See: P. Baretta, "Eenige koloniaal-economische beschouwingen", *Koloniaal Tijdschrift* XII (1923), 404 ff., and G. Gonggrijp, "Het arbeidsvraagstuk in Nederlands-Indië", *Koloniaal Tijdschrift* XIV (1925), 485–522, for two opinions that differ from Boeke on this point.

182 Van Vollenhoven, "De ontvoogding van Indië...", *op. cit.*, p. 174.

183 D. J. Hulshoff Pol, *Nationalisme in Nederlandsch-Indië: Oost tegen West* (Haarlem, 1928), pp. 1–25.

184 An American, Raymond Kennedy, in his *Ageless Indies* (New York, 1942), a Frenchman, G. H. Bousquet in his *French view of the Netherlands Indies* (London-New York, 1940), and a Japanese, Takejiro Haragoetsji, in

Contemporary Japan (1939), all, either directly or indirectly, refer to the weakness of the Indonesian political movement during the later 1930's.

185 For Minister De Graaff's views on the new Organization of the State as well as on the Constitutional changes of 1922, see: S. de Graaff, *Parlementaire geschiedenis van de Wet op de Staatsinrichting van Nederlandsch-Indië, 1925* ('s-Gravenhage, 1938), *passim.*

186 A. B. Cohen Stuart, "De nieuwe constitutie", *Koloniale Studiën* XI (1927), 1–4.

187 Oud, *op. cit.*, p. 256. Through political manipulations of Minister De Graaff the business of the Volksraad was placed in the hands of a Committee of Delegates from its midst. This arrangement insured control to a nucleus of European or Western oriented 'professional legislators'. This was what the left wing groups unsuccessfully opposed.

188 J. Drijvers, *De praktijk der conflictenregeling tusschen Volksraad en Regeering* (Leiden, 1934), p. 81 ff.

189 Speech of Dr. R. Soepomo to Budi Utomo quoted in Petrus Blumberger, *op. cit.*, p. 287.

190 Furnivall, *Progress and welfare... op. cit.*, pp. 52–3.

191 The magnum opus of A. D. A. de Kat Angelino, *Staatskundig beleid en bestuurszorg in Nederlandsch-Indië* 2 volumes ('s-Gravenhage, 1930) will always remain a monument to the syncretic-cultural solution to the colonial problem which was evolved in the 1920's. Nothing so clearly illustrates the fate of the new policy as clearly as the low esteem in which this book is held today.

BIBLIOGRAPHY

DOCUMENTS; GOVERNMENT REPORTS; and OFFICIAL SPEECHES

Annuaire de Documentation Coloniale Comparée 1927. (Bibliothèque Coloniale Internationale) Bruxelles: Etablissements Généraux d'Imprimerie, 1928.

Archive. Jean Paul graaf van Limburg Stirum, Rijksarchief. The Hague.

Archive, Secret. Ministerie van Koloniën. The Hague.

Bescheiden betreffende de vereeniging "Sarekat Islam". Zeer geheime missive van den Adviseur voor Inlandsche Zaken aan den Gouverneur Generaal 13 Mei 1913, No. 46. Batavia: Landsdrukkerij, 1913.

Fievez de Malines van Ginkel, H. and J. W. Meijer Ranneft, *Verslag van den economischen toestand der Inlandsche bevolking 1924,* 2 volumes. Weltevreden: Landsdrukkerij, 1913.

Handelingen Volksraad... (en Bijlagen), 1918–1925. Batavia: Landsdrukkerij, 1918.

Hasselman, C. J., *Eindverslag over het onderzoek naar den druk der desadiensten op Java en Madoera,* 1902. Weltevreden: Landsdrukkerij, 1905.

Hollandsch-Inlandsch Onderwijs-Commissie, Publicaties. Batavia: H–I O–C, 1929 —.

Indisch Verslag. Prior to 1930 this appeared as *Koloniaal Verslag.* Batavia: Landsdrukkerij.

Laceulle, F. A. E., *Eindverslag over het desa-autonomie-onderzoek op Java en Madoera:* samengesteld ingevolge het gouvernementsbesluit van 8 Mei 1926 No. 3x. (With supplement). Weltevreden: Landsdrukkerij, 1929.

La main-d'oeuvre aux Colonies. Documents officiels sur le contrat de travail et le lonage d'ouvrage aux Colonies. Bibliothèque Coloniale Internationale. 1re Serie Tome I. Paris: Armand Colin et Cie., 1895.

Mededeelingen van het Centraal Kantoor voor de Statistiek te Bataviacentrum. Batavia: Landsdrukkerij.

Mededeelingen der Regeering Omtrent Enkele Onderwerpen van Algemeen Belang. Weltevreden: Landsdrukkerij.

Meijer Ranneft, J. W. en W. Huender, *Onderzoek naar den belastingdruk op de Inlandsche bevolking.* Weltevreden: Landsdrukkerij, 1926.

Officieel Rapport der Nederlandsch-Indische Regeering over de Communistische Woelingen in November 1926. (Published as supplement to *Ik Zal Handhaven,* May 1927).

Onderzoek naar de Mindere Welvaart der Inlandsche Bevolking op Java en Madoera. 10 volumes. Batavia: Ruygrok & Co., 1905–1914.

Overzicht van de Gestie der Centraal Sarikat Islam in het jaar 1921. Weltevreden: Landsdrukkerij, 1922.

"De Rede van den Gouverneur-Generaal", (May 18, 1920), *De Indische Gids* XLII (1920).

"Rede van den Regeeringsgevolmatigde, den Heer W. Muurling, in den vergadering van den Volksraad van 2 Juli 1918", *De Indische Gids* XLI (1919), 1258–67.

"Redevoering van Zijne Excellentie den Gouverneur-Generaal bij gelegenheid van het openbaar gehoor op 1 September 1919", *De Indische Gids* XLI (1919), 1438–40.

Le Régime foncier aux Colonies. Bibliothèque Coloniale Internationale 3me Serie Tome IV. Indes Orientales Néerlandaises. Bruxelles: Institut Colonial International, 1899.

Le Régime des protectorats. Bibliothèque Coloniale Internationale 4me Serie, Tome I. Bruxelles: Institut Colonial International, 1899.

Sarekat-Islam Congres (1e Nationaal Congres) 17–24 Juni 1916 te Bandoeng. [Behoort bij de Geheime Missive van den Wd. Adviseur voor Inlandsche Zaken dd. 29 September 1916 No. 226.] Batavia: Landsdrukkerij, 1916.

Sarekat-Islam Congres (2e Nationaal Congres) 20–27 October 1917 te Batavia. [Behoort bij de Geheime Missive van den Regeeringscommissaris voor Inlandsche en Arabische Zaken van 23 Augustus 1918 No. 416.] Batavia: Landsdrukkerij, 1919.

Sarekat-Islam Congres (3e Nationaal Congres) 29 Sept.–6 Oct. 1918 te Soerabaja. [Behoort bij de Geheime Missive van den Regeeringscommissaris voor Inlandsche en Arabische Zaken van 9 December 1918 No. 599.] Batavia: Landsdrukkerij, 1919.

Schrieke, B., *Het Communisme ter Sumatra's Westkust.* (Overdruk uit het Rapport van de Commissie van Onderzoek, ingesteld bij het Gouvernementsbesluit van 13 Februari 1927 No. 1a.) Weltevreden: Landsdrukkerij, 1928.

Staatsblad van Nederlandsch-Indië... (met Bijbladen). Weltevreden: Landsdrukkerij.

Verslag omtrent de verdere voorbereiding eener hervorming van het bestuurswezen in Nederlandsch-Indië. Weltevreden: Landsdrukkerij, 1914.

Verslag van de arbeidscommissie betreffende de wettelijke vaststelling van minimumloonen voor werknemers op Java en Madoera. Weltevreden: Landsdrukkerij, 1920.

Verslag van de Commissie tot Herziening van de Staatsinrichting van Nederlandsch-Indië. Ingesteld bij Gouvernementsbesluit van 17en December 1918 No. 1. Weltevreden: Landsdrukkerij, 1920.

BOOKS; BROCHURES and PAMPHLETS

Adam, L., *De autonomie van het Indonesisch dorp*. Amersfoort: S. W. Melchior, 1924.

Alimin Prawirodirdjo, *Louteren Wij Ons! — Open Brief aan elk lid van de Sarekat Islam*. Bandoeng: "De Nationale Bibliotheek", 1919.

Amelz, H. O. S. *Tjokroaminoto, hidup dan perdjuangannja*, 2 volumes. Djakarta: "Bulan Bintang", 1952.

Angoulvant, G., *Les Indes Néerlandaises leur role dans l'économie internationale*, 2 volumes. Paris: Le Monde Nouveau, 1926.

Arx, A. von, *L'Évolution politique en Indonésie de 1900 à 1942*. Fribourg: Artigianelli-Mouza, 1949.

Baars, A. en H. Sneevliet, *Het proces Sneevliet: de Sociaal-democratie in Nederlandsch-Indië*. Semarang: no publisher, 1917.

Balfas, M., *Dr. Tjipto Mangoenkoesoemo: demokrat sedjati*. Djakarta/Amsterdam: Djambatan, 1952.

Ballendux, A. H., *Bijdrage tot de kennis van de Credietverlening aan de "Indonesische Middenstand"*. 's-Gravenhage: Excelsiors Foto-offset, 1951.

Boeke, J. H., *Dorp en desa*. Leiden: E. J. Brill, 1934.

———, *The Structure of the Netherlands Indian Economy*. New York: I.P.R., 1942.

Bousquet, G. H., *A French View of the Netherlands Indies*. New York: I.P.R., 1940.

Brooshooft, P., *De ethische koers in de koloniale politiek*. Amsterdam: J. H. de Bussy, 1901.

———, *Memorie over den toestand in Indië*, ter begeleiding van den open brief op 7 Maart 1888 door 1255 ingezetenen van Nederlandsch-Indië gezonden aan 12 Nederlandsche Heeren.

Burger, D. H., *De Ontsluiting van Java's binnenland voor het wereldverkeer*. Wageningen: H. Veenman and Zonen, 1939.

Cabaton, A., *Java, Sumatra, and the other islands of the Dutch East Indies*. London: T. Fisher Unwin, 1911.

Carpentier Alting, J. H. and W. de Cock Buning, *The Effect of the War upon the Colonies*. The Netherlands and the World War, Volume III. New Haven: Yale University Press, 1928.

Chailley-Bert, J., *Java et ses habitants*. Paris: Armand Colin et Cie., 1900.

Colenbrander, H. T. en J. E. Stokvis, editors, *Leven en Arbeid van Mr. C. Th. van Deventer*; 3 volumes in one. Amsterdam: P. N. van Kampen and Zoon, 1916.

Colijn, H., editor, *Neerlands Indië, Land en Volk; Geschiedenis en Bestuur; Bedrijf en Samenleving*. Amsterdam: Elsevier, 1912.

———, *Staatkundige Hervormingen in Nederlandsch Indië*. Kampen: J. H. Kok, 1918.

Collet, Octave J.-A., *L'Évolution de L'Esprit Indigène aux Indes Orientales Néer-landaises*. Bruxelles: Librairie Falck Fils, 1921.

Dagverhaal van Mr. Dr. H. H. A. van Gijbland Oosterhoff over de periode 8–15 November 1918. 's-Gravenhage: Privately printed, 1918.

Day, Clive, *The policy and administration of the Dutch in Java*. New York: Macmillan, 1904.

Deventer, C. T. van, *Overzicht van de economischen toestand der Inlandsche bevolking van Java en Madoera*. (Met aanhangsel: De voornaamste industrieën der Inlandsche bevolking van Java en Madoera door C. P. Rouffaer) 's-Gravenhage: M. Nijhoff, 1904.

Dewantara, Ki Hadjar (Soewardi Soerianingrat), *Een en ander over 'Nationaal Onderwijs' en het Instituut 'Taman Siswā' te Jogjakarta*, Brochuren-Serie-Wasita No. NII–1935. Jogjakarta: "Wasita", 1935.

Djajadiningrat, Pangeran Aria Achmad, *Herinneringen van...* Amsterdam/Batavia: G. Kolff, ca. 1936.

Douwes Dekker, E. F. E., *Aansluiting tusschen Blank en Bruin* (Rede uitgesproken te Batavia op 12 (17?) December 1911). Batavia: G. Kolff, 1912.

————, *De Indische Partij, haar wezen en haar doel* (Herdrukt uit *De Express*) gevolgd door de op 25 December 1912, gearresteerde Statuten der Partijen en het verslag der Constitutie-vergadering op dien datum. Bandoeng: "Fortuna", 1913.

————, *Het Jaar 1913 in zijn beteekenis voor de Indische Beweging*. Schiedam: "De Toekomst", 1914.

————, *Een Sociogenetische Grondwet: één der hoeksteenen voor het gebouw onzer revolutionaire maatschappij beschouwing*. Semarang: "De Indonesische Boek-en Brochurehandel, n.d.

————, (Danudirdja Setiabuddhi), *70 Jaar Konsekwent* (Samengesteld uit notities, annotaties en enige commentaar met de hulp van Harumi Wanasita). Bandung: A. C. Nix, 1950.

Douwes Dekker, E. F. E., Tjipto Mangoenkoesoemo en R. M. Suardy Suryaningrat, *Mijmeringen van Indiers over Hollands Feestvierderij in de Kolonie* (Vlugschriften v. h. Comité Boemi Poetra No. 2). Schiedam: "De Toekomst", 1913.

Drewes, G. W. J., *Drie Javaansche Goeroe's, hun leven, onderricht en messiasprediking*. Leiden: A. Vros, 1925.

Drijvers, J., *De praktijk der conflictenregeling tusschen Volksraad en Regeering*. Leiden: "Luctor et Emergo", 1934.

Duyvendak, J. P., *Inleiding tot de ethnologie van de Indonesische Archipel*. Groningen/Batavia: J. B. Wolters, 1946.

Eerde, J. C. van, *Ethnologie coloniale (L'Européen et l'Indigène)*. Paris: Le Monde Nouveau, 1927.

Emerson, Rupert, *Malaysia; a study in direct and indirect rule*. New York: Macmillan, 1937.

Fock, D., *Beschouwingen en voorstellen ter verbetering van den economischen toestand der Inlandsche bevolking van Java en Madoera*. 's-Gravenhage: M. Nijhoff, 1904.

Fokkens, F., *Bescheiden wenken voor de verbetering van den economischen toestand der Inlandsche bevolking op Java en daar buiten*. 's-Gravenhage: M. M. Couvée, 1904.

Fromberg, P. H., *Verspreide Geschriften*. Leiden: Leidsche Uitgeversmaatschappij, 1926.

Furnivall, John S., *Netherlands India; a study of plural economy*. Cambridge: University Press, 1944.

——, *Progress and Welfare in Southeast Asia*. New York: I.P.R., 1941.

Gedenkboek M.O.S.V.I.A. 1879–1929. Bandoeng: no publisher, ca. 1929.

Gedenkboek 1908–1923 Indonesische Vereeniging. No place: No publisher, No date.

Gonggrijp, G., *Over de invloed van het westerse grootbedrijf op de inheemse samenleving in Nederlands-Indië*. Haarlem: H. D. Tjeenk Willink and Zoon, 1930.

——, *Schets eener economische geschiedenis van Nederlandsch-Indië*. Haarlem: F. Bohn, 1928.

Gonggrijp Sr., G. L., *Honderd Brieven van Opheffer aan de Redactie van het Bataviaasch Handelsblad*. Batavia: Ruygrok, 1913.

Graaf, H. J. de, *Geschiedenis van Indonesië*. 's-Gravenhage/Bandung: W. van Hoeve, 1949.

Graaff, S. de, *Parlementaire geschiedenis van de Wet op Staatsinrichting van Nederlandsch-Indië, 1925*. 's-Gravenhage: M. Nijhoff, 1938.

——, *Parlementaire Geschiedenis van de Wet tot hervorming der grondslagen van het gewestelijk en plaatselijk bestuur in Nederlandsch-Indië, 1922*. 's-Gravenhage: M. Nijhoff, 1939.

Haga, B. J., *Indonesische en Indische Democratie*. Den Haag: "De Ster", 1924.

Hamka (Haji Abdul Malik Karim Amrullah), *Sedjarah Islam di Sumatera*. Medan: Pustaka Nasional, 1950.

Harahap, Parada, *Riwajat Dr. A. Rivai*. Medan: Indische Drukkerij, 1939.

Helsdingen, W. H. van, ed., *Daar Werd Wat Groots Verricht...: Nederlandsch-Indië in de XXste eeuw*. Amsterdam: Elsevier, 1941.

Hoëvell, W. R. van, *Parlementaire Redevoeringen over Koloniale Belangen 1849–1859*, 4 volumes. Zaltbommel: J. Noman en Zoon, 1862–5.

Huender, W., *Overzicht van den economischen toestand der Inheemse bevolking op Java en Madoera*. 's-Gravenhage: M. Nijhoff, 1921.

Hulshoff Pol, D. J., *Nationalisme in Nederlandsch Indië: Oost tegen West*. Haarlem: H. D. Tjeenk Willink, 1928.

——, *De strijd tegen het Communisme in Nederlandsch-Indië en het gewijzigde Regeeringsreglement*. Haarlem: H. D. Tjeenk Willink, 1925.

Hydrick, J. L., *Intensive Rural Hygiene work in the Netherlands East Indies*. Paper, Eighth Conference of the Institute of Pacific Relations, December 1942.

Idema, H. A., *Parlementaire geschiedenis van Nederlandsch Indië 1891–1918*. 's-Gravenhage: M. Nijhoff, 1924.

Jonkers, A., *Welvaartszorg in Indonesië*. 's-Gravenhage: W. van Hoeve, 1948.

Kahin, George McT., *Nationalism and Revolution in Indonesia*. Ithaca, New York: Cornell University Press, 1952.

Kartini, Raden Adjeng, *Door duisternis tot licht*. 's-Gravenhage: "Luctor et Emergo", 1912.

Kasteel, P., *Abraham Kuyper*. Kampen: J. H. Kok, 1938.

Kat Angelino, A. D. A. de, *Staatkundig beleid en bestuurszorg in Nederlandsch-Indië*, 2 volumes. 's-Gravenhage: M. Nijhoff, 1929–30.

Kennedy, Raymond, *The Ageless Indies*. New York: John Day, 1942.

Kern, R. A., *De Islam in Indonesië*. 's-Gravenhage: W. van Hoeve, 1947.

Kielstra, E. B., *De financiën van Nederlandsch-Indië*. 's-Gravenhage: M. Nijhoff, 1904.

Kleintjes, P., *Staatsinstellingen van Nederlandsch-Indië*, 2 volumes, 6th edition. Amsterdam: J. H. de Bussy, 1933.

Koch, D. M. G., *Indisch-koloniale vraagstukken*. Weltevreden: Javasche Boekhandel, 1919.

———, *Om de Vrijheid; de Nationalistische Beweging in Indonesië*. Djakarta: Jajasan Pembangunan, 1950.

Koks, J. T., *De Indo*. Amsterdam: Van Nijgh, 1932.

Kol, H. H. van, *Het Nederlandsch-Indisch Land-Syndicaat*. Amsterdam: "Ontwikkeling", 1921.

Kruijt, A. C., *Het animisme in den Indischen Archipel*. 's-Gravenhage: M. Nijhoff, 1906.

Lammers, G. J., *A. W. F. Idenburg: in zijn leven en werken geschetst*. Amsterdam: De Standaard, 1935.

Lette, J. R., *Proeve eener vergelijkende studie van het grondbezit in Rusland, zoals dit zich heeft ontwikkeld tot de Russische Revolutie, en op Java*. Leiden: No publisher, 1928.

Liem Twan Djie, *De distribueerende tusschenhandel der Chineezen op Java*. 's-Gravenhage: M. Nijhoff, 1947.

Lith, F. van, S. J., *De politiek van Nederland ten opzichte van Nederlandsch-Indië*. 's-Hertogenbosch-Antwerpen: L. C. G. Malmberg, n.d. (ca. 1920).

Louter, J. de, *Handleiding tot de kennis van het Staats-en Administratief Recht van Nederlandsch-Indië*, 4th edition. 's-Gravenhage: M. Nijhoff, 1895.

Mitchell, Kate Louise, *Industrialization of the Western Pacific*. New York: I.P.R., 1942.

Mook, H. J. van, *Nederland, Indonesië en de wereld*. Amsterdam: De Bezige Bij, 1949.

Multatuli (E. Douwes Dekker), *Max Havelaar, of de koffieveilingen der Nederlandsche Handelmaatschappij*. Amsterdam: Nederlandsche Bibliotheek, 1917. First edition appeared in 1860.

Nasution, M. Y., *Penghidupan dan perdjuangan Ir. Sukarno*. Djakarta: Pustaka "Aida", 1951.

Neijs, K., *Westerse acculturisatie en Oosters volksonderwijs*. Leiden: "Luctor et Emergo", 1945.

Nieuwenhuijze, C. A. O. van, *Mens en Vrijheid in Indonesië*. 's-Gravenhage/ Bandung: W. van Hoeve, 1949.

Ontwikkeling van het Geneeskundig Onderwijs te Weltevreden 1851–1926. [Uitgegeven ter herdenking van het 75-jarig bestaan van de School tot Opleiding van Indische Artsen (S.T.O.V.I.A.).] Weltevreden: G. Kolff, 1926.

Onze Verbanning. Publicatie der Officiëele Bescheiden, toegelicht met Verslagen en Commentaren, betrekking hebbende op de Gouvernements-Besluiten van den 18en Augustus 1913, nos. 1a en 2a, regelende de toepassing van artikel 47 R.R. (interneering) op E. F. E. Douwes Dekker, Tjipto Mangoenkoesoemo en R. M. Soewardi Soerjaningrat. Schiedam: "De Indiër", 1913.

Oppenheim, J., J. H. Carpentier Alting, P. Kleintjes, C. Snouck Hurgronje, C. van Vollenhoven, en Raden Oerip Kartodirdjo, *Proeve van eene staatsregeling voor Nederlandsch-Indië*. Leiden: E. J. Brill, 1922.

Oud, P. J., *Honderd jaren; hoofdzaken der Nederlandsche staatkundige geschiedenis, 1840–1940*. Assen: Van Gorcum, 1946.

Petrus Blumberger, J. T., *De Communistische beweging in Nederlandsch-Indië*. Haarlem: Tjeenk Willink, 1928.

———, *De Indo-Europeesche beweging in Nederlandsch-Indië*. Haarlem: Tjeenk Willink, 1939.

———, *De Nationalistische beweging in Nederlandsch-Indië*. Haarlem: Tjeenk Willink, 1931.

Pieters, J. M., *De zoogenaamde ontvoogding van het Inlandsch Bestuur*. Wageningen: H. Veenman, 1932.

Pringgodigdo, A. K., *Sedjarah pergerakan rakjat Indonesia*. Djakarta: Pustaka Rakjat, 1949.

Radjiman (R. T. Wedijodiningrat), *Een bijdrage tot het reconstructie-idee van de Javaansche maatschappij*. (XIIIe Congres van Boedi Oetomo te Soerakarta 24–26 December 1921) Djokja: "Mardi-Moeljo", 1921.

Rutgers, F. L., *Idenburg en de Sarekat Islam in 1913*. Amsterdam: Noord-Hollandsche Uitgevers Mij., 1939.

Rutgers, S. J., *Indonesië: het koloniale systeem in de periode tussen de eerste en de tweede wereldoorlog*. Amsterdam: "Pegasus", 1947.

Schrieke, B. J. O., et. al., *The Effect of Western Influence on Native Civilizations in the Malay Archipelago*. Batavia: G. Kolff, 1929.

———, *De inlandsche hoofden*. Weltevreden: G. Kolff, 1928.

Schrieke, J. J., *De Indische Politiek*. Amsterdam: J. H. de Bussy, 1929.

———, *Ontstaan en groei der stads- en landgemeenten in Nederlandsch-Indië*. Amsterdam: J. H. de Bussy, 1918.

Snouck Hurgronje, C., *Verspreide Geschriften*, 6 volumes. Bonn u. Leipzig: Kurt Schroeder, 1924.

Soekanto, *Het gewas in Indonesië Religieus-Adatrechtelijk beschouwd.* Leiden: M. Dubbeldeman, 1933.

Soembangsih: Gedenkboek Boedi-Oetomo 1908–20 Mei–1918. Amsterdam: Tijdschrift "Nederlandsch Indië" Oud and Nieuw, 1918.

Somer, J. M., *De korte verklaring.* Breda: "Corona", 1934.

Stokvis, J. E., *Van Wingewest naar Zelfbestuur in Nederlandsch-Indië.* Amsterdam: Elsevier, 1922.

Sumodiwirjo, Teko, *Koperasi artinja bagi masjarakat Indonesia.* Djakarta: Jajasan Dharma, 1951.

Supardi, Imam, *Dr. Soetomo: riwajat hidup dan perdjuangannja.* Djakarta/Amsterdam: Djambatan, 1951.

Tan Malaka, *Dari pendjara ke pendjara,* 2 volumes. Djakarta: Murba + Widjaya, n.d.

Vastenhouw, M., *Inleiding tot de voorlogse paedagogische problemen van Indonesia.* Indonesische Paedagogische Monografieën No. 1. Groningen/Djakarta: J. B. Wolters, 1949.

Verdoorn, J. A., *De Zending en het Indonesisch Nationalisme.* Amsterdam: Vrij Nederland, 1945.

25 Jaren Decentralisatie in Nederlandsch-Indië 1905–1930. Semarang: Vereeniging voor Locale Belangen, ca. 1930.

Vink, G. J., *De grondslagen van het Indonesische landbouwbedrijf.* Wageningen: H. Veenman, ca. 1939.

Visser, J., *Hoofdzaken van het Staatsrecht van Nederland en Nederlandsch-Indië,* 2 volumes. Batavia: Landsdrukkerij, 1931.

Vlekke, B. H. M., *Nusantara: a History of the East Indian Archipelago.* Cambridge, Mass., Harvard University Press, 1943.

Vollenhoven, C. van, *Het Adatrecht van Nederlandsch Indië,* 3 volumes. Leiden: E. J. Brill, 1918–1933.

———, *De Indonesiër en zijn grond.* Leiden: E. J. Brill, 1919.

Walraven, W., *Op de grens.* Amsterdam: G. A. van Oorschot, 1952.

Welderen Rengers, D. W. van, *The Failure of a Liberal Colonial Policy: Netherlands East Indies, 1816–1830.* The Hague: M. Nijhoff, 1947.

Wertheim, W. F., *Effects of Western Civilization on Indonesian Society.* New York: I.P.R., 1950.

———, *Herrijzend Azië.* Arnhem: Van Loghum Slaterus, 1950.

PERIODICAL and NEWSPAPER ARTICLES

Adriani, N., "De Hoofden der Toradja's van Midden-Celebes", *Indisch Genootschap,* 16 Februari 1916, pp. 107–126.

Baretta, P., "Eenige koloniaal-economische beschouwingen", *Koloniaal Tijdschrift* XII (1923), 396–416.

Benjamin, J. J., "Opmerkingen over de suikercultuur en omtrent hetgeen ge-
daan kan worden, om de inlandsche bevolking in gouvernementslanden van
Java, speciaal voor zoover zij den landbouw beoefent, vooruit te brengen",
Tijdschrift voor nijverheid en Landbouw in Nederlandsch-Indië LXXVI (1908).

Berg, C. C., "Critische beschouwingen van Neerlands cultureelen invloed
en Neerlands cultureele taak in Oost-Indië", *Indisch Genootschap*, 6 April
1934, pp. 273-297.

———, "Indonesia". Chapter in *Whither Islam*, edited by H. A. R.Gibbs,
(London, 1932).

———, "Nederland en Indonesië", *De Gids* CXV (Aug./Sept., 1952).

Berg, L. W. C. van den, "De jongste bewegingen onder de Inlanders en de
Vreemde Oosterlingen in Ned.-Indië en de betekenis daarvan voor de
Zending", *Orgaan der Nederlandsche Zendingsvereeniging* No. 6. Juni 1909,
1-24.

Bijleveld, J., "De Saminbeweging", *Koloniaal Tijdschrift* XII (1923), 10-
24.

Boeka [pseud.], "De Hoofden op Java: een studie", *De Indische Gids* XXVI
(1904), pp. 333-361.

Boeke, J. H., "Auto-activiteit naast autonomie", *Indisch Genootschap*, 13 October 1922, pp. 46-72.

———, "De begrippen dualisme, unificatie en associatie in de koloniale politiek", *Koloniale Studiën* VII, (1923), 153-169.

———, "Dorpsherstel", *Indisch Genootschap*, 20 Februari 1931, 31-63.

Burger, D. H., "Structuurveranderingen in de Javaanse samenleving", *Indonesië* II (1948/49), 381-398 and 521-537 and III (1949/50), 1-18.

Carpentier Alting, H., "Bestuursonthouding of Bestuursbemoeienis?", *Tijdschrift voor het Binnenlandsch Bestuur* XXVI (1904), 48-53.

Cock Buning, W. de, "De Indische beweging van den economischen kant",
De Opbouw (Juli 1924).

Cohen Stuart, A. B., "Hedendaagsch Decentralisatie-Werk in Nederlandsch-
Indië", *Leiding* II (1931), 208-20.

———, "De Nieuwe Constitutie", *Koloniale Studiën* XI₁ (1927), 16-44.

Creutzberg, K. F., "Enkele grepen uit de Indische onderwijspolitiek", *Indisch Genootschap*, 19 Januari 1923, pp. 1-35.

Damsté, H. T., "Bestuurscontinuiteit", *Tijdschrift voor het Binnenlandsch Bestuur*
XXVI (1904), 182-9.

Djajadiningrat, R. A. A. Achmad, "De positie van de regenten op Java en
Madoera in het huidige bestuursstelsel", *Indisch Genootschap*, 15 November
1929, 83-104.

———, "Vorst en Volk", *Djawa* III (1924), 62-3.

"Een dankbare herinnering aan wijlen Mr. J. H. Abendanon", *Oedaya* (Febr.,
1926).

Engelbert van Bevervoorde, W. F., "De vlechtindustrie in de residentie Jogjacarta", *Tijdschrift voor het Binnenlandsch Bestuur* XXIX (1905), 1–30 and 81–108.

Fock, D., "Decentralisatie in Nederlandsch-Indië", *De Indische Gids* XXII (1900), 153–173.

——, "De Algemeene Sekretarie in Nederlandsch-Indië", *De Indische Gids* XXII (1900), 832–8.

Fokkens, F., "Onze naaste plicht ten aanzien van de Inlandsche bevolking op Java en daarbuiten, naar aanleiding van de Indische begrooting voor 1903", *Indisch Genootschap*, 11 November 1902, 79–106.

——, "Voortvarendheid der Indische Regeering", *De Indische Gids* XXVI (1904), 30–2.

Gelderen, J. van, "Maatschappelijke veranderingen in Indië in de na-oorlogs-jaren", *De Vakbeweging* (Mei, 1927), 193–204.

——, "Welvaart en welvaartsmeting in Nederlandsch-Indië", *Indisch Genootschap*, 21 Januari 1927, 1–18.

Gobée, E., "Hedendaagse strijd over het chalifaat", *Koloniale Studiën* VIII (1924), 503–45.

Gonggrijp, G., "Het arbeidsvraagstuk in Nederlandsch-Indië", *Koloniaal Tijdschrift* XIV (1925), 485–522 and 618–648.

——, "The economic position of the Indigenous population", *The Asiatic Review*, XXIII (1927), 22–32.

Haar, B. ter, "Een keerpunt in de adatrecht-politiek: Toekomstbeschouwingen", *Koloniale Studiën* XII_1 (1928), 245–280.

Habbema, J., "Hollandsch voor aanstaande inlandsche ambtenaren en onderwijzers", *De Indische Gids* XXIII (1901), 837–44.

Haragoetsji, Takejiro, "Netherlands and the East", *Contemporary Japan* (1939).

Heekeren, E. A. A. van, "Nederlandsch Oost Indië in 1914", *De Indische Gids* XXXVII (1915), 145–160.

Heijting, H. G., "Staat de adel op Java nog steeds aan de spits van het volk?", *De Indische Gids* XLVII (1925), 769–800.

Hillen, W. P., "De verhouding tusschen het Inlandsche en het Europeesch Bestuur op Java en Madoera", *Indisch Genootschap*, 11 Mei 1934, pp. 299–318.

Hoekman, J. G., "Het tweede tienjarig tijdvak van het bestaan van het Landbouw Departement", *Koloniale Studiën* IX_1 (1925), 131–148.

Indische Gids, De, Persoverzichten, 1900–1925.

Jasper, J. E., "Ambachtsscholen voor Inlanders", *De Indische Gids* XXIX (1907), 673–681.

——, "Het Inlandsch Volksonderwijs op Java", *Indisch Genootschap*, 1 November 1910, pp. 1–36.

"De Javasche Bank in 1918", *De Indische Gids* XLI (1919), 1281–8.

Kennedy, Raymond, "Contours of Culture in Indonesia", *The Far Eastern Quarterly* II (1942), 5–14.

Kern, R. A., "De Inlandsche Gemeente-Ordonnantie", *De Indische Gids* XXVIII (1906), 1473–88.

Kielstra, J. C., "Betere rechtspraak voor de Inlandsche bevolking", *De Indische Gids* XXIX (1907), 1020–31.

Koch, D. M. G., "Indische Problemen", *Koloniale Studiën* III (1919), 265–304.

———, "Regeerder van Ned.-Indië, Mr. Jean Paul graaf van Limburg Stirum", *Sedar - Ontwaken* I no. 8 (Februari, 1949), 28–30.

Koesoemo Dikdo, R. T., "Nog iets over dessahoofdverkiezingen", *Tijdschrift voor het Binnenlandsch Bestuur* XXIV (1903), 1–18.

Koesoemo di Poetro, R. M. T. A., "Bestuursonthouding of (en) bestuursbemoeienis", *Tijdschrift voor het Binnenlandsch Bestuur* XXVI (1904), 347–359.

Kol, H. H. van, "Bestaat er scheiding of eenheid van Nederlandsche en Indische financieën?", *De Indische Gids* XXII (1900), 1142–9.

———, "Geen 'Indische Bijdragen' meer!", *De Indische Gids* XXII (1900), 697–708.

Koster, M. S., "De opleiding der Inlandsche administratieve en rechterlijke ambtenaren op Java en Madoera", *Indisch Genootschap*, 19 Januari 1904, pp. 1–40.

Kraemer, H., "Beschouwingen met betrekking tot de Inlandsche Beweging", *Koloniale Studiën* XI₁ (1927), 1–15.

Langie, G. S. S. J. Ratu, "Het nieuw Aziatisme", *Koloniaal Tijdschrift* VIII₁ (1919), 44–51.

"Licht en Donker: De Indisch Ontwerp", *De Locomotief*, 9, 18 and 20 Juli 1920.

Logemann, J. H. A., "Direct gebied met inheemsche rechtspraak", *Feestbundel uitgegeven door het Koninklijk Bataviaasch Genootschap van Kunsten en Wetenschappen bij gelegenheid van zijn 150 jarig bestaan 1778–1928*. Weltevreden: Kolff, 1929.

Lulofs, C., "Gezagsuitbreiding", *De Indische Gids* XXVIII (1906), 1342–54.

Lutter, W. F., "De Loemboeng-Desa in de Afdeeling Grobogan", *Tijdschrift voor het Binnenlandsch Bestuur* XXVIII (1905), 339–356.

Mangoensarkoro, S., "Het Nationalisme in de Taman Siswåbeweging", *Koloniale Studiën* XXI (1937), 287–96.

Mansvelt, W. M. F., "Onderwijs en Communisme", *Koloniale Studiën* XII₁ (1928), 203–225.

Marle, A. van, "De groep der Europeanen in Ned. Indië, iets over ontstaan en groei", *Indonesië* V (1951/2), 97–121, 314–341 and 481–507.

Meijer, G. A. M., "Een bestuursambtenaar, die veel voor den Inlander deed", *De Indische Gids* XLII (1920), 507–536.

Meijer Ranneft, J. W., "Reglementeering van zachten dwang", *Tijdschrift voor het Binnenlandsch Bestuur* IXL (1910), 57–70.

———, "Scheiding van bestuur en politierechtspraak op Java", *Koloniaal Tijdschrift* VI (1917), 897–916.

Moresco, E., "De Inlandsche zelfbesturen en de rechterlijke organisatie", *De Indische Gids* XXV (1903), 534–49.

——, "The New Constitution of the Netherlands Indies", *The Asiatic Review*, XXIII (1927), 216–224.

——, "Onze politiek ten aanzien van de Inlandsche zelfbesturen", *Indisch Genootschap*, 7 April 1908, pp. 201–236.

Nieuwenhuis, A. W., "De godsdienst op Java in zijne oeconomische en politieke beteekenis", *Indisch Genootschap*, 27 Maart 1906, pp. 127–159.

Nieuwenhuijs, J. H., "Kan het aantal Controleurs bij het Binnenlandsch Bestuur op Java en Madoera worden ingekrompen?", *De Indische Gids* XXX (1908), 581–593.

Nolst Trenité, G. J., "Verhuring van grond door Inlanders aan niet-Inlanders op Java en Madoera", *Indisch Genootschap*, 1 Maart 1910, 135–162.

"Ons Standpunt", (Interview between G. G. Idenburg and three members of the Indische Partij; 13 March 1913). Reprint from *De Expres* 1913.

Petrus Blumberger, J. T., "De Sarekat Islam, en hare beteekenis voor den Bestuursambtenaar", *Koloniaal Tijdschrift* VIII (1919), 272–95 and 435–55.

Plas, C. O. van der, "De maatschappelijke, cultureele en politieke ontwikkeling van Insulinde in heden en toekomst", *Koloniaal Tijdschrift* VIII (1919), 556–94 and 661–97.

——, "Mededeelingen over de stroomingen in de Moslimsche gemeenschap in Nederlandsch-Indië en de Nederlandsche Islampolitiek", *Indisch Genootschap*, 16 Februari 1934, pp. 253–273.

Rinkes, D. A., "Oude en nieuwe stroomingen onder de bevolking", *Indisch Genootschap*, 18 November 1916, pp. 55–78.

Sandick, R. A. van, "De Regeeringsvoorstellen betreffende de ambtenaarsopleiding", *De Indische Gids* XXIV (1920), 2–14.

Schrieke, B., "Uit de geschiedenis van het Adatgrondenrecht", *Tijdschrift voor Indische Taal-, Land- en Volkenkunde* LIX (1919–21), 122–190.

Slotemaker de Bruïne, N. A. C., "De cultureele beteekenis van het onderwijs in Ned.-Indië", *Indisch Genootschap*, 27 November 1931, pp. 111–143.

Snouck Hurgronje, C., "Een belangrijk Document betreffende den heiligen Oorlog van den Islam (1914) en eene officieele correctie", *Bijdragen tot de Taal-, Land- en Volkenkunde van Nederlandsch Indië* LXXIII (1917), 255–284.

Soerjodiningrat, P. A., "De ontwakende cultuur van Java", *Indisch Genootschap*, 18 Juni 1926, pp. 45–54.

Soetomo, R., "Onderwijsvraagstukken in Indonesië", *Indisch Genootschap*, 16 October 1936, pp. 95–107.

Stokvis, J. E., "Uitkomsten en vooruitzichten van den ethischen koers in onze Koloniale Staatkunde", *Indisch Genootschap*, 25 Maart 1919, pp. 125–155.

——, "Van Limburg Stirum", *Indonesië* II (1948/9), 19–38.

Tan Goan Po, "De vorming van een Indonesische Middenstand", *De Nieuwe Geest-Semangat Baroe* I No. 12 (April, 1946), 8.

Terhupeiory, W. K., "Iets over de Inlandsche geneeskundigen", *Indisch Ge-nootschap*, 28 Januari 1908, pp. 101–134.

Tjokro Adi Koesoemo, R. M. T., "Pengatoeran boeat menambahi kemadjoe-an bagei orang Djawa", *Tijdschrift voor het Binnenlandsch Bestuur* XXXIII (1907), 454–464.

Tjokroamiprodjo, R., "Het voornemen van de Regeering van Nederlandsch Indië om Inlanders tot het aanleeren en de studie der Hollandsche taal aan te moedigen", *Tijdschrift voor het Binnenlandsch Bestuur* XXIII (1902), 145–152.

Velsen, A. van, "Eenige opmerkingen over de cultureele verhouding Indo-nesië-Nederland", *De Gids* CX, No. 4 (1947), 164–172.

Visman, F. H., "Staatkundige ontwikkeling van Indonesië", *Vijftig Jaren: Officieel Gedenkboek* (Amsterdam, 1948).

Vleming Jr., J. L., "De financieele positie van Nederlandsch-Indië en de be-lasingpolitiek van de laatste jaren: (beschouwingen aan de hand van de begrootingsstukken voor het dienstjaar 1927)", *De Socialistische Gids* XI (November 1926), 963–975.

Vollenhoven, C. van, "Juridisch confectiewerk (eenheidsprivaatrecht voor Indië)", *Koloniale Studiën* IX (1925), 293–318.

———, "De ontvoogding van Indië, samenhang der maatregelen en plan-nen", *Indisch Genootschap*, 24 October 1919, pp. 165–197.

Wellenstein, E. P., "Het onderzoek naar den belastingdruk op de inheemsche bevolking van Nederlandsch-Indië", *Koloniale Studiën* IX, (1925), 23–46.

Wertheim, W. F., "Oude en Nieuwe Islamieten in Indonesië", *De Nieuwe Stem* VI (1951), 323–331 and 396–407.

Westerveld, D. J. A., "De vernederlandsching van het Inlandsch Onderwijs in Nederlandsch-Indië", *De Indische Gids* XXXVII (1915), 305–25.

Westra, H., "Custom and Muslim Law in the Netherlands Indies", *The Netherlands Indies* [Bulletin of the Colonial Institute Amsterdam] III (June/ Aug., 1940), 174–188.

Wolff van Westerrode, W. P. D. de, "Eene credietinstelling voor Inlanders", *Tijdschrift voor Nijverheid en Landbouw* LVI (1899), 35–69.

INDEX

The "Molenvliet" canal in Batavia.

View of Surabaya.

A Second-Class Native School in Batur.

A *Muhammadijah* School.

A village grain shed (*lumbung desa*).

A village bank.

A mobile library of the Bureau for Popular Literature.

The STOVIA building in Batavia.

Headquarters of the Theosophical Society in Batavia.

Dr. C. Snouck Hurgronje.

A. W. F. Idenburg.

J. P. Graaf van Limburg Stirum in the *Volksraad*.

D. Fock.

Raden Adjeng Kartini (right) and her sisters Karlinah and Roekmini.

Dr. Tjipto Mangoenkoesoemo, E. F. E. Douwes Dekker and R. M. Soewardi Soerianingrat (front row, from left to right), with other leaders of the *Indische Partij*, shortly before their exile.

Semaoen and Darsono.

Tan Malaka.

Alimin Prawirodirdjo.

Hadji Agus Salim.

Soewardi Soerianingrat (Ki Hadjar Dewantoro).

Dr. R. Soetomo.

Board of the *Indische Vereeniging* in 1923: Darmawan Mangoenkoesoemo, Mohammad Hatta, Iwa Koesoema Soemantri, Sastromoeljono and Sartono (from left to right).

Soekarno.

Printed in the United States
by Baker & Taylor Publisher Services